Praise on Purpose

A Year of Uplifting Words

Linda Grabeman

REDEMPTION
PRESS

Praise On Purpose: A Year of Uplifting Words
© 2014 by Linda Grabeman. All rights reserved.

Published by Redemption Press, PO Box 427, Enumclaw, WA 98022 Toll Free (844) 2REDEEM (273-3336)

Redemption Press is honored to present this title in partnership with the author. The views expressed or implied in this work are those of the author. Redemption Press provides our imprint seal representing design excellence, creative content and high quality production.

Scripture quotations marked (CEV) are from the Contemporary English Version © 1991, 1992, 1995 by American Bible Society. Used by Permission.

Scripture quotations marked (TLB) are taken from The Living Bible copyright © 1971. Used by permission of Tyndale House Publishers, Inc., Carol Stream, Illinois 60188. All rights reserved.

Scripture quotations marked (NCV) are taken from the New Century Version, Copyright © 1987, 1988, 1991 by Word Publishing, a division of Thomas Nelson, Inc. Used by permission. All rights reserved.

Scripture quotations marked (MSG) are from THE MESSAGE. Copyright © by Eugene H. Peterson 1993, 1994, 1995, 1996, 2000, 2001, 2002. Used by permission of NavPress Publishing Group.

Scripture quotations marked (NKJV) are taken from the New King James Version. Copyright © 1982 by Thomas Nelson, Inc. Used by permission. All rights reserved.

Scripture quotations marked (NLT) are taken from the Holy Bible, New Living Translation, copyright © 1996. Used by permission of Tyndale House Publishers, Inc., Wheaton, IL 60189 USA. All rights reserved.

Scripture quotations marked The Voice are taken from The Voice™. Copyright © 2008 by Ecclesia Bible Society. Used by permission. All rights reserved.

ISBN 13: 978-1-63232-580-8
ePub ISBN: 978-1-63232-581-5
Kindle ISBN: 978-1-63232-582-2
Library of Congress Catalog Card Number: 2014942891

Acknowledgments

To my sweet, faithful husband, Dave. All I can say is, "Thank you!" You put up with me during this crazy year and a half of writing and editing *Praise on Purpose*. You endured a messier house than you like, and a wife who was way too busy with deadlines. I love how God knit you together! You are a man of integrity in all things. Hard to believe, but we're about to enter the empty-nest season of life. How we will miss all of our children, but I'm so excited to have more "date nights" with you! God has blessed me immensely with you as my partner for life. I love you so.

To Christian, my long-desired, miracle first child. What fun it has been to watch you mature and spread your wings! Nashville seems to suit you well, and I am thrilled. You have always been my kind, logical son. You worked hard at Clemson University and it paid off. I am so very proud of you and all of your accomplishments. Thank you for allowing your dad and me the privilege of guiding you, even as an adult. It is an honor to still play a part in your decisions. Just continue to seek God's best for your life. He loves you more than you will ever know and His plans for your life will bring you ultimate fulfillment.

To Carey, my make-me-smile, tenderhearted son. What a treat to watch you flourish at Belmont University! Your passion for music fills my heart with joy. Exactly how God will use that talent, as well as your profound love for people, I can't wait to see. I am certain that God will give you a life that brings you joy because you seek His will above all else. Wherever He leads you, I'll be on the front row, applauding! Just relax and let Him open the proper doors for you. He is so faithful and His timing is perfect. He won't waste any of your gifts; He will bless the world through them!

To Chloe, my precious about-to-leave-the-nest daughter. I will dearly miss your companionship as you step into your college days at Lee University, so expect lots of phone calls. You are so ready for college friends who share your passions, a deeper biblical understanding of the world and new and exciting adventures. I can't wait to watch it all unfold! Your love for the neglected and overlooked in this world inspires and convicts me. Your joy in worshiping God thrills me. How He will knit together all your loves will be a beautiful tapestry for all to see, and I stand on tiptoe as it unfurls. I love you, darling.

To all of my dear friends and new *Praise on Purpose* companions, thank you from the bottom of my heart for your encouragement, love and prayers. They empowered me whenever I felt weary.

I pray for God's richest anointing and guidance on each of the wonderfully talented team at Redemption Press. I am so blessed to be a part of His ministry of the Word through y'all! A special thank you to editor Inger Logelin who patiently persevered through unexpected challenges. What a blessing to work with you.

Thank you to everyone at C.A.S.E. Solutions, for your artistic touches on my website and marketing materials. It has been such a joy to work with all of you!

To Jeff Norris of Remote Technology Services, who expertly set up my dual-screen computer system so I could most efficiently write *Praise on Purpose*, and then cheerfully and patiently answered my countless frantic calls for help. What a gift! I pray for God's richest blessings on your business and your family.

Finally, Lord Jesus, You surprised me with this book! I thought *No Prissy Shoes* was my one-and-only, but You always have bigger and better plans than I do. Be glorified in this book. Bring comfort and conviction to many through these devotions, by Your mighty hand. May Your name always be praised!

Introduction

Welcome to a new and exciting way to walk through the ups and downs of everyday life—by praising God on purpose. For the next 365 days, even in the midst of difficulties and disappointments, we will deliberately thank God for something in our day, because He is worthy of that gratitude. As we lift up our hearts and voices to the One who showers us with blessings, He will give us eyes to see His God-gifts. Yes, as we embark on this holy habit of praise, a rising-up-inside-joy will awaken in us, one not dependent on good circumstances. This praising-Him-gladness flies in the face of the one who tries to deceive, derail and depress us, because praise has power. Satan knows it. That's why God ordained it. So, step into this new, jubilant way of living. You won't be sorry. It will be a transforming 365 days!

Spread for me a banquet of praise, serve High God a feast of kept promises, and call for help when you're in trouble—I'll help you...

It's the praising life that honors me.

Psalms 50:14-15, 23
The Message

Day 1

You Are For Me!

Thank You, Lord, You are for me! Why is it easier to believe the world's lie that You are *mad* at me? Crazy! As a flower opens up to the sun, Your love and Christ-bought acceptance awaken and soothe my wounded soul. No more hiding, no more fear. You are in my corner, working for me. And You have not recently decided that I was good enough to love, but before the world even began. You set this plan in motion before time, because You didn't want me to just live, but to intimately live in a close relationship with You.

Have You Thought? Do you feel as especially loved by God right now as I do?

His Answer:

> Blessed be the Lord—day after day he carries us along. He's our Savior, our God, oh yes! He's God-for-us, he's God-who-saves-us. Oh you, his people—bless God!
>
> Psalms 68:19, 35
> The Message

Day 2

Quiet My Ways

Thank You, Lord, Your ways are so simple and free. When I seek You, I find You and I find freedom. You are always waiting for my cry…for my focus to turn to You. Sadly, some days my attention gets distracted. I get all tangled up in the things of this world. They drag me in and pull me down. Keep my eyes fixed firmly on You today, Lord, and my ears immune to the drone of the world's charms. I long to live an unhindered life before You, empowered and set free by You to be the true me You have designed me to be. But that won't happen if I am not in Your presence. You refuse to scream over the noise in my life. Quiet my ways, Lord.

Have You Thought: What's tangling me up today?

His Answer:

Light, space, zest—that's GOD!

That's the only quiet, secure place in a noisy world, the perfect getaway, far from the buzz of traffic.

Point me down your highway, GOD.

Psalms 27:1, 5, 11
The Message

Day 3

I'm Safe With You

Thank You, Lord, You are the listening ear when no one else is interested. When comfort is long exhausted or dreams I've spoken fall to the ground unopened, You hear and You care. The conversation is never over with You, Lord. Wise counsel or encouraging affirmations are never lacking at Your throne. You lift me up and take me seriously. You even let me dream or vent with no reprimands. Every word I long to speak is safe with You. Thank you for allowing me to be the true me with You, my faithful God. The next time my earthly companions fail me, remind me what a wonderful Comforter and Counselor You are. Thanks.

Have You Thought: What do I need to share with God today?

His Answer:

You've always given me breathing room, a place to get away from it all, a lifetime pass to your safe-house, an open invitation as your guest. You've always taken me seriously, God, made me welcome among those who know and love you.

Psalms 61:3-5
The Message

Day 4

In Confident Trust

Thank You, Lord, You are with me in the highs and lows of life. Don't let me get so caught up in the good times that I forget to thank You...the One who orchestrated my good times. And when bad things happen which I didn't expect or longed for results don't pan out, help me not fall into despair. Everything, good or bad, must be sifted through Your Hand before it reaches me. You ordain and allow it all to work for my good in order to perfect me into Your image. Help me to walk with confident trust in Your plans for me. All creation gives You the final word, Jesus. Today I choose to follow You that closely too.

Have You Thought? Have I given You the final word in my life?

His Answer:
> All this energy issues from Christ: God raised him from death and set him on a throne in deep heaven, in charge of running the universe, everything from galaxies to governments, no name and no power exempt from his rule. And not just for the time being, but *forever*. He is in charge of it all, has the final word on everything.

Ephesians 1:20-22
The Message

Day 5

God's Smile

Thank You, Lord, You give me more grace than I give myself. As I think about last year, I list all the things I didn't get done…and I frown. You see the times when I trusted You, or reached out to a stranger, or chose Your truth over the world's opinion… and You smile. I need to put on Your God-Glasses this year to see my way clearly. Yes, I'll mess up again, and neglect things. You, God, will love me anyway, and smile. You see all the ways You will *still* grow me into Your woman.

Have You Thought? Where do I need to relax and trust Your work in me?

His Answer:

> God bless you and keep you, God smile on you and gift you, God look you full in the face and make you prosper.
>
> Numbers 6:24-26
> The Message

Day 6

God of My Life Journey

Thank You, Lord, You are the God of our life journey. Whether that path is new and terrifying, or familiar and ho-hum, You long to be our Navigator. You did it like a pro for the Israelites, guiding them with Your cloud by day and Your fire by night. There was never a moment when You were not leading them or fighting for them. The same is true for us. Give us some quiet moments with You today to assure us of Your Fatherly care. Every bend and curve in our path has been carefully designed by You for our good.

Ask Yourself: Where am I afraid God won't guide or protect me?

His Answer:

> GOD, your God, is leading the way; he's fighting for you. You saw with your own eyes what he did for you in Egypt; you saw what he did in the wilderness, how GOD, your God, carried you as a father carries his child, carried you the whole way until you arrived here.

Deuteronomy 1:30-31
The Message

Day 7

The Real-Deal God

Lord, thank You that You are an actual Savior in the reality of our lives. You are not just an abstract, up-in-the-skies, easy-to-forget-about God. You have always portrayed Yourself as the *real deal* God. As You walked this earth with people who were in darkness without their lamps, You called yourself the Light. To those who smelled bread baking every day, You called yourself the Bread of Life. For crowds who walked everywhere, You called Yourself the Way. Be just that real and present to us as we come and go this year. Break into our lives where You have never been before.

Have You Thought? Where haven't I allowed God to break into my life?

His Answer:

So the people asked, "What miracle will you do? If we see a miracle, we will believe you. What will you do? Our fathers ate the manna in the desert. This is written in the Scriptures: 'He gave them bread from heaven to eat.'" Jesus said, "I tell you the truth, it was not Moses who gave you bread from heaven; it is my Father who is giving you the true bread from heaven."

Then Jesus said, "I am the bread that gives life. Whoever comes to me will never be hungry, and whoever believes in me will never be thirsty."

"Those who see the Son and believe in him have eternal life, and I will raise them on the last day. This is what my Father wants."

John 6:30-32, 35, 40
New Century Version

Day 8

He Loves Me Anyway

I can't fool You at all, Lord. You even want me to be brutally honest and real with You. That's a relief! Whether I act in anger or am green with envy, overwrought with anxiety or down-in-the-dumps discouraged, You never judge or get annoyed with me. Those ragged edges in my soul only evoke Your tender mercies! So, Lord help me to open up fully to You today about whatever is dragging me down, because You alone can heal those places that I hide from everyone else. Come, my Great Physician, and patiently, gently tend to all the wounded, broken places in my heart. You alone can change me. I'm Yours, Lord.

Have You Thought? Where am I not totally honest with the Lord because I fear His displeasure?

His Answer:
> GOD makes everything come out right; he puts victims back on their feet. GOD is sheer mercy and grace; not easily angered, he's rich in love. He doesn't endlessly nag and scold, nor hold grudges forever. He doesn't treat us as our sins deserve, nor pay us back in full for our wrongs.
>
> He knows us inside and out, keeps in mind that we're made of mud.
>
> Psalms 103:6, 8-10, 14
> The Message

Day 9

My Put-Me-Back-Together God

I thank You, Lord, there are no hard places in my heart and no character flaws in my soul that You can't refine, change or erase. The turning point comes when I ask for Your help! I don't always want to admit those deficiencies or faults because then I am forced to deal with them. How sad! Only when I freely admit where I am empty can You fill me. To the extent that I confess my brokenness, You are able to restore me. So Lord, I acknowledge my critical spirit, my vanity and my love of pretty things. Where I grieve or dishonor You, please convict and change me with Your Holy Spirit.

Have You Thought? Where do I need a God-overhaul?

His Answer:

> More than anything else, a person's mind is evil and cannot be healed. Who can understand it? But, I, the Lord look into a person's heart and test the mind. So I can decide what each one deserves; I can give each one the right payment for what he does.

Jeremiah 17:9-10
New Century Version

Day 10

It's All Grace

Lord, I'm grateful knowing You changes my outlook about myself and others. The ground really is level at the foot of the cross. We are all in need of redemption; all unable to save ourselves. In Your eyes, we are either saved by grace, or in need of grace. You gladly reached out to me when I had nothing to offer You. Help me see others through your eyes today. I need Your heart of compassion to reach out, instead of looking past or looking down at others. I want to display kindness to everyone I meet today.

Have You Thought? Where do I rely on myself instead of God's grace towards me?

His Answer:
> Living then, as every one of you does, in pure grace, it's important that you not misinterpret yourselves as people who are bringing this goodness to God. No, God brings it all to you. The only accurate way to understand ourselves is by what God is and by what he does for us, not by what we do for him.

> Get along with each other; don't be stuck-up. Make friends with nobodies; don't be the great somebody. Don't hit back; discover beauty in everyone. If you've got it in you, get along with everybody.

> Romans 12:3, 16-18
> The Message

Day 11

Can I Remember?

Thank You, Lord, for the realization that much of the Bible is composed of "journal entries" written by those who longed to live for You. What if they had ignored that call? How much we would have missed without David's brutally honest interactions with God, the disciples' moment-by-moment accounts of Jesus, or Paul's chronicles of the early church. As I read the recorded snippets of my life in hindsight they also teach and bless me. Thoughts and experiences not written down are too easily forgotten and the power of the Lord on my behalf may not be realized. Help me to be more faithful this year, Lord.

Have You Thought? How can I make a habit of recording God's work in my life?

His Answer:

> The Lord answered me: "Write down the vision; write it clearly on clay tablets so whoever reads it can run to tell others. It is not yet time for the message to come true, but that time is coming soon; the message will come true. It may seem like a long time, but be patient and wait for it, because it will surely come; it will not be delayed.

> Habakkuk 2:2-3
> New Century Version

Day 12

Singing a God-Song

You are the God of Hope…a Hope that has rippled throughout all history and continues to flow through us. Our lives as God-followers touch our families, friends and down the line to perfect strangers. Knowing Jesus alters our work, our language, and our behavior. People notice and their lives are changed. Our witness of God's grace never ends with us. Heaven is brought to earth for someone. Hearts are touched, spirits are lifted and hope is reborn. This world is mired in hopelessness. Rejoice that you are a Hope-giver.

Have You Thought? To whom does God want me to give a word of hope today?

His Answer:
> I'm ready, God, so ready, ready from head to toe. Ready to sing, ready to raise a God-song:
>
> I'm thanking you, GOD, out in the streets, singing your praises in town and country. The deeper your love, the higher it goes; every cloud's a flag to your faithfulness.

Psalms 108:1, 3-4
The Message

Day 13

God of My Biggest Messes

Thank You, Lord, for the power of reflection. It exposes Your redemption in the design of my life. When I take time to pause, I can see You have brought blessing even in those messy, snarled-up places where it felt like all was lost. I am able to discern how some of life's tangles have been straightened out, or at least, woven together in a new way. You show me how You have faithfully woven color and beauty into areas which I thought were just boring, gray tapestry. What a joy that my very daily life provides You with a canvas on which You display Your unfailing grace.

Have You Thought? Where has God brought solutions to seemingly hopeless situations in my past?

His Answer:
> …he saved us from all that. It was all his doing; we had nothing to do with it. He gave us a good bath, and we came out of it new people, washed inside and out by the Holy Spirit. Our Savior Jesus poured out new life so generously. God's gift has restored our relationship with him and given us back our lives. And there's more life to come—an eternity of life! You can count on this.

Titus 3:5-8
The Message

Day 14

The Answer to Every Need

Lord, You long to be involved in my struggles and decisions. My prayers for Your help are not attempts at wooing a God who is really not interested or available. I don't need to persuade You that I am worthy of Your help. You ever wait to hear my requests. As your Word says, "For the eyes of the Lord run to and fro throughout the whole earth, to show Himself strong on behalf of those whose heart is loyal to him" (2 Chron. 16:9 NKJV). You are my attentive, adoring, all-ears Answer to my every need, Lord.

Have You Thought? Are there places in my life where I don't rely on God's power for me?

His Answer:

> Watch this: God's eye is on those who respect him, the ones who are looking for his love. He's ready to come to their rescue in bad times; in lean times he keeps body and soul together. We're depending on GOD; he's everything we need.
>
> Psalms 33:18-20
> The Message

Day 15

Generous Redemption

Your Word is full of real people, broken and flawed. Individuals who lied, cheated, got mad at their church friends and thought about themselves way too much. People just like me. But the best part of the Story is Your mercy still flowed to them. You didn't write them off, nor did You say, "Too bad. You brought this on yourself. You got just what you deserve." That is the *good news* of the Gospel because, honestly, a lot of my problems are brought on by my own bad attitudes or hastily spoken words. Thank you for Your unending grace in my life, Lord.

Have You Thought: Do I ever feel God's forgiveness will run out?

His Answer:

Help, GOD—the bottom has fallen out of my life! Master, hear my cry for help! Listen hard! Open your ears! Listen to my cries for mercy. If you, GOD, kept records on wrongdoings, who would stand a chance? As it turns out, forgiveness is your habit, and that's why you're worshiped.

...with GOD's arrival comes love, with GOD's arrival comes generous redemption.

Psalms 130:1-4, 7
The Message

Day 16

Entering God's Dance

You are a patient, gentle Suitor, thank You. You never stop inviting me in. Your arms open wide, beckoning me to join in Your dance. But I hold back, afraid to give myself fully; nervous about where this holy Romance may lead. At times I play the wallflower, fearful to take that first step. Other times I enter, but I'm stiff, self-conscious and unable to relax or enjoy myself. Yet You continue to whisper, "Let Me be Lord of your dance." So, today, I gladly enter in. I'll lay my head on Your shoulder and let You lead, for once. This is an important day, but I'm scared. Hold me close.

Have You Thought? Where do I need to just relax and let God lead me?

His Answer:

I will build you up again, and you will be rebuilt. You will pick up your tambourines again and dance with those who are joyful.

They will be crying as they come, but they will pray as I bring them back. I will lead those people by streams of water on an even road where they will not stumble.

The young women of Israel will be happy and dance, the young men and old men also. I will change their sadness into happiness; I will give them comfort and joy instead of sadness.

Jeremiah 31:4, 9, 13
New Century Version

Day 17

A Clean Slate

Thank You Lord, that forgiveness is a gift not just to be received, but also to be shared. Every time You show me Your amazing grace and mercy, You make it just a little bit easier for me to pass on that forgiveness to others. As I respond to Your unmerited love, my heart is somehow softened and enlarged and my perspective is altered little by little. Your love and mercy triumph over Your judgment, as it says in James 3:13. What a gift Your love is to free me and change me. Love is victor over condemnation; forgiveness is victor over resentment and bitterness. Amazing!

Have You Thought? Has God's forgiveness for me made my heart more ready to share that grace with others?

His Answer:

> Jesus was matter-of-fact: "Embrace this God-life. Really embrace it."
>
> "Include everything as you embrace this God-life, and you'll get God's everything. And when you assume the posture of prayer, remember that it's not all asking. If you have anything against someone, forgive—only then will your heavenly Father be inclined to also wipe your slate clean of sins."

Mark 11:22, 24-25
The Message

Day 18

A Constant Connection

Thank You, Lord, for the simplicity of prayer. You read the sighs of my heart when the words of my mouth falter. If I simply lift up someone's name with just a word, or even a thought, I evoke Your power and presence in his or her life. What an astounding privilege and blessing! Lord, let more of my waiting moments throughout the day be times of staccato prayer, quietly raising those names You bring to mind. Make me ever aware of my constant connection to You, Lord. I want to increasingly press in to the God who hears, understands and acts on my behalf.

Have You Thought? Are there areas in my life where God is calling me to press in closer to Him?

His Answer:
> Meanwhile, the moment we get tired in the waiting, God's Spirit is right alongside helping us along. If we don't know how or what to pray, it doesn't matter. He does our praying in and for us, making prayer out of our wordless sighs, our aching groans. He knows us far better than we know ourselves, knows our pregnant condition, and keeps us present before God. That's why we can be so sure that every detail in our lives of love for God is worked into something good.
>
> Romans 8:26-28
> The Message

Day 19

Peace in Turmoil

I thank You, Lord, for the peace You provide. This world can be a very threatening place. Structures we once thought could never fail are tottering. We worry about terrorists, bankruptcy and the dissolution of the family. Our lives don't feel safe anymore. But You speak Your truth into the turmoil of our lives, Your peace into our panic. We just need to step away from the commotion and commune with You. You are waiting to soothe our ruffled nerves, if we will enter into Your Presence. I certainly need to go to that place of quiet daily, to be reminded that my peace is not dependent on carefree scenarios, but on the One who will take my cares and carry them Himself.

Have You Thought? Where do I need God to whisper His peace to my soul today?

His Answer:
> GOD the wicked get away with murder—how long will you let this go on? They brag and boast and crow about their crimes! They walk all over your people, GOD, exploit and abuse your precious people.
>
> Well, think again, you idiots, fools—how long before you get smart? Do you think Ear-Maker doesn't hear, Eye-Shaper doesn't see?
>
> How blessed the man you train, GOD, the woman you instruct in your Word, providing a circle of quiet within the clamor of evil…
>
> Rest assured that justice is on its way…
>
> Psalms 94:3-6, 8-9, 12-13, 15
> The Message

29

Day 20

The Power Behind it All

Thank You, Lord, You are the Strong One. I need to consistently lean into Your power. How many times have I felt capable enough to perform whatever was required…good enough in my own strength? *What's wrong with that? I* am. My *self-*reliance is the problem. When I do things in *my* own power with no thought of asking for divine help or blessing, I get none. But, when I realize my weakness and need of You in everything—*everything*—then You can work in Your supernatural way. So, come, Lord, be the Power behind all I do; give it eternal worth.

Have You Thought? Where have I slipped into self-reliance instead of receiving God's power?

His Answer:

May all the gifts and benefits that come from God our Father, and the Master, Jesus Christ, be yours.

The Message that points to Christ on the Cross seems like sheer silliness to those hellbent on destruction, but for those on the way of salvation it makes perfect sense.

Christ is God's ultimate miracle and wisdom all wrapped up in one. Human wisdom is so tinny, so impotent, next to the seeming absurdity of God. Human strength can't begin to compete with God's "weakness."

1 Corinthians 1:3, 18, 24-25
The Message

Day 21

In His Name

Thank You, Lord, that "Your Kingdom come" can be lived out through each of us. We can be a part of Your *eternal story.* What an awesome thought! When Jesus touched people and healed them, forgave them or blessed them, He spoke of His Kingdom and how it had come near to them. I want to embrace the reality that as a believer in this Risen One, I am also an agent of His Kingdom to our broken world. Each of our words of encouragement, comfort, blessing or healing can miraculously resound with Jesus' voice. Lord, make us Your hands and voice to the waiting harvest!

Have You Thought? How has God used me in the past, and how is He calling me to bless others in His Name?

His Answer:

Jesus traveled through all the towns and villages, teaching in their synagogues, preaching the Good News about the kingdom, and healing all kinds of diseases and sicknesses. When he saw the crowds, he felt sorry for them because they were hurting and helpless, like sheep without a shepherd. Jesus said to his followers, "There are many people to harvest but only a few workers to help harvest them. Pray to the Lord, who owns the harvest, that he will send more workers to gather his harvest."

Matthew 9:35-38
New Century Version

Day 22

Our Big-Picture God

Thank You, Lord, for including in Your Word Abraham's early, not-so-obedient walk. It gives us hope about the paths we walk. We remember Abraham's incredible, I-couldn't-do-that-faith when he placed his promised son, Isaac, on the altar. But, when God initially called him, He told him to leave his country, his family and his father's house. Abram (his name then) obeyed two of those parts, but he took his father, his family and his nephew with him. He only partially obeyed. God saw his emerging faith though, and gave him grace when he was not there yet. He sees our nearly-got-it faith in the same way and gives us grace.

Have You Thought? How has God been gentle with me as I have struggled to fully obey Him?

His Answer:

> The Lord said to Abram, "Leave your country, your relatives, and your father's family and go to the land I will show you."

> So Abram left Haran as the Lord had told him, and Lot went with him. At this time Abram was 75 years old. He took his wife Sarai, his nephew Lot, and everything they owned, as well as all the servants they had gotten in Haran. They set out from Haran, planning to go to the land of Canaan, and in time they arrived there.

> Genesis 12:1, 4-5
> New Century Version

Day 23

Your Altar

Thank You, Lord, that the story of Abraham and Isaac teaches us more than we see on the surface. His journey up Mount Moriah to the altar lasted three days, the same as the three days between Jesus' death and resurrection. Emotionally and spiritually, Abraham endured the "death" of his son as he traveled to the altar. By his arrival, he *knew* that even if Isaac died, God would raise him up again. That trip was also a testing time for Isaac. He willingly lay on that altar! Lord, grow that same faith in me so I can willingly lay things on Your altar which are important to me.

Have You Thought? How has God shown me His blessings when I have obeyed Him?

His Answer:

> Take your dear son Isaac whom you love and go to the land of Moriah. Sacrifice him there as a burnt offering on one of the mountains that I'll point out to you.
>
> On the third day he looked up and saw the place in the distance. Isaac said to Abraham his father, "Father?" "Yes, my son." "We have flint and wood, but where's the sheep for the burnt offering?"
>
> Abraham said, "Son, God will see to it that there's a sheep for the burnt offering." ... They arrived at the place to which God had directed him. Abraham built an altar. He laid out the wood. Then he tied up Isaac and laid him on the wood. Abraham reached out and took the knife to kill his son. Just then an angel of God called to him out of Heaven, "Abraham! Abraham!" "Yes, I'm listening." "Don't lay a hand on that boy! Don't touch him! Now I know how fearlessly you fear God; you didn't hesitate to place your son, your dear son, on the altar for me."

Genesis 22: 2, 4, 8-12
The Message

Day 24

Unending Praise

Thank You, Lord, for the new salvation-life You bought for us. Turn our hearts in praise to You as we remember our lives before we knew Your saving grace. I can never say *thank you* enough. You redeemed my self-centered life and purchased my pardon. You brought mercy, grace and hope when I deserved none of these. Even now, You tenderly comfort my broken and disconnected places, and You bring unmerited redemption. Help me to realize my overwhelming debt to You, precious Savior. Let me live a thank-you-note life to show the world that I owe You everything!

Have You Thought? Lord, never let me forget the deep joy of knowing I am Yours!

His Answer:
> Hallelujah! It's a good thing to sing praise to our God; praise is beautiful, praise is fitting.
>
> He heals the heartbroken, and bandages their wounds. GOD puts the fallen on their feet again and pushes the wicked into the ditch.
>
> Those who fear GOD get GOD's attention; they can depend on his strength.
>
> Psalms 147:1, 3, 11
> The Message

Day 25

Overcoming One

Lord, I thank You that you died to free me from fear—even the fear of death itself. Sometimes I still let it grab me in its clutches. But then I remind myself I have trusted You for my eternity, and can certainly trust Your method of getting me there! Isn't it amazing that our Adversary can still wreak havoc in our hearts about the way we'll get to heaven? He's been using that same line for over two thousand years, and we still fall for it! The next time he tries to torment me with his lies from the pit, I'm going to remind him that I belong to the Overcoming One who knows me best, loves me most and who has perfect plans for me from now until eternity!

Have You Thought? Lord, show me where I believe Satan's lies, and free me from the power of his scare tactics.

His Answer:
> By embracing death, taking it into himself, He destroyed the Devil's hold on death and freed all who cower through life, scared to death of death.

> Hebrews 2:15
> The Message

Day 26

God of Hard Journeys

You understand the "big picture" and Your perspective is always precisely right in the long haul. Thank you, Lord! Help me to trust that truth in my daily walk, even when I don't see things Your way. You recognized the eternal benefits of dying on the cross, even while You were suffering. You can also see the long-term blessings of those hard journeys that I am trudging through right now. But You are my trustworthy Savior, my Safe Shelter during storms. Help me to trust in Your goodness and reverently bow to Your work-in-progress in my life and in the lives of those I love.

Have You Thought? Jesus, would You be Lord of all the hard places in my life right now?

His Answer:
God, the one and only—I'll wait as long as he says. Everything I hope for comes from him, so why not?

So trust him absolutely, people; lay your lives on the line for him. God is a safe place to be.

Psalms 62:5, 8
The Message

Day 27

Second-Chances God

You are a God of second chances. And third. And more. You showed it to Your disciple Peter, and even more, to the thief on the cross. He had made poor choices and gone down wrong paths all his life. But, with nearly his last breath, he chose You, and You said "Yes!" You love us even though we deny You, forsake You, or walk away from You. To the very end, You are ready to rewind, reload and restart our lives for Your glory. So the next time Satan screams loudly how we have failed, remind us that Your amazing grace is always just a cry away. Thank you, Lord. There are no better words.

Have You Thought? Am I in need of a fresh start somewhere? Do I believe God will give it to me?

His Answer:

> GOD is all mercy and grace—not quick to anger, is rich in love. GOD is good to one and all; everything he does is suffused with grace.
>
> GOD gives a hand to those down on their luck, gives a fresh start to those ready to quit.

Psalms 145:8-9, 14
The Message

Day 28

The Gift

Thank You, Lord, that Your death and resurrection purchased the most precious Gift ever given. It's a gift to be shared, but sometimes I stuff it deep into my pockets instead. *My present...for me.* Then I think of the many people I run into during my day. I imagine how their lives would change if they knew You...if I would share the Gift. Help my words to always brim over with Jesus-life. Let them just naturally, joyfully tell of the deep, abiding peace that is so foreign to the many heart-weary folks who brush past me. Speak through me today. Let me give away the Gift to someone else.

Have You Thought? Lord, make me more ready to share You with others.

His Answer:

> We saw it, we heard it, and now we're telling you so you can experience it along with us, this experience of communion with the Father and his Son, Jesus Christ. Our motive for writing is simply this: We want you to enjoy this, too. Your joy will double our joy!

1 John 1:3-4
The Message

Day 29

Unending Love

Thank You, Lord, for the depth and width and breadth and height of Your love for us. There is no surpassing or outrunning Your love. That is such good news for this emotional, up-and-down girl! How comforting to understand that in the depth of pain or the height of joy, You, my compassionate Father, see and care. You never say, "Get over it." You never get tired of the drama. Instead, You wrap us in Your arms, whisper how much You care and then work on our behalf. You are our shelter whenever we feel broken. Be our Abba, Daddy, today.

Have You Thought? Help me to run to You more quickly, my compassionate Father.

His Answer:

> God made my life complete when I placed all the pieces before him. When I got my act together, he gave me a fresh start. Now I'm alert to God's ways; I don't take God for granted.
>
> I feel put back together, and I'm watching my step. God rewrote the text of my life when I opened the book of my heart to his eyes.
>
> Psalms 18:20-21, 23-24
> The Message

Day 30

Persistent Prayer

Thank You, Lord, for the lessons in Your Word on the power of persistent prayer. Let me be more like the widow who relentlessly prayed until she had an answer. Even when I feel as if I have prayed long and hard enough for something, keep me faithful. *My* timetable *always* requires immediate answers. *Yours* doesn't. You see details I can't even imagine. You work with a perfect knowledge of every accompanying circumstance that I see dimly or not at all. Help me to trust You with the prayers that demand patience. Guard and guide my prayers today, Lord.

Have You Thought? Where do I need to be more faithful in prayer?

His Answer:

> I waited and waited and waited for GOD. At last he looked; finally he listened. He lifted me out of the ditch, pulled me from deep mud. He stood me up on a solid rock to make sure I wouldn't slip. He taught me how to sing the latest God-song, a praise-song to our God. More and more people are seeing this: they enter the mystery, abandoning themselves to GOD.

Psalms 40:1-4
The Message

Day 31

No Measuring Up Required

Thank You, Lord, for the understanding that I can't work for Your love. No mission trips, altar guild or any other duty I perform for You will make You love me more. This matters, for if I can earn Your love, then I can also lose it, and that's not good news. The world's idea of getting into heaven is based on earning it, and we often buy into that mindset. But the Redemption Story says our value comes not from what we do, but from what has been done for us—by Jesus. Only because of Him have we been redeemed and restored to fellowship with God. No measuring up needed.

Have You Thought? Are there any places where I feel I don't measure up to God's expectations?

His Answer:

Let me put this question to you: How did your new life begin? Was it by working your heads off to please God? Or was it by responding to God's Message to you? Are you going to continue this craziness? For only crazy people would think they could complete by their own efforts what was begun by God.

The person who lives in right relationship with God does it by embracing what God arranges for him. Doing things for God is the opposite of entering into what God does for you.

Galatians 3:2-3, 11
The Message

Day 32

God of Endings and New Beginnings

Lord, You are in all my beginnings and endings. What starts and stops have You planned for me this year? In what ways will I stand amazed at Your design when this year is over? How will You heal me, lead me, empower me or make me just a little bit more like You? What new experiences and new friends will You bring into my life even when I am afraid to walk through those doors? How will You nudge me to trust You more deeply as I leave my comfort zones? Thank You in advance for Your gentle leading of my year which has just begun. You are a great God!

Have You Thought? Lord, help me to once again lay down my plans and trust Your path for me.

His Answer:

No one can see God, but Jesus Christ is exactly like him. He ranks higher than everything that has been made. Through his power all things were made—things in heaven and on earth, things seen and unseen, all powers, authorities, lords, and rulers. All things were made through Christ and for Christ.

He is the head of the body, which is the church. Everything comes from him. He is the first one who was raised from the dead. So in all things Jesus has first place. God was pleased for all of himself to live in Christ. And through Christ, God has brought all things back to himself again—things on earth and things in heaven. God made peace through the blood of Christ's death on the cross.

Colossians 1:15-16, 18-20
New Century Version

Day 33

God's Got it Covered

Thank You, Lord, You care about the things that worry me. But, even better, You actually orchestrate the outcome of events long before I can see Your Hand at work. You've got it all covered, put together and lined up in just the right way for my highest good. You even have wonderful blessings in store for me, planned and held in waiting to be revealed at just the perfect moment. Help me to live life as a precious, adored daughter, who trusts her Abba Daddy to do the right thing for her at just the right time. You've proven Yourself worthy of that trust time and time again.

Have You Thought? Lord, help me to once again lay down my plans and trust Your path for me.

His Answer:
> That's right. Because I, your GOD, have a firm grip on you and I'm not letting go. I'm telling you, "Don't panic. I'm right here to help you."

> Isaiah 41:13
> The Message

Day 34

Relentlessly Wooed

Thank You, Lord, Your love for unbelievers is deeper than I could ever imagine and more persistent than I could ever comprehend. Sometimes I get discouraged because I have prayed for so many years that those whom I love would come to know You. Then you remind me how You *relentlessly* draw and woo each of them to Yourself with perfect understanding of their lives and their hearts, because You knit them together. My responsibility is not to convince them of their need, with my words, but rather to intercede on their behalf, with my prayers. Help me to be a faithful intercessor.

Have You Thought? Are there any unbelievers whom I have written off? Lord, help me to intercede for them instead.

His Answer:

> God didn't set us up for an angry rejection but for salvation by our Master, Jesus Christ. He died for us, a death that triggered life. So speak encouraging words to one another. Build up hope so you'll all be together in this, no one left out, no one left behind. I know you're already doing this; just keep on doing it.

1 Thessalonians 5:9-10
The Message

Day 35

Scattered or Settled

Thank You, Lord, that You are infinitely focused. I am not. Sometimes I spread myself too thin or take on projects not designed for me. I either try to do too much too fast and get overwhelmed, or I never really get on board and I feel guilty. Neither of these paths follow Your way. While You were on earth, You never ran out of time or got frazzled with all that You had to do. If I would just listen to You, my paths and timing would be less frantic and more fulfilling. You trusted Your Father for every moment of Your journey. Help me to do that more and more, and let me sense the difference that it makes.

Have You Thought? Settle me down today, Lord, and show me the difference that makes.

His Answer:

But what happens when we live God's way? He brings gifts into our lives, much the same way that fruit appears in an orchard—things like affection for others, exuberance about life, serenity. We develop a willingness to stick with things, a sense of compassion in the heart, and a conviction that a basic holiness permeates things and people. We find ourselves...able to marshal and direct our energies wisely.

Galatians 5:22-23
The Message

Day 36

His

Thank You, Lord, for accepting us! Even when we don't say yes to Your will and Your plans for us. Not just when we say, *Okay, Lord, I'm all Yours.* And it's not a just-by-the-skin-of-my-teeth acceptance, either. I mean an angels-singing, sit-right-here-by-Me welcome! We don't always act like that because we love conditionally…You don't. Hard for us to believe, but that is Your heart. So today, if you are beating yourself up over not feeling worthy of His love, *get over it!* You are amazingly, continuously, and no-matter-what loved by God because you are HIS…through JESUS! Woo-hoo!

Have You Thought? Forget the regrets. Live in His unconditional love instead.

His Answer:
> We all did it, all of us doing what we felt like doing, when we felt like doing it, all of us in the same boat. It's a wonder God didn't lose his temper and do away with the whole lot of us. Instead, immense in mercy and with an incredible love, he embraced us. He took our sin-dead lives and made us alive in Christ. He did all this on his own, with no help from us! Then he picked us up and set us down in highest heaven in company with Jesus, our Messiah. Now God has us where he wants us, with all the time in this world and the next to shower grace and kindness upon us in Christ Jesus.

> Ephesians 2:3-7
> The Message

Day 37

Never-Changing Love

Thank You, Lord, for seeing and understanding me as a woman and a mother. Life in both of those arenas is changing, and that is not easy for me. Children are leaving the nest that I have lovingly hovered over for more than two decades. And on top of that, I hardly recognize the woman I see in the mirror anymore. But in the midst of these upheavals, I know that You are changeless, and Your character is from everlasting. You ordain every season of my life. So in the ebb and flow of life, mercifully give me the grace to walk through each season in a way that honors You, my solid, steadfast Shelter.

Have You Thought? How comforting that in the midst of life's crises and chaos God remains changeless.

His Answer:
> I've been carrying you on my back from the day you were born, and I'll keep on carrying you when you're old. I'll be there, bearing you when you're old and gray. I've done it and will keep on doing it, carrying you on my back, saving you.

Isaiah 46:3-4
The Message

Day 38

Gentle Molding

Thank You, Lord, for Your correction. It only reminds me that I am Your beloved child. You don't discipline strangers, only family members. I don't like being scrutinized. When You correct me, I get defensive…even when I know deep down Your ways are right. My way comes much more naturally. It's the potter and the clay thing. The truth is You are molding me little by little into the woman You want me to be. I really do want to be pliable. Thank you for Your gentle hands. Your intention is not to break me, but to beautify me. I give You permission again today, Lord.

Have You Thought? Lord, show me where You long to correct me.

His Answer:

> My child, do not reject the Lord's discipline, and don't get angry when he corrects you. The Lord corrects those he loves, just as parents correct the child they delight in.

> Proverbs 3:11-12
> New Century Version

Day 39

Never-Ending Affection

Thank You, Lord, for Your matchless grace and mercy. In this present world we experience betrayal, rejection, and not much mercy, especially in personal relationships. Not so with God. Once we accept His gracious join-the-family invitation, there is no chance of ever being banished from His love or excluded from His blessings. But, despite His repeated attempts to convince us, we sometimes fear losing that never-ending affection. That saddens Him. So today, confidently celebrate God's abiding love for you. It will be an effervescent undercurrent of joy that will energize your days.

Have You Thought? Set right—because of Jesus! Let that wash over you today.

His Answer:
> Out of sheer generosity he put us in right standing with himself. A pure gift. He got us out of the mess we're in and restored us to where he always wanted us to be. And he did it by means of Jesus Christ...God sets things right. He also makes it possible for us to live in his rightness."

Romans 3:24-26
The Message

Day 40

Ordered Days

Thank You, Lord, for the wisdom that You so freely give us—if we ask. When I get in my own self-appointed, this-is-what-I'm-doing mode for the day, I totally ignore any input from You. But on good days, I send up a quick-and-easy, "Lord, order my day today." It is incredible how much more efficient and less stressed I am on those days! Not to mention, I'm actually *doing Your* will! Creator and Sustainer of the Universe, I want to live guided by You every day, all day long. In Your mercy, prick my memory daily to remember You in my comings and goings. That's Your design for my life.

Have You Thought? Lord, as I lay my head down tonight, let my steps have been directed by You.

His Answer:
> Happy are those who live pure lives, who follow the Lord's teachings. Happy are those who keep his rules, who try to obey him with their whole heart.
>
> Psalms 119:1-2
> New Century Version

Day 41

Our Watch-Me-Work God

Lord, circumstantial facts have never held much weight with You. Noah's contemporaries scoffed at the idea of rain and they got washed away. The residents of Jericho trusted in their wall until a God-ordered shout brought it down. Ahab's prophets paid little attention to Elijah's prayers for fire from heaven and ended up as burnt offerings. Paul's shackles and guards were no match for the earthquake that freed him. Even Satan's delight on Good Friday proved false on Easter. And we wonder if God can help us in our trying situations? Really?

Have You Thought? Show me how small my version of You is today.

His Answer:

> Do you think I've forgotten how to help? Am I so decrepit that I can't deliver? I'm as powerful as ever, and can reverse what I once did: I can dry up the sea with a word, turn river water into desert sand, and leave the fish stinking in the sun, stranded on dry land…turn all the lights out in the sky and pull down the curtain.

Isaiah 50:2-3
The Message

Day 42

Always God, Always Good

Thank You, Lord, there is no place where Your presence and Your goodness do not dwell. Let that be my firm footing. There are no unexpected situations or unforeseen circumstances with You. In every trial or tragedy, You plan some type of blessing—some evidence of Your redemption and salvation. Your Light *always* dispels darkness, regardless of its enormity. I praise You, holy-God-of-the-universe for the miracles You do which may remain unknown to us until we see Your face. Your sovereign rule and reign over this world is coming, and every knee will bow to You. *Every* one. Hallelujah!

Have You Thought? Be reassured today that there is no place in your life where He is not able to bring redemption.

His Answer:
> Oh, how great is your goodness to those who publicly declare that you will rescue them. For you have stored up great blessings for those who trust and reverence you. So cheer up! Take courage if you are depending on the Lord.

Psalms 31:19, 24
The Living Bible

Day 43

Help Me, Lord!

You are always bigger than any difficulty or situation I find myself jammed in. Whenever I allow a problem or a demanding circumstance to fill my thoughts, frighten me or make me feel helpless, I have made You far too small. How faithless is that after all the times You have intervened in my life in the past? You give me surprise occurrences and not-even-imagined sequences of events because of Your faithful promises to me. That's the kind of God You are! So help me to be a have-no-fear kind of daughter today. I know You are near, Lord and I thank You.

Have You Thought? How unending Your love; how amazing Your tenderness. Remind me again today.

His Answer:

God met me more than halfway, he freed me from my anxious fears. Look at him; give him your warmest smile. Never hide your feelings from him. When I was desperate, I called out, and God got me out of a tight spot. God's angel sets up a circle of protection around us while we pray.

Is anyone crying for help? God is listening, ready to rescue you. If your heart is broken, you'll find God right there; if you're kicked in the gut, he'll help you catch your breath. Disciples so often get into trouble; still, God is there every time.

Psalms 34:4-7, 17-19
The Message

Day 44

Redeemed and Redirected

Thank You, Lord, there is no misstep—intentional or accidental—that You can't redeem. No matter what wrong turn I've taken, or direction I've misunderstood, You can still handle it! And You redirect me without a lecture! Isn't that just the most comforting thought? We've all walked down the wrong path at some time. But, instead of saying, "Too bad. You blew it. You're on your own," our gracious, loving Father says, "Here's the way to go. Just follow Me." Help me to walk in the certainty of Your ever-ready compass which will direct and re-direct my way until I step into Your eternal home.

Have You Thought? There is no limit to Your patience, Lord. Let that be my quiet refrain today.

His Answer:

Keep me safe, O God, I've run for dear life to you. I say to GOD, "Be my Lord!" Without you, nothing makes sense.

The wise counsel GOD gives when I'm awake is confirmed by my sleeping heart. Day and night I'll stick with GOD; I've got a good thing going and I'm not letting go.

Now you've got my feet on the life path, all radiant from the shining of your face. Ever since you took my hand, I'm on the right way.

Psalms 16:1-2, 7-8, 11
The Message

Day 45

God of the Difficult

Life is not always easy. But, honestly, isn't it in the hard times that we diligently search for God? When things are going well, we tend to rely on ourselves, and we miss His presence and His power. So, thank you, Lord, for difficult people and trying circumstances that cause us to fall on our knees before You. That's where we should always be. Today, when things don't go quite as planned, or something unexpected happens, remind me to invite You into the situation. Then I'll watch you demonstrate You really are our All-in-All God.

Have You Thought? That difficult situation needs Your touch. Come, Lord Jesus.

His Answer:
> When things were going great I crowed, "I've got it made. I'm God's favorite. He made me king of the mountain." Then you looked the other way and I fell to pieces. I called out to you, God; laid out my case before you:
>
> You ripped off my black mourning band and decked me with wildflowers. I'm about to burst with song; I can't keep quiet about you. God, my God, I can't thank you enough.
>
> Psalms 30:6-8, 11-12
> The Message

Day 46

Fingerprints of God

I thank You today, Lord, that You can't be explained, You have to be experienced—first with our eyes, then with our hearts. Because You are not an impersonal, irrelevant deity, but a gracious, reveal-Yourself-to-us God. Sometimes You show Your Hand in creation, or through Your Word; other times through a song, a sermon or in a conversation with a friend. You love to unfold Your goodness to us because then Your name is glorified. So delight us with Your fingerprints on our lives today. Open our eyes to see and our mouths to praise You for Your nearness, our Emmanuel-God-with-us.

Have You Thought? Open my eyes to see Your Hand at work in my life today.

His Answer:
> There's no one quite like you among the gods, O Lord, and nothing to compare with your works.
>
> From the bottom of my heart I thank you, dear Lord; I've never kept secret what you're up to.
>
> You've always been great toward me—what love!
>
> So look me in the eye and show kindness…

Psalms 86:8, 12-13, 15-16
The Message

Day 47

Canvas of My Life

Thank You, Lord, You make sense of our lives when we trust the long-range plan to You. When circumstances catch us off guard or the course of events takes our breath away, You remain unwavering. Except for our eternal security, there is no greater comfort than to know that nothing is random in our lives. Seemingly arbitrary happenings or out-of-the-blue experiences are really purposeful and beneficial when seen in the larger landscape. Lord, help me to trust Your broad, sweeping brushstrokes as well as the minute details of Your pen on the canvas of my life. Be Lord of it all.

Have You Thought? Give me a trusting heart, Lord, even when I don't understand Your ways.

His Answer:

Who do you think "spoke and it happened"? It's the Master who gives such orders. Doesn't the High God speak everything, good things and hard things alike, into being?

If he works severely, he also works tenderly. His stockpiles of loyal love are immense.

God proves to be good to the man who passionately waits, to the woman who diligently seeks him. It's a good thing to quietly hope, quietly hope for help from GOD.

Lamentations 3:37-38, 32, 25-26
The Message

Day 48

Your Will, Lord

Lord, Your plans are always bigger and better than I could ever imagine. Then why do I still try to impose *my* will on You? You have shown me repeatedly that Your purposes have broader and deeper blessings and meaning than my puny, shortsighted ideas. You understand every future implication of actions taken today. Your perfect understanding gives You wisdom about things I can't possibly know…things which need to be considered. So, Lord, teach me to trust Your design, details and timing for my life. It's always right.

Have You Thought? Letting go. Where do I need to do that today?

His Answer:

> God can do anything, you know—far more than you could ever imagine or guess or request in your wildest dreams! He does it not by pushing us around but by working within us, his Spirit deeply and gently within us.

Ephesians 3:20
The Message

Day 49

My Rescuer

Thank You, Lord, that You are a rescuing God. I need Your divine deliverance with ridiculous regularity. For while I want to follow You with all my heart, time after time my actions derail me. I follow my own plans, for my own selfish desires. For a while, life seems good. But inevitably, I realize that I am far from You, lonely and lost. So I cry out from yet another winding back road, nowhere near Your desired destination for me. But, You lovingly retrieve me every time! Lord of my circuitous journey, get me back on track and show me the way to go. Maybe this time I will stay on course a little longer.

Have You Thought? Where have I wandered this time? Rescue me there, Lord.

His Answer:

It seems to be a fact of life that when I want to do what is right, I inevitably do what is wrong. I love God's law with all my heart. But there is another law at work within me that is at war with my mind. This law wins the fight and makes me a slave to the sin that is still within me. Oh, what a miserable person I am! Who will free me from this life that is dominated by sin? Thank God! The answer is in Jesus Christ our Lord.

Romans 7:21-25
New Living Translation

Day 50

Followers and Friends

God's Word is a treasure beyond comparison. It is my greatest joy, my most faithful guide and tender comfort. For the next forty days, let's mine just a fraction of the treasure stored in the Gospels. To get to know about someone, who better to ask than those who spent the most time with Him? Let's begin with John's Gospel. John was the one who proudly proclaimed he was "the disciple Jesus loved" (21:20 MSG). He wrote with a specific purpose: "that you will believe that Jesus is the Messiah, the Son of God and…have real and eternal life…" (20:31 MSG) Lord, draw us closer to You as we learn more.

Have You Thought? Have I ever thought that I, too, am a disciple whom Jesus loves?

His Answer:

God's Word is better than a diamond, better than a diamond set between emeralds…

There's more: God's Word warns us of danger and directs us to hidden treasure. Otherwise how will we find our way? Or know when we play the fool? Clean the slate, God, so we can start the day fresh! Keep me from stupid sins, from thinking I can take over your work; then I can start this day sun-washed, scrubbed clean of the grime of sin. These are the words in my mouth; these are what I chew on and pray. Accept them when I place them on the morning altar, O God, my Altar-Rock, God, Priest-of-My-Altar.

Psalms 19:10-14
The Message

Day 51

Jesus, Bread of Life

Jesus showed so clearly that He was the Son of God with His words and His works, His statements and His signs. His seven (number of perfection) statements were very clear to His Jewish hearers because He began them with "I AM"—the same words His Father spoke to Moses (Exodus 3:14) These statements were always spoken in context, like a show-and-tell lesson, for greatest impact. His first, *"I am the Bread of Life,"* was said after He miraculously fed the five thousand. Bread perishes, as do people. Christ gives eternal food to those who receive Him into themselves, those who believe He is the Bread of Life, sent from God.

Have You Thought? Be as real to me as the food I eat today, Lord.

His Answer:
> "I am the bread that gives life! Your ancestors ate manna in the desert, and later they died. But the bread from heaven has come down, so that no one who eats it will ever die. I am that bread from heaven! Everyone who eats it will live forever. My flesh is the life-giving bread that I give to the people of this world."

John 6:48-51
Contemporary English Version

Day 52

Your Light for Dark Places

"I am the light of the world," the Lord proclaimed at the Feast of Tabernacles, a joyous pilgrim celebration in Jerusalem. The Jews had marched around the temple for seven days, and the large lampstands had been lit, commemorating the light that guided them in the wilderness. Jesus had also just healed a blind man. Both of these show-and-tell lessons gave Jesus a stage to announce that He fulfilled all the Old Testament promises. In creation, God said, "Let there be Light." Now, God Incarnate, Jesus the Messiah had come to bring light into those dark and blind places in our lives. I invite You, Lord, to shine Your Light into those dark or empty places in my life today.

Have You Thought? Where am I in need of Your Light today, Lord? Where am I blind?

His Answer:
> "I am the world's Light. No one who follows me stumbles around in the darkness. I provide plenty of light to live in."

> All these God-signs he had given them and they still didn't get it, still wouldn't trust him.

John 8:12, John 12:37
The Message

Day 53

My Shepherd's Sheep

Jesus proclaimed, "I am the Good Shepherd." Surely, Jesus had just passed a sheep pen, and was thinking about the blind man whom He had healed. The Pharisees kicked the now-joyfully-seeing man out of the temple. Jesus called them hired men, who have no care for the sheep. Many shepherds use one sheep pen, but the sheep know their own shepherd's voice, and only follow him. Jesus knows us, His sheep, and He calls us. Lord, help me to listen to Your voice, staying when You tell me to stay, and going where You lead me with no fear, my Good Shepherd.

Have You Thought? The shepherd/lamb analogy is so tender. Do you see Jesus as your loving, Good Shepherd?

His Answer:
"I am the Good Shepherd. The Good Shepherd puts the sheep before himself, sacrifices himself if necessary. A hired man is not a real shepherd. The sheep mean nothing to him."

"I know my own sheep and my own sheep know me."

"My sheep recognize my voice. I know them, and they follow me. I give them real and eternal life."

John 10:11-12, 14, 27
The Message

Day 54

All For Us

Today I thank you, Lord, for Your proclamation: "I am the Gate." Jesus was probably still looking at the sheep pen, pointing to the opening. There was no door or gate that could be closed or opened. How would the sheep keep from wandering out, getting lost or hurt? What would keep wild animals or thieves from coming in to attack the sheep? The shepherd! He would lie down at the opening to the pen, making *himself* the gate. The shepherd would lay down his life for his sheep, before he would allow them to be harmed. What a precious visual of all that You are for us, Jesus!

Have You Thought? Everything in our lives goes through Him before it gets to us. What an astounding, comforting thought.

His Answer:
> "I tell you the truth, I am the door for the sheep. All the people who came before me were thieves and robbers. The sheep did not listen to them. I am the door, and the person who enters through me will be saved and will be able to come in and go out and find pasture. A thief comes to steal and kill and destroy, but I came to give life—life in all its fullness."

John 10:7-10
New Century Version

Day 55

Deliberate Delays

Thank You, Lord, that You proclaimed, "I am the resurrection and the life," after You called Lazarus from the grave. You showed Your power over death, even after four days. This was when the Jews believed the spirit left the body and decay began. Four vital things happened here: Lazarus was raised from the dead, God was glorified, many Jews believed, and the plot to kill Jesus was formed. His delay to go see Lazarus meant He missed the chance to heal him, but gained the opportunity to bring him back to life! That delay was loving and deliberate. Lord, help me to trust Your delays.

Have You Thought? I want what I want, when I want it. Teach me in my delays.

His Answer:

So the sisters sent word to Jesus, "Master, the one you love so very much is sick." When Jesus got the message, he said, "This sickness is not fatal. It will become an occasion to show God's glory by glorifying God's Son."

Then he shouted, "Lazarus, come out!" And he came out, a cadaver, wrapped from head to toe, and with a kerchief over his face. Jesus told them, "Unwrap him and let him loose." That was a turnaround for many of the Jews who were with Mary. They saw what Jesus did, and believed in him. But some went back to the Pharisees and told on Jesus.

John 11:3-4, 43-46
The Message

Day 56

The Bridegroom

When Jesus said, "I am the way, the truth, and the life," the time for His death was near. When He said He was going to prepare a place for us and He would come back to get us, it was His last will and testament. This is a Jewish wedding ritual which the Jews knew well. The future bridegroom leaves to add on a room to his father's home, then comes back to take his bride there to live. Jesus, our Eternal Bridegroom, has prepared our way and our room in heaven. He is the Truth of God, showing the Way, to bring us real Life, and He will return for us.

Have You Thought? How does this Jewish wedding custom change your idea of Heaven?

His Answer:
> Jesus said to his disciples, "Don't be worried! Have faith in God and have faith in me. There are many rooms in my Father's house. I wouldn't tell you this, unless it was true. I am going there to prepare a place for each of you. After I have done this, I will come back and take you with me. Then we will be together. You know the way to where I am going." Thomas said, "Lord, we don't even know where you are going! How can we know the way?" "I am the way, the truth, and the life!" Jesus answered. "Without me, no one can go to the Father. If you had known me, you would have known the Father. But from now on, you do know him, and you have seen him."

John 14:1-7
Contemporary English Version

Day 57

Attached

Thank You, Lord, for proclaiming, "I am the True Vine." This is Jesus' final I AM, spoken just hours before His arrest. With grapevines present all around, He concludes His most important teaching on vines and abiding. Israel had often been called God's vine in the Old Testament, but they produced no fruit. Jesus came, as the True Vine, to graft us in as branches on that Vine. As His life flows through us, fruit will naturally come. Jesus provides all we need, if we will just abide in Him, the Vine. I forget that often and I think having results depends on *my* work, when I just need to rest on *His work*.

Have You Thought? Keep me close, Jesus. Let me bear fruit for You.

His Answer:

Yes, I am the vine; you are the branches. Those who remain in me, and I in them, will produce much fruit. For apart from me you can do nothing. Anyone who does not remain in me is thrown away like a useless branch and withers. Such branches are gathered into a pile to be burned. But if you remain in me and my words remain in you, you may ask for anything you want, and it will be granted! When you produce much fruit, you are my true disciples. This brings great glory to my Father.

John 15:5-8
New Living Translation

Day 58

Everyday Miracles

Thank You, Lord, that You give us signs. You spoke seven proclamations of Your deity, but You also gave seven signs to back them up. What is the scope and significance of these signs today? In the very last verse of John's gospel, he says, "There are so many other things Jesus did. If they were all written down, each of them, one by one, I can't imagine a world big enough to hold such a library of books" (John 21:25 MSG). These miracles caused many to believe in Jesus. He still does things only God could do. Do *we* even notice? Or do we believe because of these signs?

Have You Thought? What miraculous things has Jesus done in your life?

His Answer:

Philip said to him, "Lord, show us the Father. That is all we need." Jesus answered, "I have been with you a long time now. Do you still not know me, Philip? Whoever has seen me has seen the Father. So why do you say, 'Show us the Father'? Don't you believe that I am in the Father and the Father is in me? The words I say to you don't come from me, but the Father lives in me and does his own work. Believe me when I say that I am in the Father and the Father is in me. Or believe because of the miracles I have done."

John 14:8-11
New Century Version

Day 59

Filled with the Best

The Lord's first sign was turning water into wine at the wedding in Cana. The wording indicates that Mary was in charge; when the wine ran low, she came to Jesus with her need. That's a great lesson for all of us! Jesus ordered the six clay pots (the number "six" and "clay pots" both refer to mankind in the Bible) to be filled with water. These were purification pots, which each held twenty to thirty gallons of water. Jesus miraculously turned the water into fine wine. This was symbolic of how He purifies us, taking the ordinary and filling us with the supernatural. This miracle led his disciples to believe in Him. Lord, fill the ordinary parts of me with Your supernatural life, joy, and peace today. Be glorified in all that I do.

Have You Thought? Where am I empty and in need of the Lord's filling?

His Answer:

Two days later there was a wedding in the town of Cana in Galilee. Jesus' mother was there, and Jesus and his followers were also invited to the wedding. When all the wine was gone, Jesus' mother said to him, "They have no more wine."

Jesus said to the servants, "Fill the jars with water." So they filled the jars to the top.

When the master of the feast tasted it, the water had become wine. He did not know where the wine came from, but the servants who had brought the water knew. The master of the wedding called the bridegroom and said to him, "People always serve the best wine first. Later, after the guests have been drinking awhile, they serve the cheaper wine. But you have saved the best wine till now." So in Cana of Galilee Jesus did his first miracle. There he showed his glory, and his followers believed in him.

John 2:1-3, 7, 9-11
New Century Version

Day 60

New Life

The Lord's second sign was the healing of the son of the nobleman. The son was in Capernaum, and Jesus was in Cana of Galilee, but Jesus told the father that his son would live. Two miracles happened here: the son was healed, which meant Jesus was divine; but also, Jesus transcended space. He spoke the word for the boy's healing from a different town. The father believed in both miracles. In verse 50, it says he believed that Jesus *could* heal. In verse 53, he realized that at the very moment Jesus' healing word was spoken, his boy revived. Healing received, glory given!

Have You Thought? Where do I feel empty and in need of new life?

His Answer:

As he traveled through Galilee, he came to Cana, where he had turned the water into wine. There was a government official in nearby Capernaum whose son was very sick. When he heard that Jesus had come from Judea to Galilee, he went and begged Jesus to come to Capernaum to heal his son, who was about to die.

Then Jesus told him, "Go back home. Your son will live!" And the man believed what Jesus said and started home. While the man was on his way, some of his servants met him with the news that his son was alive and well. He asked them when the boy had begun to get better, and they replied, "Yesterday afternoon at one o'clock his fever suddenly disappeared!" Then the father realized that that was the very time Jesus had told him, "Your son will live." And he and his entire household believed in Jesus.

John 4:46-47, 50-53
The Living Bible

Day 61

Lord of the Sabbath

The Lord's third sign was the healing of the invalid man at the pool of Bethesda. This man spoke no plea for help, had not an inking of faith, yet our compassionate Lord healed him and he could walk. The Pharisees were upset that this man picked up his mat on the Sabbath! Really? They were upset that their religious rules were broken. A miracle had just happened! What hard hearts! Lord, never let my heart get calloused or caught up in "proper" religion! Help me to reflect Your mercy and grace to others today because You have so lavishly shown it to me.

Have You Thought? Are any of my religious traditions too important to me?

His Answer:

Inside the city, near the Sheep Gate, was Bethesda Pool, with five covered platforms or porches surrounding it. Crowds of sick folks—lame, blind, or with paralyzed limbs—lay on the platforms (waiting for a certain movement of the water, for an angel of the Lord came from time to time and disturbed the water, and the first person to step down into it afterwards was healed).

Jesus told him, "Stand up, roll up your sleeping mat and go on home!" Instantly, the man was healed! He rolled up the mat and began walking! But it was on the Sabbath when this miracle was done. So the Jewish leaders objected. They said to the man who was cured, "You can't work on the Sabbath! It's illegal to carry that sleeping mat!"

John 5:2-4, 8-10
The Living Bible

Day 62

Beyond Hope

Thank You, Lord, for the second lesson You teach us from Your healing of the invalid man. He had been waiting for the miraculous stirring of the water for thirty-eight years. Maybe he had lost hope. Maybe he had gotten used to his life being like that? Could that be why Jesus asked him if he *wanted* to be healed? The Lord knew exactly how long it had been—and He didn't leave him there. Do you ever feel as if your difficulties have gone on so long that maybe God doesn't even care? He does. Lord, help us to be honest with You about every circumstance in our lives that might need Your healing change. Come, Lord.

Have You Thought? Is there any situation in my life that feels beyond the touch of Jesus?

His Answer:

One of the men lying there had been sick for thirty-eight years. When Jesus saw him and knew how long he had been ill, he asked him, "Would you like to get well?" "I can't," the sick man said, "for I have no one to help me into the pool at the movement of the water. While I am trying to get there, someone else always gets in ahead of me." Jesus told him, "Stand up, roll up your sleeping mat and go on home!"

John 5:5-8
The Living Bible

Day 63

God of My Future

The Lord's fourth sign was feeding the five thousand. The crowds had been listening to Jesus for a long time, and everyone was hungry and tired. Jesus cared that they needed food. The disciples just wanted them all to go home. They were stressing about how to feed everyone. But the five loaves and two fishes just keep coming until there are twelve baskets left over. I am just like the disciples—I worry about my provision in the future. Forgive me Lord, and help my unbelief. You have proven Your faithfulness time and time again in my life. I know You can still turn small lunches into banquets, Almighty One.

Have You Thought? Does considering my future cause me stress? Do I not think Jesus will be there for me?

His Answer:
"There's a little boy here who has five barley loaves and two fish. But that's a drop in the bucket for a crowd like this." Jesus said, "Make the people sit down." There was a nice carpet of green grass in this place. They sat down, about five thousand of them. Then Jesus took the bread and, having given thanks, gave it to those who were seated. He did the same with the fish. All ate as much as they wanted. When the people had eaten their fill, he said to his disciples, "Gather the leftovers so nothing is wasted." They went to work and filled twelve large baskets with leftovers from the five barley loaves. The people realized that God was at work among them in what Jesus had just done. They said, "This is the Prophet for sure, God's Prophet right here in Galilee!"

John 6:9-14
The Message

Day 64

God of the Storm

The Lord's fifth sign was walking on the water and calming the waves. All four Gospels tell this story, with so many lessons. One "aha" moment for me was that they were out on the lake by Jesus' command. He *told* them to go to Bethsaida and they obeyed. I often assume that I have missed God's will when I am in a storm. Not always. He may have a vital lesson to teach, so He allows it. Mark tells us that He saw them…in the pitch black, from many miles away! Are you in a storm right now, by Jesus' design? He sees and He will come to help. Allow Him in. He'll bring His calm to your wind and waves.

Have You Thought? What storm do I need Jesus to calm? Do I believe He can…and will?

His Answer:

Immediately after this Jesus instructed his disciples to get back into the boat and strike out across the lake to Bethsaida, where he would join them later. He himself would stay and tell the crowds good-bye and get them started home. Afterwards he went up into the hills to pray. During the night, as the disciples in their boat were out in the middle of the lake, and he was alone on land, he saw that they were in serious trouble, rowing hard and struggling against the wind and waves. About three o'clock in the morning he walked out to them on the water. He started past them, but when they saw something walking along beside them, they screamed in terror, thinking it was a ghost, for they all saw him. But he spoke to them at once. "It's all right," he said. "It is I! Don't be afraid." Then he climbed into the boat and the wind stopped! They just sat there, unable to take it in!

Mark 6:45-51
The Living Bible

Day 65

Unfathomable

When Jesus walked on the water it echoed Old Testament depictions of God. Psalm 107:24, 29-30 says, "Out at sea you saw GOD in action, saw his breathtaking ways with the ocean:…He quieted the wind down to a whisper, put a muzzle on all the big waves. And you were so glad when the storm died down, and he led you safely back to harbor." I wonder if the disciples ever reflected on this psalm when they remembered His rescue that day? Thank you, Lord, that in every type of chaos in our lives, You are not only the Rescue, but You are also the Safe Harbor, the Destination.

Have You Thought? Lord, let me stand in awe of You today.

His Answer:
> The next day the crowd that had stayed on the far shore saw that the disciples had taken the only boat, and they realized Jesus had not gone with them. Several boats from Tiberias landed near the place where the Lord had blessed the bread and the people had eaten. So when the crowd saw that neither Jesus nor his disciples were there, they got into the boats and went across to Capernaum to look for him. They found him on the other side of the lake and asked, "Rabbi, when did you get here?"

John 6:22-25
New Living Translation

Day 66

Humility

The Lord's sixth sign was giving sight to the man born blind. But, how He did it! Ugh! I would much rather be healed with something other than spit and mud! But think, what do spit and mud make? Clay. When God *formed* Adam out of dust as we read in Genesis, the word means the potter's shaping of a pot. What if Jesus was showing His deity by reshaping this man? What if he was originally shaped without sight in order to display Jesus' power? And on top of that, Jesus sends him to wash in the Pool of Siloam (which means "sent"). Jesus was the Sent One. Will I let God show my weaknesses in order to proclaim His glory? I pray my pride would not keep me from allowing that!

Have You Thought? Let me not miss Your healing because of my pride getting in the way.

His Answer:

>   As he was walking along, he saw a man blind from birth.

>   Then he spat on the ground and made mud from the spittle and smoothed the mud over the blind man's eyes, and told him, "Go and wash in the Pool of Siloam" (the word *Siloam* means "Sent"). So the man went where he was sent and washed and came back seeing!

>   John 9:1, 6-7
>   The Living Bible

Day 67

Circumstances

The most spectacular sign was the seventh—raising Lazarus from the dead! I have much to learn here: first, from Mary and Martha. They sent him a message saying, "Master, the one you love so very much is sick." As Jesus' mother did at the wedding in Cana, they simply presented Jesus with the problem. Mary, Jesus' mother, said, "No wine." Mary and Martha said, "Sick friend." No *suggestions* about *how* Jesus should respond—just simple faith He would do the very best thing. But when Jesus said He was going back to Judea, the disciples said, "Rabbi, you can't do that. The Jews are out to kill you, and you're going back?" Their actions were determined by circumstances. Lord, make me more like Mary and Martha and less like the disciples!

Have You Thought? Lord, let not my circumstances dictate my faith.

His Answer:

Do you remember Mary, who poured the costly perfume on Jesus' feet and wiped them with her hair? Well, her brother Lazarus, who lived in Bethany with Mary and her sister Martha, was sick. So the two sisters sent a message to Jesus telling him, "Sir, your good friend is very, very sick."

Finally, after the two days, he said to his disciples, "Let's go to Judea." But his disciples objected. "Master," they said, "only a few days ago the Jewish leaders in Judea were trying to kill you. Are you going there again?"

John 11:1-3, 7-8
The Living Bible

Day 68

On Purpose

Two miracles of Jesus surpass any of the seven singled out by John: Jesus' incarnation and His resurrection. These miracles begin and end John's Gospel. First it was the Divine becoming dependent, then the Almighty One becoming accessible. He did it on purpose, for us. Because God knew the only way to save us was to become one of us. He didn't just come; He came to die. The second miracle was that He didn't stay in that grave—He rose again. Because He was not only man, He was God. So, what do you say to this Jesus? He wants you to call Him "My Lord, and my God" as Thomas did.

Have You Thought? Who is Jesus to me? Lord? God?

His Answer:

So the Word became human and made his home among us. He was full of unfailing love and faithfulness. And we have seen his glory, the glory of the Father's one and only Son.

John 1:14
New Living Translation

Eight days later, his disciples were again in the room. This time Thomas was with them. Jesus came through the locked doors, stood among them, and said, "Peace to you." Then he focused his attention on Thomas. "Take your finger and examine my hands. Take your hand and stick it in my side. Don't be unbelieving. Believe." Thomas said, "My Master! My God!"

John 20:26-28
The Message

Day 69

Insiders

The Gospel of John finishes with the sweetest ending—the restoration of Peter. He had betrayed his Friend; turned his back on his Lord. Surely, he relived those three "I-don't-know-Him" statements a million times. But Jesus wanted him to move past that night, to live an unburdened life for Him. Jesus met one-on-one with Peter. "He was seen by Cephas [Peter], then by the twelve," 1 Corinthians 15:5 (NKJV) says. No details are given, but it must have been a tender reunion. There was forgiveness, freeing and empowering. Do you know this reality in your life? We all need it at some point. This is what Jesus offers.

Have You Thought? Be amazed by Jesus' forgiveness today.

His Answer:

> Entering into this fullness is not something you figure out or achieve. It's not a matter of being circumcised or keeping a long list of laws. No, you're already in—insiders—not through some secretive initiation rite but rather through what Christ has already gone through for you, destroying the power of sin.

> When you were stuck in your old sin-dead life, you were incapable of responding to God. God brought you alive—right along with Christ! Think of it! All sins forgiven, the slate wiped clean, that old arrest warrant canceled and nailed to Christ's cross.

Colossians 2:11, 13-14
The Message

Day 70

Celebration

Thank You, Lord, for the first four books of the New Testament, the Gospels. Gospel really means "celebration." These wonderful books are by God's design, different on purpose, each written from a different perspective for a different audience. What if our parents, spouse, children and friends described us? Their views would each be different, but they would all be correct. Together, the snapshots give the big picture of who we are. Join me and see how the Gospel writers teach us of this precious, multifaceted, salvation-for-all Jesus, and celebrate who He is to each of us!

Have You Thought? Lord, where my initial joy of knowing You is waning, revive me.

His Answer:
> Celebrate God all day, every day. I mean, revel in him! Make it as clear as you can to all you meet that you're on their side, working with them and not against them.
>
> Receive and experience the amazing grace of the Master, Jesus Christ, deep, deep within yourselves.

Philippians 4:4-5, 23
The Message

Day 71

Included

Matthew was a disciple of Jesus and the writer of the first celebration Gospel. A tax collector whose name was once Levi, the Jews considered him a traitor because he had sold out to Rome for his own gain. Jesus changed his name to Matthew, which means, "gift of God." God's gift to him? Once banned from the temple, he became friends with the God of that temple! Not surprisingly, mercy stories fill his Gospel. Just like Matthew, I praise You, Lord, for those places where I feel included instead of being an outcast because of Your grace to me. Anyone with me?

Have You Thought? Lord, let Your welcoming love overwhelm me.

His Answer:
> God picked you out as his from the very start. Think of it: included in God's original plan of salvation by the bond of faith in the living truth. This is the life of the Spirit he invited you to…in which you get in on the glory of our Master, Jesus Christ.
>
> 2 Thessalonians 2:13-14
> The Message

Day 72

For Everyone

The Gospel written by Matthew shows Jesus as the promised King and Messiah. As a Jew, Matthew wrote to the Jews, and his favorite word was "fulfilled." He began his claims about Jesus with a genealogy in which he calls Jesus the "Son of David." Matthew focused on what Jesus *said*, and he incorporated five of His teachings in blocks within his Gospel. He welcomed the Gentiles by including stories of the wise men, the Roman centurion and others. Matthew understood that this Messiah was for everyone. In the story of my life, Lord, help me to also proclaim that truth!

Have You Thought? Lord, give me Your heart for others.

His Answer:
> Your new life, which is your real life—even though invisible to spectators—is with Christ in God. He is your life.
>
> Now you're dressed in a new wardrobe. Every item in your new way of life is custom-made by the Creator, with his label on it. Words like Jewish and non-Jewish, religious and irreligious, insider and outsider, uncivilized and uncouth, slave and free, mean nothing. From now on everyone is defined by Christ, everyone is included in Christ.
>
> Colossians 3:3, 10-11
> The Message

Day 73

Good News

The Gospel writer Mark, was not a disciple of Jesus, but a disciple of Peter. He was possibly the young man in the linen cloth who followed Jesus after His arrest (Mark 14:51). He was the son of Mary, at whose home Peter announced his miraculous prison escape (Acts 12:12). He was the cousin of Barnabas, and his name was really John Mark. In his short, fast-paced Gospel, Mark used his favorite word, "immediately," forty times. His audience was the church in Rome, under persecution by Nero. Peter supervised his writing. His urgent message was: God is here and He is on our side! Thank you, Jesus, for that truth in each of our lives today and every day! What a promise!

Have You Thought? Does the knowledge that God is with me even on my toughest days make a difference in my life?

His Answer:

When I get really afraid I come to you in trust. I'm proud to praise God; fearless now, I trust in God. What can mere mortals do?

You've kept track of my every toss and turn through the sleepless nights, each tear entered in your ledger, each ache written in your book. If my enemies run away, turn tail when I yell at them, then I'll know that God is on my side. I'm proud to praise God, proud to praise GOD.

Psalms 56:3-4, 8-10
The Message

Day 74

Real

I'm grateful that the Gospel of Mark portrays Jesus as the Suffering Servant. There are no genealogies to begin this Gospel, as in Matthew. Why? No one cares about the ancestry of a servant! Mark focuses on what Jesus *did*. He loves the number three (maybe because of the Trinity?) and emphasizes Jesus' *actions* and *achievements*, revealing His *authority*. He shows Him as Savior, servant and sacrifice, with power over disease, demons and death. Mark is realistic about the faults and failings of the disciples, which shows us following Jesus does not demand perfection. What an encouragement that is to each of us now! Lord, make me more like Mark—honest and open about my failings and never ho-hum about You!

Have You Thought? Lord, let me never be ho-hum about You.

His Answer:

Companions as we are in this work with you, we beg you, please don't squander one bit of this marvelous life God has given us.

Our work as God's servants gets validated—or not—in the details. People are watching us as we stay at our post, alertly, unswervingly… in hard times, tough times, bad times;

when we're telling the truth, and when God's showing his power; when we're doing our best setting things right, when we're praised, and when we're blamed.

2 Corinthians 6:1, 4, 7-8
The Message

Day 75

Set Right

Thank God for Luke, "the beloved physician" who never knew Jesus, was not even a Jew, yet chose to follow Him (see Col. 4:14). Luke was probably a convert from Paul's first missionary journey to Antioch. He was a member of the upper class, but had a tender heart for the oppressed. He delves into the feelings of Jesus, his disciples, Jesus' mother and Elizabeth, the mother of John the Baptist. His Gospel is the only one with a sequel, the book of Acts, which focuses on the spread of Jesus' Gospel of grace. Like Luke, make me quick to show grace to those who cross my path today, Lord.

Have You Thought? Lord, set me right today and let me shout Your praise.

His Answer:

> By entering through faith into what God has always wanted to do for us—set us right with him, make us fit for him—we have it all together with God because of our Master Jesus. And that's not all. We throw open our doors to God and discover at the same moment that he has already thrown open his door to us. We find ourselves standing where we always hoped we might stand—out in the wide open spaces of God's grace and glory, standing tall and shouting our praise.

Romans 5:1-2
The Message

Day 76

Rejoice!

Thank You, Lord, for the Gospel of Luke, which embraces the least, the lost and the lowest. Where Matthew loved the word "fulfilled," and Mark "immediately," Luke's word was "rejoice." As a Greek, Luke portrayed Jesus as the Perfect Man…the man before the Fall in the Garden. He focuses on what Jesus *felt*, showing Jesus' everyday life: time fishing, entertaining, and cooking. His Gospel is actually a letter to a friend, Theophilus, encouraging him to follow Jesus. The impact of this letter is immeasurable, causing many to rejoice. Lord, give us hearts like Luke, always eager to share Your joy.

Have You Thought? Fill me up with Your joy and peace, Lord.

His Answer:

So, reach out and welcome one another to God's glory. Jesus did it, now you do it! Jesus, staying true to God's purposes, reached out in a special way to the Jewish insiders so that the old ancestral promises would come true for them. As a result, the non-Jewish outsiders have been able to experience mercy and to show appreciation to God. Just think of all the Scriptures that will come true in what we do!

Oh! May the God of green hope fill you up with joy, fill you up with peace, so that your believing lives, filled with the life-giving energy of the Holy Spirit, will brim over with hope!

Romans 15:7-9, 13
The Message

Day 77

Transformed

Thank You, Lord, for John, "the disciple whom You loved." First a disciple of John the Baptist, Jesus called him and his brother, James, "the sons of thunder." As a younger man, his hot-headed temper may have damaged some of his relationships. He obviously cherished the fact that Jesus loved him anyway, and what a transformation Jesus made in his life! John was known in his later years as the disciple of love. He wrote four other books, and nurtured the church at Ephesus. Lord, let Your love touch me as deeply as it did John.

Have You Thought? Lord, may Your loving touch on my life transform me.

His Answer:

I've loved you the way my Father has loved me. Make yourselves at home in my love. If you keep my commands, you'll remain intimately at home in my love. That's what I've done—kept my Father's commands and made myself at home in his love.

John 15:9-10
The Living Bible

Day 78

Categories

The Gospel of John was written for the largest audience—the world! John's favorite word was "believe," which he used over ninety-nine times. He didn't spend time on historical events. No nativity scenes or stories of Jesus' youth. John dealt with spiritual realities. He portrayed Jesus as the Son of God, with his focus on who Jesus *is*. John separated his Gospel into two portions: the first half written to those who don't believe, and the last half to those who do. How sobering to think that God has those same two categories when He looks at us and determines our eternity.

Have You Thought? Keep eternity a reality to me, Lord.

His Answer:
> Answer this question: Does the God who lavishly provides you with his own presence, his Holy Spirit, working things in your lives you could never do for yourselves, does he do these things because of your strenuous moral striving or because you trust him to do them in you? Don't these things happen among you just as they happened with Abraham? He believed God, and that act of belief was turned into a life that was right with God.
>
> Galatians 3:5-6
> The Message

Day 79

Chosen

Today I'm thankful for the baptism of Jesus. He stood in line to be baptized by John the Baptist *for* us, *as* us. All of our sins would soon be placed on His head. His Father spoke words of favor to Him and gave Him a sign of His Spirit's filling—the dove. A preacher described it like this: God said, "I *love* You, let's do stuff together." He longs to say that to each of us. Those words that began Jesus' ministry are available for our daily-life ministry too. He is waiting to fill us and walk with us. Lord, I need You to change me from the inside out, mark me with Your love and walk with me through my life today!

Have You Thought? Contemplate being chosen and marked as God's.

His Answer:
This messenger was John the Baptist.

Here is a sample of his preaching: "Someone is coming soon who is far greater than I am, so much greater that I am not even worthy to be his slave. I baptize you with water but he will baptize you with God's Holy Spirit!" Then one day Jesus came from Nazareth in Galilee, and was baptized by John there in the Jordan River. The moment Jesus came up out of the water, he saw the heavens open and the Holy Spirit in the form of a dove descending on him, and a voice from heaven said, "You are my beloved Son; you are my Delight."

Mark 1:4, 7-11
The Living Bible

Day 80

Mighty Warrior

Thank You, Lord, for Your temptations and the lesson You taught us through them. You showed us how to fight temptation with the Word of God. Adam had failed in his test, but You won. You give us the power to defeat Satan just as You did. You countered the prince of darkness and his lies with the powerful truth of the Bible. Paul calls the Word of God the Sword of the Spirit, and You used it as a Mighty Warrior! We have to know this Word in order to access its power. Help me to spend quiet time in that "steady stream of words from God's mouth" so that I am not defenseless when a test comes. The weapons are at my disposal, so I need not fear. I just need to be prepared!

Have You Thought? Do I know Your Word well enough to defeat Satan and his lies?

His Answer:
> Then Jesus was led out into the wilderness by the Holy Spirit, to be tempted there by Satan. For forty days and forty nights he ate nothing and became very hungry. Then Satan tempted him to get food by changing stones into loaves of bread. "It will prove you are the Son of God," he said. But Jesus told him, "No! For the Scriptures tell us that bread won't feed men's souls: obedience to every word of God is what we need." Then Satan took him to Jerusalem to the roof of the Temple.
>
> "Get out of here, Satan," Jesus told him. "The Scriptures say, 'Worship only the Lord God. Obey only him.'" Then Satan went away, and angels came and cared for Jesus.

> Matthew 4:1-5, 10-11
> The Living Bible

Day 81

Paid in Full

Thank You, Lord, for the joy of receiving Your forgiveness. I can't even begin to comprehend its vastness in the Matthew 18 parable. The servant owed the king the equivalent of sixty million days' wages! In other words, the debt was totally impossible to repay. Lord, I never want to underestimate how much I once owed You. But I never want to be tormented by Satan about that debt either, for it was paid in full on the Cross. Psalm 103:12 says that Jesus separated my sins from me "as far as sunrise is from sunset" (MSG). He will continue to cover my guilt and shame until He brings me Home where sin can never harass me any more. Let the bliss of that freedom and bright future wash over my life today just as You color the sky at dawn and dusk.

Have You Thought? Forgive me for digging up past sins, long forgotten by You.

His Answer:

> This story will show you what the kingdom of heaven is like: One day a king decided to call in his officials and ask them to give an account of what they owed him. As he was doing this, one official was brought in who owed him fifty million silver coins. But he didn't have any money to pay what he owed. The king ordered him to be sold, along with his wife and children and all he owned, in order to pay the debt. The official got down on his knees and began begging, "Have pity on me, and I will pay you every cent I owe!" The king felt sorry for him and let him go free. He even told the official that he did not have to pay back the money.

Matthew 18:23-27
Contemporary English Version

Day 82

Generosity

Thank You, Lord, for the joy of giving forgiveness to others. You who gave me my freedom from debt, guilt and shame expect me to return the favor to others. You don't see it as a burden, but rather, a privilege, because I am acting as You would. Somehow I think of it as something I *have* to do, when you think it is something I *get* to do. The King expects his kindness, mercy and forgiveness to change me, so the new me can give that same mercy to others. He demands that I offer to others what I have so freely received from Him. I want to walk in that God-sent generosity today.

Have You Thought? Change my heart with Your extravagant love, Lord.

His Answer:

As the official was leaving, he happened to meet another official, who owed him a hundred silver coins. So he grabbed the man by the throat. He started choking him and said, "Pay me what you owe!" The man got down on his knees and began begging, "Have pity on me, and I will pay you back." But the first official refused to have pity. Instead, he went and had the other official put in jail until he could pay what he owed. When some other officials found out what had happened, they felt sorry for the man who had been put in jail. Then they told the king what had happened. The king called the first official back in and said, "You're an evil man! When you begged for mercy, I said you did not have to pay back a cent. Don't you think you should show pity to someone else, as I did to you?" The king was so angry that he ordered the official to be tortured until he could pay back everything he owed. That is how my Father in heaven will treat you, if you don't forgive each of my followers with all your heart.

Matthew 18:28-35
Contemporary English Version

Day 83

Faithful

Thank You, Lord, that You designed each of us with different passions and giftings—ones You mean for us to use for You! The world judges our success based on our productivity. You, on the other hand, review our performance by our faithfulness. Whether You gave us much or little, did we use it for You? Did we glorify Your Name with our talents and aptitudes? The man with the $5,000 capability and the one with only a strength worth $2,000 both earned the very same praise from the master. Lord, make me faithful with what You have given me, whether I consider it big or small. Use me, Lord.

Have You Thought? Lord, in small and large callings, make me faithful.

His Answer:

Again, the Kingdom of Heaven can be illustrated by the story of a man going into another country, who called together his servants and loaned them money to invest for him while he was gone. He gave $5,000 to one, $2,000 to another, and $1,000 to the last—dividing it in proportion to their abilities—and then left on his trip.

The man to whom he had entrusted the $5,000 brought him $10,000. His master praised him for good work. "You have been faithful in handling this small amount," he told him, "so now I will give you many more responsibilities. Begin the joyous tasks I have assigned to you." Next came the man who had received the $2,000, with the report, "Sir, you gave me $2,000 to use, and I have doubled it." "Good work," his master said. "You are a good and faithful servant. You have been faithful over this small amount, so now I will give you much more."

Matthew 25:14-15, 20-23
The Living Bible

Day 84

Priorities

Thank You, Lord, for the unparalleled value and power of spending time with You. You taught us by showing us Your prayer life. It was successful because it was planned, private and prolonged. You got up early enough, got far away enough, and stayed at it long enough. Sometimes my prayers treat You more like a drive-through: I make my order and drive away. Ugh! The time of day matters little; my faithfulness to take that time is what matters. You long to order my days, for my good, for the good of others, and for Your glory. Make this my highest priority, Lord. Order my days.

Have You Thought? Lord, I want You to be higher on my to-do list.

His Answer:
> Before daybreak the next morning, Jesus got up and went out to an isolated place to pray. Later, Simon and the others went out to find him. When they found him, they said, "Everyone is looking for you."

Mark 1:35-37
New Living Translation

Day 85

Undeterred

Thank You, Lord, for the lessons we learn from Zaccheus, the short of stature tax collector who wanted to see Jesus. He was willing to swallow his pride and act like a child so he climbed a tree to see the Savior. He also ignored the mean catcalls from the Jews around him. I want to be like Zaccheus but You need to do some work on me. I'm not so quick to throw off my pride, and I allow others' opinions to intimidate me. You loved his heartfelt determination, and You rewarded it. Make me focused on Your opinion only, Lord, so regardless of the obstacles or objections, I press on to see You.

Have You Thought? Lord, let Your opinion matter most to me.

His Answer:

> As Jesus was passing through Jericho, a man named Zacchaeus, one of the most influential Jews in the Roman tax-collecting business (and, of course, a very rich man), tried to get a look at Jesus, but he was too short to see over the crowds. So he ran ahead and climbed into a sycamore tree beside the road, to watch from there. When Jesus came by, he looked up at Zacchaeus and called him by name! "Zacchaeus!" he said. "Quick! Come down! For I am going to be a guest in your home today!"

> But the crowds were displeased. "He has gone to be the guest of a notorious sinner," they grumbled.

> Jesus told him, "This shows that salvation has come to this home today. This man was one of the lost sons of Abraham, and I, the Messiah, have come to search for and to save such souls as his."

> Luke 19:1-5, 7, 9-10
> The Living Bible

Day 86

A Step Ahead

Thank You, Lord, for Your lessons about hard times.
You are always a step ahead of us as we walk through
them. On the road to Jerusalem, Jesus knew He would become
the Sacrifice, endure separation from His Father
and horrible suffering. The disciples followed behind Him,
feeling puzzled and afraid. Jesus also goes ahead of us to those
places where we anticipate sacrifice, separation or suffering…
our "Jerusalem Roads." The fear and dread can drive us crazy,
but what a comfort to know that Jesus has already been there.
He will bring His perfect will and way for our future.

Have You Thought? How comforting to know that nothing
about my life surprises You.

His Answer:
> Back on the road, they set out for Jerusalem. Jesus had
> a head start on them, and they were following, puzzled
> and not just a little afraid. He took the Twelve and
> began again to go over what to expect next: "Listen to
> me carefully. We're on our way up to Jerusalem. When
> we get there, the Son of Man will be betrayed to the
> religious leaders and scholars. They will sentence him to
> death. Then they will hand him over to the Romans, who
> will mock and spit on him, give him the third degree, and
> kill him. After three days he will rise alive."

Mark 10:32-34
The Message

Day 87

Hold On!

Thank You, Lord, that You are still way ahead of us when we are actually in the midst of hard times, feeling either sacrifice, suffering or separation. You bring Your good in the midst of evil and loss. When there are more questions than answers, or when the answers are full of gloom, You still make Your presence plain. You send comfort and encouragement in the smallest details of our story to assure us You are still in control, working things out for the best for us, Your beloved children. Lord, wherever we are in the midst of a battle in this broken world, wherever we are feeling abandoned, lost or beyond Your help, show up with Your grace to remind us that You have won the victory.

Have You Thought? Remind me again that You are the God of details. Reveal Your grace to me today.

His Answer:

Early on Sunday morning, as the new day was dawning, Mary Magdalene and the other Mary went out to the tomb.

And as they were running, suddenly Jesus was there in front of them! "Good morning!" he said. And they fell to the ground before him, holding his feet and worshiping him. Then Jesus said to them, "Don't be frightened! Go tell my brothers to leave at once for Galilee, to meet me there."

Matthew 28:1, 9-10
The Living Bible

Day 88

Every Chapter

Thank You, Lord, for Your glorious end to the Story. Some days when the trials of this life and the harassment of the devil seem overwhelming, we need to hear this encouragement. In 1 Peter 5:10 (NKJV), Peter prays that the "God of all grace" will "perfect, establish, strengthen, and settle us." He promises to mend us where we were once broken, strengthen us where we are worn out from the battle, stabilize or establish us with the certainty that He is with us, and settle us. He gives us a firm foundation so we can be steadfast and unmovable through every chapter of our own life's story. Thank you, Jesus, that You are not only the Author of our stories, but the Finisher, too. Amen!

Have You Thought? Some seasons of life are tough, Lord. Be my Firm Foundation.

His Answer:

> So keep a firm grip on the faith. The suffering won't last forever. It won't be long before this generous God who has great plans for us in Christ—eternal and glorious plans they are!—will have you put together and on your feet for good. He gets the last word; yes, he does."

> 1 Peter 5:9-11
> The Message

Day 89

Real and Eternal Life

Thank you, Lord, for making the entrance requirement to Heaven so plain and simple. Maybe it seems too good to be true to many, and unnecessary to others. I can't imagine anyone rejecting this message of Life and Redemption, because doing so means choosing to be rejected by God. So all I can do is thank You, God, for Your generosity. For, by accepting Jesus, I am accepted by You, His Father. Let me both cherish and share this unsurpassed Gift with those who have no knowledge of its worth. It brings not only comfort and counsel in this world, but "real and eternal life" in the next.

Have You Thought? Thank You for obeying…all the way to the Cross.

His Answer:
> "I will not judge those who hear me but don't obey me, for I have come to save the world and not to judge it. But all who reject me and my message will be judged on the day of judgment by the truth I have spoken. I don't speak on my own authority. The Father who sent me has commanded me what to say and how to say it. And I know his commands lead to eternal life; so I say whatever the Father tells me to say."

John 12:47-50
The Living Bible

Day 90

Head to Toe

Thank You, Lord, for the impulsiveness of Peter and Your tender correction when he was wrong. You do the same thing for us! At the Last Supper, when You were washing the feet of the disciples, Peter first refused, but then said to wash him all over. You explain our "washing," or forgiveness, so clearly. There are two parts to this cleansing. First, there is the all-over bathing (Greek word, *louo*), which You did once and for all with Your Blood. Then, there is the foot washing from the dirt of the world (Greek word, *nipto*). Lord, thank You for both washings. Make me clean and fresh again today.

Have You Thought? Your ever-flowing fountain never runs dry. Hallelujah!

His Answer:

> So he got up from the supper table, took off his robe, wrapped a towel around his loins,[a] poured water into a basin, and began to wash the disciples' feet and to wipe them with the towel he had around him. When he came to Simon Peter, Peter said to him, "Master, you shouldn't be washing our feet like this!"

> "No," Peter protested, "you shall never wash my feet!" "But if I don't, you can't be my partner," Jesus replied. Simon Peter exclaimed, "Then wash my hands and head as well—not just my feet!" Jesus replied, "One who has bathed all over needs only to have his feet washed to be entirely clean. Now you are clean—but that isn't true of everyone here."

John 13:4-6, 8-10
The Living Bible

Day 91

What If?

Thank You, Lord, that You already know my future. None of it surprises You. So why do I wander down the *what-if* haunted trail so often and end up running scared? When I catch my breath, I remember You are the same yesterday, today and forever. In all my days to come You will still be there, hovering as close as I will allow, ready to guide, empower and if needed, redirect. My tomorrows are distant yesterdays in Your mind. They were specifically conceived and constructed long ago for my ultimate wellbeing by my Divine Designer. This realization calms my heart every time.

Have You Thought? No more running scared, Lord. You've calmed my heart again.

His Answer:

You're God, and on the throne for good, your rule makes everything right.

Since God assured us, "I'll never let you down, never walk off and leave you," we can boldly quote, "God is there, ready to help; I'm fearless no matter what. Who or what can get to me?"

Hebrews 1:18, 13:6
The Message

Day 92

Promise Keeper

Thank You, Lord, You are a Promise Keeper! I am a promise maker, but the follow through often remains undone. I realize that at times I have cast You in that same bad light, but that is a lie. You really are faithful to your Word. You can't be otherwise because Your pledges flow from your character. They are set in stone from before time even began. Open my eyes to see Your faithfulness in a new way. Encourage me in some very tangible way to assure me of Your steadfast care. Let me walk expectantly today because of who You have always been and will remain forever.

Have You Thought? Are there any places where I am not anticipating God's faithfulness?

His Answer:
I will keep on obeying your instructions forever and ever.

I honor and love your commands. I meditate on your decrees. Remember your promise to me; it is my only hope. Your promise revives me; it comforts me in all my troubles.

You have done many good things for me, Lord, just as you promised.

Psalms 119:44, 48-50, 65
New Living Translation

Day 93

Attitude Adjustment

Thank You, Lord, Your Presence changes my attitude. When all seems chaotic and noisy in my life, the atmosphere changes if I just get away with You for a little while. You remind me again Who You are and that I am Yours. Like warm sunshine, You bathe me in Your love. Your promises wash over me and soothe my tangled jumble of emotions. *"You will never leave me...Your plans for me give me a future and a hope...No one can snatch me out of Your hand."* Your quiet voice and Your promises silence the clatter of my circumstances. You calm me down like no other, and I am so grateful.

Have You Thought? Lord, help me to give You all the cluttered, chaotic places in my life.

His Answer:
> And this is the reason: God lives forever and is holy. He is high and lifted up. He says, "I live in a high and holy place, but I also live with people who are sad and humble. I give new life to those who are humble and to those whose hearts are broken.
>
> I have seen what they have done, but I will heal them. I will guide them and comfort them and those who felt sad for them. They will all praise me. I will give peace, real peace, to those far and near, and I will heal them," says the Lord.

Isaiah 57:15, 18-19
New Century Version

Day 94

Re-twisted Thorns

Lord, You can transform anything. You re-twisted the circle of thorns on Your brow into a crown of glory. You reformed a brash fisherman named Peter into the charismatic leader of Your Church. With just a light and a voice from Heaven, you redesigned Paul from a martyr-maker into the preeminent manuscript writer of the New Testament. With one word You brought the dead to life, changed five loaves into a mass feeding, and reduced huge squalls on the lake into a glassy sea. So why do I think for one moment that You can't change my situation? Forgive me, Lord.

Have You Thought? How amazing that You never stop working out Your good plans for me.

His Answer:
> Oh, blessed be GOD! He didn't go off and leave us. He didn't abandon us defenseless, helpless as a rabbit in a pack of snarling dogs. We've flown free from their fangs, free of their traps, free as a bird. GOD's strong name is our help, the same GOD who made heaven and earth.

Psalms 124:6-8
The Message

Day 95

God's Friend

Thank You, Lord, that the sign on the door of Your throne room always says "welcome." We have fallen for the lie that either God doesn't care about us, or even worse, that He is angry with us, so we feel distant from Him. The truth is He cares passionately about everything in our lives, and He is longing for us to come and pour out our hearts to Him. He is not *mad* at us…He is madly *in love* with us! So today, come! Begin to talk to your Father as if He is your best friend. Then, day by day, those conversations will feel a little more comfortable and safe. Begin today!

Have You Thought? Do I really believe God is my Friend?

His Answer:
> Become friends with God; he's already a friend with you. How? you ask. In Christ. God put the wrong on him who never did anything wrong, so we could be put right with God.

> "I'll be their God and they'll be my people…I'll be a Father to you; you'll be sons and daughters to me."

> 2 Corinthians 5:20-21; 2 Corinthians 6:16, 18
> The Message

Day 96

Honor and Help

*Thank You, Lord, for walking me through my last crisi*s. You did things I could never have imagined. How awesome You are! Well, I'm in a new predicament now. Because of Your past faithfulness, I know that I can trust You with this problem too. Show me Your earth-shaking power again, wonder-working God. I know You never change. So, until I see Your hand at work on my behalf, I will gratefully sing Your praises, and tell everyone of the promises You have already kept. You are my Shelter in the storm; my Rock and my Fortress; and You are worthy to be praised.

Have You Thought? Thank You for Your past faithfulness to me. I will never stop praising You.

His Answer:
> "Spread for me a banquet of praise, serve High God a feast of kept promises, and call for help when you're in trouble—I'll help you, and you'll honor me."

> "It's the praising life that honors me. As soon as you set your feet on the Way, I'll show you my salvation."

Psalms 50:14-15, 23
The Message

Day 97

Squeaky Clean

Thank You, Lord, You are my Ever-Flowing Fountain. You wait at Your cleansing stream to free me from the guilt of my newest stains. You understand how quickly my heart and my mind can end up in a sin mud puddle. With an I-wish-I-hadn't-said-that remark, or a dagger-through-your-heart thought, I am grimy again. But without a moment's hesitation, You offer to make me squeaky clean. Such compassion and grace! Not one word of "This is your last chance," or "You did that *again*?" Just Your total forgiveness! Did I tell You how much that means to me, Lord?

Have You Thought? Where do I need a fresh start?

His Answer:

Generous in love—God give grace! Huge in mercy—wipe out my bad record.

Soak me in your laundry and I'll come out clean, scrub me and I'll have a snow-white-life.

God, make a fresh start in me, shape a Genesis week from the chaos of my life.

Psalms 51:1, 7, 10
The Message

Day 98

God-Gifts

Thank You, Lord, the Ultimate Gift Giver. Daily You provide an endless succession of favors for me, piled high and spilling over. Not generic one-size-fits-all gifts either. Individually tailored, lovingly detailed, perfect-fit presents. Some days I walk right by them unaware because I am so caught up in the chaos of the day. How sad when You send me tokens of Your love to make me smile and I am clueless. But, when I do recognize these tender remembrances, my heart is lifted and my spirit soars. Open my eyes to recognize Your God-gifts for me today, Lord. And I will say, "Thank You!"

Have You Thought? Let me see Your blessings today. I thank You for them, Lord.

His Answer:
> It is wonderful to be grateful and to sing your praises, Lord Most High! It is wonderful each morning to tell about your love and at night to announce how faithful you are.

Psalms 92:1-2
Contemporary English Version

Day 99

Inexplicable Love

Thank You, Lord, Your love for us overrode Your love for your Son. As a parent, I can't fully grasp the depth of that. I don't love anyone enough to sacrifice one of my children. And if I were God, I certainly wouldn't give up my Child for a rebellious, sneering bunch of God-haters! But Your love for us is inexplicable. Above all, You wanted us to be Your friends, not Your enemies, so You were willing to pay the deepest price for that friendship. Let the joy of the Cross—that costly companionship purchased for us—wash over us. Deepen our love for You, our Father, Redeemer, Savior and Friend.

Have You Thought? For me. You did it for me.

His Answer:
> But God put his love on the line for us by offering his Son in sacrificial death while we were of no use whatever to him…there is no longer a question of being at odds with God in any way.

> Now that we have actually received this amazing friendship with God…we sing and shout our praises to God through Jesus, the Messiah!

> Romans 5:8-9, 11
> The Message

Day 100

Permanent

Thank You, Lord, Your Word never changes. The facts about my life can be altered in an instant, because nothing in this world is permanent. But, when all else is falling apart or proving itself false, You remain. Your promises, your Word, your character remain. So I choose to build my life and base my hope on You, for You are eternal and Your Word is trustworthy. I place my life in Your safekeeping, Faithful One. Hold me close in your arms, and nourish me with Your promises so that even when the course gets rocky, my feet won't slip as I follow Your perfectly planned paths.

Have You Thought? Is my life and my hope based on You, Lord, or on temporary world things?

His Answer:
> Forever, O LORD, your word stands firm in heaven. Your faithfulness extends to every generation, as enduring as the earth you created.

> If your law hadn't sustained me with joy, I would have died in my misery. I will never forget your commandments, for you have used them to restore my joy and health.

> Remember your promise to me, for it is my only hope.

Psalms 119:89-90, 92-93, 49
New Living Translation

Day 101

One

Lord, You can remove the blinders from our eyes and give us new sight. You, who are the Healer of the Breach, can mend whatever has previously been shattered, discarded or forgotten. You have done this in my own life. When our feelings get hurt and walls go up, relationships get strained. Friendships are damaged, possibly even discarded, until You change hearts and bring harmony. Reconciling God, continue to bring unity where there is discord. I praise You that You alone can create renewed, restored relationships out of divided, detached ones.

Have You Thought? Lord, are there any relationships in my life that need your healing touch?

His Answer:
"I want all of them to be one with each other, just as I am one with you and you are one with me. I also want them to be one with us. Then the people of this world will believe that you sent me."

John 17:21
Contemporary English Version

Day 102

He Clothed Himself

Thank You, Lord, our Warrior! Satan relentlessly battles for our hearts, our minds and our very lives. But You planned our salvation from before time. You saw evil coming, and no one capable of rectifying the situation, and it broke Your heart. So, you planned a Warrior-Redeemer, Your only Son. He alone was righteous enough to bring salvation. He gladly dressed Himself for sacrifice and battle. He still hears; He still saves. He brings His salvation to us and for us, even now. Lord, show us Your passionate heart for our rescue from all that wars against us.

Have You Thought? How amazing to think Almighty God fights for me.

His Answer:

Listen now! The Lord isn't too weak to save you. And he isn't getting deaf! He can hear you when you call!

Yes, truth is gone, and anyone who tries a better life is soon attacked. The Lord saw all the evil and was displeased to find no steps taken against sin. He saw no one was helping you and wondered that no one intervened. Therefore he himself stepped in to save you through his mighty power and justice. He put on righteousness as armor and the helmet of salvation on his head. He clothed himself with robes of vengeance and of godly fury.

Isaiah 59:1, 15-17
The Living Bible

Day 103

Forever Purposes

Thank You, Lord, that You want to include us in Your holy plans. You are eager for us to participate in Your forever-purposes. You long for us to experience the joy You feel in doing eternal things. They may be small, seemingly insignificant actions done one-on-one, but they point to You and show Your everlasting heart of love. Give us hands outstretched to those in need and soft words of encouragement to lift up a burdened soul. By doing so we have embraced and entered into the work of God. Include us in Your supernatural solace today, Lord. Lift up our souls as we refresh others.

Have You Thought? Lord, make me an instrument of Your peace today.

His Answer:
> But you are the ones chosen by God, chosen for the high calling of priestly work, chosen to be a holy people, God's instruments to do his work and speak out for him, to tell others of the night-and-day difference he made for you—from nothing to something, from rejected to accepted.
>
> Then they'll be won over to God's side and be there to join in the celebration when he arrives.

1 Peter 2:9-10, 12
The Message

Day 104

Darkness Dispelled

Thank You, Lord, you are the Light of the world. You are the Bearer of Brightness wherever we are experiencing darkness, not only for the world, but in each of our lives. The gloom of every sin, sickness, or sadness that gets us down just provides us another invitation to ask God's radiance to dispel the darkness we are feeling. Where His Light appears, there is no darkness. So today, Lord, we ask for Your illuminating Presence in the dark details of our day. From Your vantage point, all darkness is light. So come, Lord Jesus, shine in our darkness, and bring Your light and Your salvation.

Have You Thought? Bring Your Light into my life today, Jesus.

His Answer:
> For God, who said, "Let there be light in the darkness," has made this light shine in our hearts so we could know the glory of God that is seen in the face of Jesus Christ.

2 Corinthians 4:6
New Living Translation

> Jesus spoke to the people once more and said, "I am the light of the world. If you follow me, you won't have to walk in darkness, because you will have the light that leads to life."

John 8:12
New Living Translation

Day 105

A New Name

Thank You, Lord, for the new names You give us when we claim Your Name. None of those old labels apply any longer. What a relief! The nicknames that always caused pain or those critical descriptions which we even possibly embraced—*gone*! No longer *wounded* or *rejected*. *Left out*? Not any more! *Afraid*? No way. "I can do all things through Christ who strengthens me." It is high time we walk away from those old stale monikers and welcome in our glorious God-given names: *Overcomer, Chosen, Beloved, Redeemed, Forgiven*. Such a great salvation, Lord!

Have You Thought? Do I live as one redefined by You, Lord?

His Answer:
> You'll get a brand-new name straight from the mouth of God. You'll be a stunning crown in the palm of God's hand, a jeweled gold cup held high in the hand of your God. No more will anyone call you Rejected…You'll be called Hephzibah (My Delight)…
>
> …Holy People, God-Redeemed, Sought-Out, City-Not-Forsaken.
>
> Isaiah 62:2-4, 12
> The Message

Day 106

Sustained

Thank You, Lord, for modeling endurance for us on the Cross. You could have just called down that legion of angels to save You, but You didn't. You endured…for us. Some of us are walking through really hard times right now, and honestly, we'd rather they just go away. But You are allowing these trials for some reason, so we also must learn endurance. Unfortunately, the only way to learn it is to walk through the pain. Sustain us with Your Presence and Your Peace, Lord, as we cling to You during our adversities, whatever they are. Bring Your deliverance in Your way and in Your time. We trust You.

Have You Thought? Have I piled all my troubles on Jesus, or am I still bearing them?

His Answer:

I wish I had wings like a dove, so I could fly far away and be at peace.

I ask for your help, Lord God, and you will keep me safe.

Our Lord, we belong to you. We tell you what worries us, and you won't let us fall.

Psalms 55:6, 16, 22
Contemporary English Version

Day 107

Set Free

Thank You, Lord, for gently, lovingly showing us where we have wrong attitudes or actions. No bony-finger wagging for You! Help us to never mistake those accusatory attacks from the pit of Hell for Your sweet voice. You are not a slandering God. You convict us in a gracious way, not ever attacking our character, and then You promise Your counsel to help us change. As You were gentle with the woman caught in adultery, You are with us. You desire holiness for us, but You don't achieve it with a guilt trip, for You bore all of our guilt on the cross. What freedom You bought for us!

Have You Thought? Thank You for Your gentle ways with us.

His Answer:
> Could it be any clearer? Our old way of life was nailed to the Cross with Christ, a decisive end to that sin-miserable life—no longer at sin's every beck and call!
>
> All your lives you've let sin tell you what to do. But thank God you've started listening to a new master, one whose commands set you free to live openly in his freedom!
>
> Romans 6:6, 16-18
> The Message

Day 108

Fears

Thank You, Lord, that You heal afflictions. Mine is fear. It doesn't bother me all the time, but when it flares up, I am captured by it. What is fear but projecting into my future and forgetting that You will be there to help or relieve or save. Honestly? Do I really believe that could ever happen? No, I don't. So, when Satan has me reeling with apprehension, falling for his lies, I remember Your faithfulness. I thank You that there is no situation in my future where You will not be right beside me, to bless, comfort or empower me. I am Yours. Forever. And that's all I need to know.

Have You Thought? When I am afraid, remind me who You are, Lord.

His Answer:
Live under the protection of God Most High and stay in the shadow of God All-Powerful. Then you will say to the Lord, "You are my fortress, my place of safety; you are my God, and I trust you."

He will spread his wings over you and keep you secure. His faithfulness is like a shield or a city wall.

The Lord Most High is your fortress. Run to him for safety.

Psalms 91:1-2, 4, 9
Contemporary English Version

Day 109

Striking Resemblance

Thank You, Lord, that You embody mercy and grace. Occasionally we may act graciously or mercifully, but those actions are behaviors we have learned from You, for they are the essence of who You are. Your gracious hand bestows on us things that we don't really deserve, and Your merciful heart withholds from us those bad things which we certainly do have coming. Your character is loving, faithful, compassionate, forgiving. Could we ever thank You enough, except by imitating Your heart to others? Please Lord, give us open eyes and a willing heart to treat others that way today.

Have You Thought? Lord, help me to imitate You today.

His Answer:
> Watch what God does, and then you do it, like children who learn proper behavior from their parents. Mostly what God does is love you. Keep company with him and learn a life of love. Observe how Christ loved us. His love was not cautious, but extravagant. He didn't love in order to get something from us but to give everything of himself to us. Love like that.

Ephesians 5:1-2
The Message

Day 110

Join the Chorus

Thank You, Lord! All creation sings Your praises! Early in the morning the bird's chorus in joy as the earth wakes up. They sing to You, their Creator and give grateful voice to all Your goodness. You are Maker and Keeper, Protector and Provider. Not one sparrow falls without Your knowledge. I confess sometimes I am not a part of that glorious melody. Some days I let my circumstances steal Your applause. I'm sorry. Help me to live the life of unending worship that You deserve, most Holy God. This day, and every day, let me sense Your glorious hand in all that I see.

Have You Thought? Give me a God-song today, Lord.

His Answer:
> You are wonderful, Lord, and you deserve all praise, because you are much greater than anyone can understand. Each generation will announce to the next your wonderful and powerful deeds.

Psalms 145:3-4
Contemporary English Version

Day 111

Uncomfortable Places

Thank You, Lord, for all those comfortable places and times where I can easily sense Your presence: early morning hours on my screened porch as all creation wakes, or quiet talks over coffee with friends who love You or are searching for You. But how about those nerve-racking moments when I feel overwhelmed, out of place or totally inadequate? You promise to be in those dreaded situations too. In fact, You are already there, waiting for me to arrive so You can empower and guide me through them. Help me to really believe that and walk confidently in my difficult times this week, Lord.

Have You Thought? Lord, comfort me where I feel beaten-up or beaten-down.

His Answer:

GOD has comforted his people. He has tenderly nursed his beaten-up, beaten-down people. But Zion said, "I don't get it. GOD has left me. My Master has forgotten I even exist." Can a mother forget the infant at her breast, walk away from the baby she bore? But even if mothers forget, I'd never forget you—never. Look, I've written your names on the backs of my hands."

Isaiah 49:13-15
The Message

Day 112

All My Sins

Thank You, Lord, that Your cross is enough for all my sins. All of them. Even the one that always comes to mind when I am feeling hard on myself…which I have asked forgiveness for so many times. Because if Your redemption doesn't cover every one of my sins, it is not sufficient for any of them. But it does and it is. And even better, you don't even remember those sins. They are forgiven and forgotten, forever. So if *You* don't remember them, why in the world should I? That's the wonder of the cross that Satan is hoping we never realize. Disappoint him and believe it once and for all!

Have You Thought? Impress the wonder of the Cross on me again today, Lord.

His Answer:

He forgives your sins—every one. He redeems you from hell—saves your life!

As high as heaven is over the earth, so strong is his love to those who fear him. And as far as sunrise is from sunset, he has separated us from our sins.

Psalms 103:3-4, 11-12
The Message

Day 113

No Scales

Thank You, Lord, that we can't earn Your love. Anything admirable or worthy we do is just a response to that love, not a qualification for it. When we really think about what we bring to the table, it is only brokenness and need, fear and doubt. These are the things we hypothetically place on our side of the scales. You weigh in with your wholeness, fulfillment and salvation. Your offering wins hands-down, which is why You don't play the worthiness game. So, Father, help us to accept Your extravagant love for what it truly is...priceless, instead of trying to earn it with our "good works."

Have You Thought? Lord, I'm glad You don't play the worthiness game.

His Answer:

> But if you see that the job is too big for you, that it's something only God can do, and you trust him to do it—you could never do it for yourself no matter how hard and long you worked—well, that trusting-him-to-do-it is what gets you set right with God, by God. Sheer gift....the one who trusts God to do the putting-everything-right without insisting on having a say in it is one fortunate man.

> Romans 4:5-6
> The Message

Day 114

Broken Hallelujahs

Thank You, Lord, for reminding me that life has seasons. I am well aware that my life-song won't always be those exquisite high notes. Sometimes the melody will just drone on in somber bass tones. The crucial factor during those dark nights of the soul is whether I cling more closely to You or choose to walk away. Do I curse God as Job's wife did, or do I worship you even with my broken hallelujahs? Those seemingly unfruitful times are just as ordained by God as the abundant ones. So in *all* my seasons, Lord, may my song consistently be "Praise God From Whom All Blessings Flow."

Have You Thought? Teach me to trust You even in life's darker times, Lord.

His Answer:

I am not complaining about having too little. I have learned to be satisfied with whatever I have. I know what it is to be poor or to have plenty, and I have lived under all kinds of conditions. I know what it means to be full or to be hungry, to have too much or too little. Christ gives me the strength to face anything.

Philippians 4:11-13
Contemporary English Version

Day 115

Ammunition

Thank You, Lord, that our prayers, praises and time spent in Your Word impact heavenly realms and are all more beneficial than we can imagine. In our world, we are empowered, sustained and encouraged by that time and those words. In the spiritual world, those words and that time ambush Satan. How cool is that? Every time we exalt our Almighty God, or spend time in His Word, dwelling on it and making it our reality, we denounce and defeat the enemy and his hordes. I love that, and I purposely praise Him just to cause them more consternation. Join me today in making Satan unhappy!

Have You Thought? Let praise rise from my lips, Lord.

His Answer:

> God is strong, and he wants you strong. So use everything the Master has set out for you, well-made weapons of the best materials. And put them to use so you will be able to stand up to everything the Devil throws your way.

> Take all the help you can get, every weapon God has issued, so that when it's all over but the shouting you'll still be on your feet.

> Ephesians 6:10-11, 13
> The Message

Day 116

Final Product

Thank You, Lord, every day is a new beginning with You. When I get exasperated with myself, You remind me again that Your perspective is long-term. I see my flaws so clearly, but You envision the final product at the end of Your purifying assembly line. You only make beautiful things, so even my flaws and scars can be made glorious in Your redeeming Hands. Whatever personal disappointments I have today, I will lay them at Your feet. I trust in Your perfect knowledge of me. You will use every part of my makeup, history and even the future events in my life for my best good and Your best use.

Have You Thought? Lord, teach me to be patient with Your work in me.

His Answer:

> I'm an open book to you; even from a distance, you know what I'm thinking.
>
> You know everything I am going to say before I start the first sentence.
>
> Like an open book, you watched me grow from conception to birth; all the stages of my life were spread out before you. The days of my life all prepared before I'd even lived one day.
>
> Psalms 139:2, 4, 16
> The Message

Day 117

Every Moment

Thank You, Lord, that You are always thinking about me. Often I don't think of You. It is sad how easily my mind gets preoccupied with projects or fun activities and I totally forget about You. When things are going well, I'm easily distracted. But when I am in need I think of You often! How astounding that You understand all my fleeting obsessions, and You still love me. How pleased You would be if my thoughts turned to You more often. Teach me to reciprocate the delight that You have in me. Stay on my mind in the hard times and the good.

Have You Thought? Stay on my mind more today, Lord.

His Answer:

I look behind me and you're there, then up ahead and you're there, too—your reassuring presence, coming and going. This is too much, too wonderful—I can't take it all in!

Your thoughts—how rare, how beautiful! God, I'll never comprehend them! I couldn't begin to count them—any more than I could count the sand of the sea. Oh, let me rise in the morning and live always with you!

Psalms 139:5-6, 17-18
The Message

Day 118

Comforter and Counselor

Lord, You are the best secret keeper and guidance giver. I can run to You with my deepest hurts and silliest feelings, and always find Your compassionate heart and reassuring embrace. You never tire of tending to my wounded spirit. I can let down all of my walls with You, Lord, and reveal my ugliest emotions, because I know You will love me unconditionally. No wonder Isaiah calls You the Wonderful Counselor! You bring such healing truth to any confusing situation or relationship if I will just pour out my heart to You. No one compares to You, Compassionate Friend!

Have You Thought? Comfort me wherever I am weary, Lord.

His Answer:

Our God has said: "Encourage my people! Give them comfort."

The Lord gives strength to those who are weary. Even young people get tired, then stumble and fall. But those who trust the Lord will find new strength. They will be strong like eagles soaring upward on wings; they will walk and run without getting tired.

Isaiah 40:1, 29-31
Contemporary English Version

Day 119

Deepest Longings

Thank You, Lord, You alone give ultimate satisfaction. When I follow Your lead and pursue enduring, eternal goals, I experience joy and fulfillment. When I fall for this world's temporary highs—pretty things, exciting activities—they come up short every time! Yes, it is true that You have given us everything to enjoy. The problem comes when I expect these trinkets or trips to fill my deepest longings. Only You can do that, Lord. So keep me ever aware of the value I place on perishable things. Help me to long for and value what You treasure most so that I can live a life of lasting significance.

Have You Thought? Lord, let me not buy into the world's priorities. I need Your help on this.

His Answer:
"That is why I tell you not to worry about everyday life—whether you have enough food and drink, or enough clothes to wear. Isn't life more than food, and your body more than clothing?"

"So don't worry about these things, saying, 'What will we eat? What will we drink? What will we wear?' These things dominate the thoughts of unbelievers, but your heavenly Father already knows all your needs. Seek the Kingdom of God above all else, and live righteously, and he will give you everything you need."

Matthew 6:25, 31-33
New Living Translation

Day 120

Commander of the Heavenly Armies

Thank You, Lord, You are all I need. You gave so many incredible visual evidences of that fact throughout the Old Testament. You purposely recorded Your miraculous dealings with Your people in order to encourage us on *our* journeys. You were their cloud by day to shelter them from the heat of the sun, their fire by night to guide them in the dark. When they cried out for water, You sent enough water (from a rock!) to quench their thirst, and water all of their herds. And I wonder if You can handle my problems? You are truly all I need. I thankfully rest in that today, Lord.

Have You Thought? Lord, You are powerful and wonderful at the same time.

His Answer:

For who in all of heaven can be compared with God? What mightiest angel is anything like him? The highest of angelic powers stand in dread and awe of him. Who is as revered as he by those surrounding him? O Jehovah, Commander of the heavenly armies, where is there any other Mighty One like you? Faithfulness is your very character.

Psalms 89:6-8
The Living Bible

Day 121

Stooping-Down God

Thank You, Lord, that You came not just to inspire us, but to inhabit us. That is what makes Christianity different from every other religion in the world. It is not an us-seeking-You relationship, but rather a You-stooping-down-to-us relationship. And even better, after Pentecost, it became a You-living-in-us friendship. You don't want us to admire You, but to accept You as the Lord of our lives. You don't merely want to change us, You want to show off Your amazingly compassionate, powerful, joyful life through us for the world to see! We just need to let You have Your way in us daily. Do it today, Lord.

Have You Thought? Live fully in me today, Lord.

His Answer:

But for you who welcome him, in whom he dwells—even though you still experience all the limitations of sin— you yourself experience life on God's terms. It stands to reason, doesn't it, that if the alive-and-present God who raised Jesus from the dead moves into your life, he'll do the same thing in you that he did in Jesus, bringing you alive to himself?

This resurrection life you received from God is not a timid, grave-tending life. It's adventurously expectant, greeting God with a childlike "What's next, Papa?" God's Spirit touches our spirits and confirms who we really are.

Romans 8:10-11, 15-16
The Message

Day 122

No Lost Causes

Thank You, Lord, for the many stories of redemption in Your Word. Paul, Peter, Jonah, Moses—the list goes on and on. There is a specific reason for these accounts in Your holy Scripture. These depictions of dramatically changed lives build hope in our hearts for the situations and people we worry about. They remind us again of Your transforming touch whenever we feel discouraged about wayward loved ones or hard experiences. You can change any rebellious person or rearrange any desperate situation. You have no category labeled "Lost causes." What an encouraging God!

Have You Thought? Is there anyone on my "lost cause" list?

His Answer:
"I am the Lord, the God of every person on the earth. Nothing is impossible for me."

"I will make an agreement with them that will last forever. I will never turn away from them; I will always do good to them. I will make them want to respect me so they will never turn away from me. I will enjoy doing good to them."

Jeremiah 32:27, 40-41
New Century Version

Day 123

Reconciling God

Thank You, Lord, for the power of forgiveness, which You graciously offered us on the cross. We have all felt the elation of burdens relieved, guilt washed away and pardon freely given. You call us to imitate that loving attitude to others because You understand the overwhelming strain of broken relationships. So, it is time to be honest. No more sweeping under the rug bad behavior or rotten attitudes. God wants to freshen up our friendships and mend our family feuds. Whether we need to offer forgiveness or ask for pardon, now is the time to do it. Give us grace to respond as You do today.

Have You Thought? Bring reconciliation in my life wherever it is needed, Lord.

His Answer:

So, chosen by God for this new life of love, dress in the wardrobe God picked out for you: compassion, kindness, humility, quiet strength, discipline. Be even-tempered, content with second place, quick to forgive an offense. Forgive as quickly and completely as the Master forgave you. And regardless of what else you put on, wear love. It's your basic, all-purpose garment. Never be without it.

Colossians 3:12-14
The Message

Day 124

No Worries

Thank You, Lord, that every one of my problems is Your problem too, because I am Yours. The difference is that my problems are not difficulties to You—they are just redeemed situations that have not yet been revealed. From Your perspective, You have my life totally figured out, so worry is unnecessary. The big question then is this: If I trust You and You don't worry, then why do I? All I need to do is pray for Your perfect will, in Your perfect timing. You tried to teach me this with the prayer we call The Lord's Prayer. Help me to rely on You, Father, just as Jesus taught and lived. I want to relax in Your care.

Have You Thought? You have the solution to my problems, Lord. Thank You!

His Answer:

"This is your Father you are dealing with, and he knows better than you what you need. With a God like this loving you, you can pray very simply. Like this: Our Father in heaven, reveal who you are. Set the world right; do what's best—as above, so below."

"Here's what I want you to do: Find a quiet, secluded place so you won't be tempted to role-play before God. Just be there as simply and honestly as you can manage. The focus will shift from you to God, and you will begin to sense his grace."

Matthew 6:8-10, 6
The Message

Day 125

Waiting

Thank You, Lord, You are with us in the waiting periods of our lives. Those times where we long for the phone to ring or that letter to come in the mail. We just want to know how everything is going to work out! Maybe it's an anxiously-awaited medical diagnosis, a child's college acceptance notification or an appraisal on a house. Those are sitting-on-the-edge-of-our-seats times when we can't see our future clearly. The good news is—You can! You are working everything out in the best possible way, at the most perfect time. Teach us to be patient when everything feels up in the air.

Have You Thought? Help me to trust You for Your perfect timing.

His Answer:

You are my King and my God. Answer my cry for help because I pray to you. Each morning you listen to my prayer, as I bring my request to you and wait for your reply.

Because of your great mercy, I come to your house, Lord, and I am filled with wonder as I bow down to worship at your holy temple. You do what is right, and I ask you to guide me. Make your teaching clear…

Psalms 5:2-3, 7-8
Contemporary English Version

Day 126

God-Confidence

Thank You, Lord, for Your power at work in us. We are so prone to panic when we get into new, uncomfortable situations. We're like Moses, who repeatedly doubted his ability to do the job God gave him to do. Just as he did, we quickly recite our inadequacies when God calls us out of our comfort zones. We define ourselves by our weaknesses. Maybe God wants us to lose our self-confidence so we can develop our God-confidence? When He empowers us, our shortcomings are totally irrelevant, aren't they? If He calls us to a task, He will enable us to do it. Lord, convince us of that today!

Have You Thought? Your power erases my inadequacies when I depend on You.

His Answer:

But Moses said, "They won't believe me! They won't do what *I* tell them to. They'll say, 'Jehovah never appeared to you!'"

But Moses pleaded, "O Lord, I'm just not a good speaker. I never have been, and I'm not now, even after you have spoken to me, for I have a speech impediment." "Who makes mouths?" Jehovah asked him. "Isn't it I, the Lord? Who makes a man so that he can speak or not speak, see or not see, hear or not hear? Now go ahead and do as I tell you, for I will help you to speak well, and I will tell you what to say."

Exodus 4:1, 10-12
The Living Bible

Day 127

Precious Promises

Thank You, Lord, Your promises become even more precious as our situations intensify. Your commitment to comfort, redeem, forgive, and most of all, be with us, stands firm in the darkest night. This is the hope that we joyfully wrap around ourselves to feel protected and cherished. Without this Light to guide our way, there would be only dark despair. But Your truth illuminates our path like the stars You flung across the sky. They dimly shine at dusk, but dazzle our eyes in the deepest night. This eternal hope endures despite hard circumstances. It sustains us, Lord, and we are so grateful.

Have You Thought? Be the Hope I cling to today, Lord.

His Answer:

So we're not giving up. How could we! Even though on the outside it often looks like things are falling apart on us, on the inside, where God is making new life, not a day goes by without his unfolding grace. These hard times are small potatoes compared to the coming good times, the lavish celebration prepared for us. There's far more here than meets the eye. The things we see now are here today, gone tomorrow. But the things we can't see now will last forever.

2 Corinthians 4:16-18
The Message

Day 128

Come Home

Thank you, Lord, that You don't play fair. Tit-for-tat is not Your rule. Extreme "Mother, May I?" is more Your style. Feeble steps towards You bring Your giant leap of response! You came to redeem our broken world. All those sinful, disgraced, Prodigal-Son places in our lives elicit Your forgiving, accepting, run-to-meet-us Father's heart. Where are You estranged from God? Where are you feeling the guilt of your sin? He is ever ready to place His signet ring on your finger, His shoes on your feet, and His glorious robes of righteousness on your shoulders to cover your shame. Just come Home.

Have You Thought? You want me to find my home in You.

His Answer:

So he returned home to his father. And while he was still a long distance away, his father saw him coming, and was filled with loving pity and ran and embraced him and kissed him. His son said to him, "Father, I have sinned against heaven and you, and am not worthy of being called your son—" But his father said to the slaves, "Quick! Bring the finest robe in the house and put it on him. And a jeweled ring for his finger; and shoes! And kill the calf we have in the fattening pen. We must celebrate with a feast, for this son of mine was dead and has returned to life. He was lost and is found." So the party began.

Luke 15:20-24
The Living Bible

138

Day 129

New Normals

*Thank You, Lord, there is no location where You are not...*except where You haven't been invited. Would You come and fill some places in me which need Your Presence? There are holes in my heart that once were filled with loved ones and their activities. My house is quiet, and my heart is broken. But I know that Your plans for me are still good, Lord. Remind me of Your love and revive me with Your Word while I am adjusting to my new normal. How comforting to know You understand and You are with me through all the changes in this life. My Faithful One, give me a new start.

Have You Thought? Where my life has changed, Lord comfort me.

His Answer:

Hear my cry to you, Lord. Let your word help me understand.

Give me your helping hand, because I have chosen your commands. I want you to save me, Lord. I love your teachings. Let me live so I can praise you, and let your laws help me.

Psalms 119:169, 173-175
New Century Version

Day 130

In the Dumps

Thank You, Lord, You can quiet my soul like no other. I needed it again today. With my familiar routine changed I was left wondering which way to go. I needed to be still and focus on You and Your goodness. I asked You to orchestrate my day and give me back the song in my heart. And You did, Lord! Change is always perceived as loss. But how awesome it is that You transcend the changes in our lives, and bring true contentment in any season. Thank you that regardless of our circumstances, You are able to bring us joy...even when life shifts and everything feels different and new.

Have You Thought? No blues, today, Lord. Give me Your new song.

His Answer:
> Why am I discouraged? Why is my heart so sad? I will put my hope in God! I will praise him again—my Savior and my God! Now I am deeply discouraged, but I will remember you—
>
> But each day the Lord pours his unfailing love upon me, and through each night I sing his songs, praying to God who gives me life.
>
> Psalms 42:5-6, 8
> New Living Translation

Day 131

Lost Bearings

Lord, You never tire of reminding us who we are in Your sight! The world blurs that vision every day. We lose our bearings when we listen to the voices around us, but Your voice steadies us. You remind us that we are unquestionably Yours. No striving, no straining is ever necessary to keep Your love. We can just rest in Your constant care and everlasting devotion. We run to other places for this peace, but only You provide it. Draw us near again to hear Your love-whispers, Lord. They give us back our true identity. On earth there is no sound quite as soothing.

Have You Thought? Help me to give in to You today, Lord.

His Answer:

> Give in to God, come to terms with him and everything will turn out just fine. Let him tell you what to do; take his words to heart. Come back to God Almighty and he'll rebuild your life.
>
> You'll take delight in God, the Mighty One, and look to him joyfully, boldly. You'll pray to him and he'll listen; he'll help you do what you've promised.

Job 22:21-23, 26-27
The Message

Day 132

Follow Me!

Thank You, Lord, that Christianity is just a simple "Follow Me," spoken by Jesus to each one of us. That old covenant of "shoulds" and "oughts" was replaced by the Cross! Now we decide whether to receive the graceful invitation from the One who loves us and wants to be with us—day by day in this life, and forever in the life to come. It's a hold-My-hand-and-walk-with-Me joyful intimacy. It is free and easy whispers back and forth with your Best Friend all day long. We make it too formal and, well, impersonal. Jesus called us friends, remember? Lord, help us to act like Your friends today!

Have You Thought? Lord, let me enjoy free and easy whispers with You today.

His Answer:

I didn't want some petty, inferior brand of righteousness that comes from keeping a list of rules when I could get the robust kind that comes from trusting Christ—God's righteousness.

I'm not saying that I have this all together, that I have it made. But I am well on my way, reaching out for Christ, who has so wondrously reached out for me.

Philippians 3:9, 12
The Message

Day 133

Abundant Life

Thank You, Lord, that Your desire and plan for us is to live abundant lives. No meager existences or just getting by for Your children. Sound too good to be true? It's not. Life lived open to the Lord's daily call brings ultimate fulfillment. It is how Jesus lived. That didn't mean great riches or a lack of hard times for Him, and it very well may not for us either. It is simply a daily "What's next, Father?" life, joyfully blessing others and glorifying God in the process. This God-designed life is what we all long for, but don't find anywhere but in Jesus. Lord, help us to live abundantly today.

Have You Thought? Let me live joyfully in You today.

His Answer:
> "Yes, I am the Vine; you are the branches. Whoever lives in me and I in him shall produce a large crop of fruit. For apart from me you can't do a thing."

> "I have told you this so that you will be filled with my joy. Yes, your cup of joy will overflow!"

> "I no longer call you slaves, for a master doesn't confide in his slaves; now you are my friends, proved by the fact that I have told you everything the Father told me."

John 15:5, 11, 15
The Living Bible

Day 134

Equipped

Thank You, Lord, You are everything I am not. In every detail of my life that has an edge to it or needs refining, You are Perfection. You don't get your feelings hurt, and You don't have thin skin. You are always patient and You always see the good in people or situations. You don't get weary of doing good, and You never want to run away. I do all of these! Where I am weary or worn down, I need You to fill me. Remind me of Your strength and power at work in me, Lord. Today, don't let me attempt to live my life in my own strength. Keep my eyes on *You*, and my ears open to Your voice.

Have You Thought? Equip me for my race today, Lord.

His Answer:
> Keep your eyes on *Jesus,* who both began and finished this race we're in. Study how he did it. Because he never lost sight of where he was headed—that exhilarating finish in and with God—he could put up with anything along the way: cross, shame, whatever. And now he's *there*, in the place of honor, right alongside God. When you find yourself flagging in your faith, go over that story again... That will shoot adrenaline into your souls!

Hebrews 12:2-3
The Message

Sweet Sleep

Thank You, Lord, for modeling a prayerful, decisive life for us. Your decisions and actions were always confidently made because You had already talked to Your Father about them. I seem to do that for the big questions and problems, but not always in the little, everyday decisions. So why am I surprised when Satan attacks me there in the middle of the night? I've spent wide-awake hours rethinking or regretting my words spoken or actions taken spontaneously without prayer! Remind me to keep chatting with You all day long, so I can sleep more soundly tonight.

Have You Thought? Lord, guide my thoughts and actions today.

His Answer:

But Lord, you are my shield, my glory, and my only hope. You alone can lift my head, now bowed in shame. I cried out to the Lord, and he heard me from his Temple in Jerusalem. Then I lay down and slept in peace and woke up safely, for the Lord was watching over me.

For salvation comes from God. What joys he gives to all his people.

Psalms 3:3-5, 8
The Living Bible

Day 136

Past

Thank You, Lord, You are a forever God! Our stresses and burdens come in all three tenses: past, present, and future. You, the Eternal One, are the answer in every timeframe of our lives. Today we thank You that as our Savior and the Perfect Lamb, You covered all the sins of our past with Your precious blood. They are cast away as far as the east is from the west. So, the next time Satan tries to take us down memory lane, we can remind him the road has been detoured forever! Thank you for buying us so great a freedom. There is no more guilt from any of our yesterdays! Hallelujah!

Have you Thought? You are Lord of every bad memory.

His Answer:
> God paid a ransom to save you from the impossible road to heaven which your fathers tried to take, and the ransom he paid was not mere gold or silver as you very well know. But he paid for you with the precious lifeblood of Christ, the sinless, spotless Lamb of God.

1 Peter 1:18-19
The Living Bible

Day 137

Present

Thank You, Lord, You are not only the answer to our problems from the past, but You bring healing and redemption for the brokenness and trials which we experience today. You are the Perfect Lamb, but You are also the Loving Shepherd. You guide us to still waters to refresh us. You lead us to secure places so we can rest. And when we are totally spent and ready to drop, You lovingly pick us up and hold us close. Sometimes we seek shelter in earthly things that cannot bring relief for long. For the troubles we find today, help us instead to rest in the safety of Your arms, Loving Shepherd.

Have You Thought? Be my Loving Shepherd this day.

His Answer:
> GOD holds the high center, he sees and sets the world's mess right. He decides what is right for us earthlings, gives people their just deserts. GOD's a safe-house for the battered, a sanctuary during bad times. The moment you arrive, you relax, you're never sorry you knocked.

Psalms 9:7-10
The Message

Day 138

Future

As our reigning King, You even have our futures all figured out. When our questions all begin with "What if...?", remind us about Your perspective. You see all of time at once, and You are the Sovereign Ruler of it all. You have shown us Your faithfulness about our past, and have proved Your lovingkindness in our everyday present lives. So, now Lord, give us glimpses of Your Almighty Hand at work on our behalf for our days to come. You promise to guide us in the way we should go. You are steadfast and true, and we love and trust You, Lord.

Have You Thought? My future is secure with You. Let that give me peace today.

His Answer:
> And don't forget the many times I clearly told you what was going to happen in the future. For I am God—I only—and there is no other like me who can tell you what is going to happen. All I say will come to pass, for I do whatever I wish.

Isaiah 46:9-10
The Living Bible

Day 139

Priests

Thank You, Lord, for Your high calling for each of our lives. So many of us spend our lives wondering what God's will is. Well, here it is—to be Your priests! We are His representatives on this earth, bringing God to people and people to God. Each of us has a unique manner and mode for doing that task, but the calling is always the same. We are to tell what God has done for us, bring hope to the hurting, and grace to the afflicted. I like to think of it as being Jesus' hands and heart to those whom God parades across our paths. There is no more meaningful job, and no special training is required!

Have You Thought? Wherever I go, Lord, let me be Your representative today.

His Answer:

All praise to him who always loves us and who set us free from our sins by pouring out his lifeblood for us. He has gathered us into his Kingdom and made us priests of God his Father. Give to him everlasting glory! He rules forever! Amen!

Revelation 1:5-6
The Living Bible

Day 140

Love Hungry

Thank You, Lord, that You are a loving God, for we are a love-hungry people. We search for affirmation and affection everywhere, oftentimes in superficial activities or relationships. We surround ourselves with those who will stroke us, and we seek validation in every situation. What we actually need is a deeper realization of Your love for us. Teach us to quiet our lives of their incessant noise, so we can recognize Your tender voice. You know and understand us completely. When we are still, and listening, Your words of comfort fill every empty place in our hearts and lives. Quiet our lives today.

Have You Thought? Let Your love be my reality today, Lord.

His Answer:

Don't love the world's ways. Don't love the world's goods. Love of the world squeezes out love for the Father. Practically everything that goes on in the world— wanting your own way, wanting everything for yourself, wanting to appear important—has nothing to do with the Father. It just isolates you from him. The world and all its wanting, wanting, wanting is on the way out—but whoever does what God wants is set for eternity.

1 John 2:15-17
The Message

Day 141

Doing My Part

Thank You, Lord, for the power of prayer—that partnership with You that we often misunderstand or underestimate. Here's the best explanation I've heard: If God is the CEO, then His corporate checkbook requires two signatures. His name is already signed. What is needed is ours, as His partner—in the form of prayer. What an amazing privilege and responsibility! Lord, make us quick to pray for the people and situations You place on our hearts today. If we don't do our part, You can't do Yours. So stir us, Lord, to always be Your faithful partners in prayer.

Have You Thought? Lord, help me to be Your partner today.

His Answer:

> One day Jesus told his disciples a story to illustrate their need for constant prayer and to show them that they must keep praying until the answer comes. "There was a city judge," He said, "a very godless man who had great contempt for everyone. A widow of that city came to him frequently to appeal for justice against a man who had harmed her. The judge ignored her for a while, but eventually she got on his nerves. 'I fear neither God nor man,' he said to himself, 'but this woman bothers me. I'm going to see that she gets justice, for she is wearing me out with her constant coming!'" Then the Lord said, "If even an evil judge can be worn down like that, don't you think that God will surely give justice to his people who plead with him day and night? Yes! He will answer them quickly! But the question is: When I, the Messiah, return, how many will I find who have faith and are praying?"

Luke 18:1-8
The Living Bible

Day 142

Loosed Chains

Thank You Lord, You came to free us from the bondage of religious rules! Instead of commands to do or not to do, You established a new covenant with Your shed blood. Those meet-the-requirements chains were forever loosed. But, on our bad days, we wrap them snugly around ourselves all over again! Lord, You came to unlock those self-imposed shackles. You died to begin a new order, one based on relationship, not rules. You are not interested in our achievements; You want our allegiance. So help us live in the freedom Jesus bought for us—a life of faith in *His* works and not our own!

Have You Thought? Let me live freely before You today.

His Answer:

Christ has set us free to live a free life. So take your stand! Never again let anyone put a harness of slavery on you. I am emphatic about this. The moment any one of you submits to…any…rule-keeping system, at that same moment Christ's hard-won gift of freedom is squandered.

For in Christ, neither our most conscientious religion nor disregard of religion amounts to anything. What matters is something far more interior: faith expressed in love.

Galatians 5:1-2, 6
The Message

Day 143

One of a Kind

Thank You, Lord, You came to free us from the bondage of comparison. How easily we fall into that destructive trap, which has no winner! We measure ourselves against others and end up either prideful or humiliated. God detests either of these situations, calling them unwise. Lord, help us to rejoice in the one-of-a-kind persons God created each of us to be. We are unique, never-to-be-duplicated expressions of God's artistry. We are specifically gifted and wired to bless the world as no one else ever could or ever will. What a gift…if we embrace it. Help us to do that, Lord, for Your glory!

Have You Thought? Let me embrace who I am in You, Lord.

His Answer:

If we are living now by the Holy Spirit's power, let us follow the Holy Spirit's leading in every part of our lives. Then we won't need to look for honors and popularity, which lead to jealousy and hard feelings.

Let everyone be sure that he is doing his very best, for then he will have the personal satisfaction of work well done and won't need to compare himself with someone else. Each of us must bear some faults and burdens of his own. For none of us is perfect!

Galatians 5:25-26, Galatians 6:4-5
The Living Bible

Day 144

Purified

Lord, You are more interested in my holiness than my happiness. That is a very hard sentence to write! I would much rather have You indulge my every whim for a great marriage, productive kids, paid bills, and perfect health. But, You don't want pampered children, You want purified ones. You teach us patience through annoyances, peace through unsettled circumstances, and self-control through trying people and tough situations. Help me realize that today, Lord. In every little irritation, remind me that You are purifying me. Then show me why You are also called the Comforter.

Have You Thought? Continue to shape my life, Lord.

His Answer:

So prepare your minds for service and have self-control. All your hope should be for the gift of grace that will be yours when Jesus Christ is shown to you. Now that you are obedient children of God do not live as you did in the past. You did not understand, so you did the evil things you wanted. But be holy in all you do, just as God, the One who called you, is holy. It is written in the Scriptures: "You must be holy, because I am holy."

1 Peter 1:13-16
New Century Version

Day 145

All Things

Thank You, Lord, for three vital words in Romans 8:28: know and all things. Here's the phrase: "And we know that all things work together for good to those who love God…" (NKJV). What doesn't that verse say? It doesn't say we *hope* or we *feel* or even that we *pray*. It says we *know!* And what do we know? That *some* things work for good? No. *All* things. That includes past mistakes. That's a tough one to swallow, isn't it? We can believe circumstances out of our control or things done to us can eventually be turned around for good. But, believing God will even redeem our wrong, willful choices… that's tough! And, that's grace!

Have You Thought? What a promise, Lord! Help me to believe it.

His Answer:

And we know that all that happens to us is working for our good if we love God and are fitting into his plans.

For I am convinced that nothing can ever separate us from his love. Death can't, and life can't. The angels won't, and all the powers of hell itself cannot keep God's love away. Our fears for today, our worries about tomorrow, or where we are—high above the sky, or in the deepest ocean—nothing will ever be able to separate us from the love of God demonstrated by our Lord Jesus Christ when he died for us.

Romans 8:28, 38-39
The Living Bible

Day 146

Every Detail

Thank You, Lord, that Your timing is always perfect. My here-and-now faulty human understanding makes my decisions lucky guesses at best. You, on the other hand, understand every present and future implication, so You never act precipitously or after the fact. When I do seek You first, You guide my ways and ordain my steps. In fact, You actually delight in arranging the smallest little details of my life! It is such a joyful thing to see Your Hand at work. My most carefree days are those surrendered completely to Your will. Lord, I'm asking, nudge me to do that every single day!

Have You Thought? Lord, show me Your Hand in the details today.

His Answer:

That is what is meant by the Scriptures which say that no mere man has ever seen, heard, or even imagined what wonderful things God has ready for those who love the Lord.

No one can really know what anyone else is thinking or what he is really like except that person himself. And no one can know God's thoughts except God's own Spirit. And God has actually given us his Spirit (not the world's spirit) to tell us about the wonderful free gifts of grace and blessing that God has given us.

1 Corinthians 2:9, 11-12
The Living Bible

Day 147

Whoever

Thank You, Lord, that "whoever calls upon the name of the Lord will be saved" (Romans 10:13 NKJV). Those of us who know that statement to be true need to be reminded of two things. First, we did *nothing* to bring about that redemption; it was God's work from start to finish. That fact keeps us from becoming *arrogant*. Second, regarding those we love who don't understand His saving grace yet, the Good News is that God isn't done pursuing them. Until their last breath, He will be drawing them to Himself. That keeps us from becoming *discouraged*, yet always lifting them in prayer.

Have You Thought? Come, Lord Jesus, bring Your salvation today.

His Answer:
Say the welcoming word to God—"Jesus is my Master"—embracing, body and soul, God's work of doing in us what he did in raising Jesus from the dead. That's it. You're not "doing" anything, you're simply calling out to God, trusting him to do it for you. That's salvation.

Romans 10:9
The Message

Day 148

Gracious Words

Thank You, Lord, that You have given us the God-like power of words! But oh, Lord Jesus, how we misuse them! Every morning that You have graciously given to me, discipline me to lay my day at Your feet—every thought, word, and action. My days ordered by You bring such fulfillment because of their Designer. Give me the mind of Christ, by Your grace. You are gentle, insightful, compassionate. Just as You brought healing wherever You went, let my words bear the imprint of Your heart, speaking encouragement, comfort and peace to a world unfamiliar with these.

Have You Thought? Guide my words today, Lord.

His Answer:
The right word at the right time—beautiful!

Prayerful answers come from God-loyal people; the wicked are sewers of abuse.

An undisciplined, self-willed life is puny; an obedient, God-willed life is spacious. Fear-of-God is a school in skilled living—first you learn humility, then you experience glory.

Proverbs 15:23, 28, 32-33
The Message

Day 149

God With Us

The "I am with you" bookends that begin and end the Gospel of Matthew are not a random coincidence. From Jesus' birth to His ascension, His message was always the same—I am here. That makes all the difference. I want every chapter of my life to proclaim that truth—not just the times in my life that I breeze through, but also those chapters with tear-stained pages. May they all record Your presence as the repetitive footnote. Remind us all today in a very tangible way that You are truly Immanuel, "God with us," for every day of our lives.

Have You Thought? Day after day, after day, You are with me.

His Answer:

> *"Listen! The virgin shall conceive a child!* She shall give birth to a Son, and he shall be called "Emmanuel" (meaning "God is with us")."

> "…and then teach these new disciples to obey all the commands I have given you; and be sure of this—that I am with you always, even to the end of the world."

Matthew 1:23, Matthew 28:20
The Living Bible

Day 150

Look Up

Thank You, Lord, that this life is not all there is. I know that in my heart, but so often my actions sing a different song. Many days I try to dress up my here-and-now life to look like Heaven, but I am quickly reminded that it is not. This is a broken world, and we all have fragmented places in our bodies, our hearts and our relationships. Only Your wisdom and eternal perspective will show us how to hold loosely the soon-gone things of the present and revere and hold up the truly forever ones. I need Your help to do that, Lord. Set my mind less on the visible, perishable things and more on the eternal treasures.

Have You Thought? Give me Your perspective today, Lord.

His Answer:
> Since you became alive again, so to speak, when Christ arose from the dead, now set your sights on the rich treasures and joys of heaven where he sits beside God in the place of honor and power. Let heaven fill your thoughts; don't spend your time worrying about things down here.

Colossians 3:1-2
The Living Bible

Day 151

Noise

Thank You, Lord for quiet... those times when I only hear the cooing of the doves or scampering of the squirrels. When I am out on my porch, reading Your Word, I sense You. I am refreshed and renewed in those moments and my soul soars. The sad truth is that You call me regularly to those tranquil times, but so often I don't hear You over the noise in my day. Would You show me those activities which make my life loud and uneasy? Maybe I have even gotten accustomed to that turbulence. If so, forgive me. Restore me again as I turn away from the world and choose You instead.

Have You Thought? Take me to Your quiet place today, Lord.

His Answer:

> The one thing I want from God, the thing I seek most of all, is the privilege of meditating in his Temple, living in his presence every day of my life, delighting in his incomparable perfections and glory. There I'll be when troubles come. He will hide me. He will set me on a high rock out of reach of all my enemies. Then I will bring him sacrifices and sing his praises with much joy.

Psalms 27:4-6
The Living Bible

Day 152

Just Ask

Thank You, Lord, for the power of prayer. You love to "show up and show off" when we come to You with our needs. You do what we can't do. You open doors we could never unlock. You bring about solutions we never would have imagined. There is no end to Your power available to us. We just need to invite You in…instead of leaving You a brokenhearted bystander. How sad that we run other places, to frail, human resources for our answers. They can satisfy the superficial problems. You fulfill the deep longings of our hearts. Do we doubt that You will do the very best for us? Forgive us, Lord and draw us to our knees more quickly.

Have You Thought? Lord, help me to worry less and pray more.

His Answer:
> "And besides, what's the use of worrying? What good does it do? Will it add a single day to your life? Of course not! And if worry can't even do such little things as that, what's the use of worrying over bigger things? Look at the lilies! They don't toil and spin, and yet Solomon in all his glory was not robed as well as they are. And if God provides clothing for the flowers that are here today and gone tomorrow, don't you suppose that he will provide clothing for you, you doubters?"

Luke 12:25-28
The Living Bible

Day 153

Holy Requests

Thank You, Lord, for the sacred bond You form when we pray for someone, or they pray for us. Whether they are well-spoken prayers, heartfelt written pleas or even silent whispers in the dark, they hold us in an unbreakable connection with each other. Poured out for dearly loved family members, cherished friends or just-met strangers, there is something about lifting up one another to the Lord. It grabs our hearts and won't let go. Those petitions bring God's will in heaven into the realm of earth, and life is changed. Battles are won. Breakthroughs achieved. Lord, draw us more into prayer. Anytime. Anywhere.

Have You Thought? Who are You calling me to pray for today, Lord?

His Answer:
Every time I say your name in prayer—which is practically all the time—I thank God for you, the God I worship with my whole life...

2 Timothy 1:3
The Message

Day 154

Refilled

Thank You, Lord, that our oft-repeated prayer of "Lord, fill me again" is the answer to the fatigue and frustration of a worn-down-to-the-bone soul. When I'm either ready to drop or to explode, I know it's past time to be refilled. And no one does that like Jesus. He draws me away from the rat race and the unreal to the important and the eternal…to be with Him… just the two of us. There is time to cry or vent or just be, with the One who knows and understands and helps. The One who formed me. The only One who can truly fill me. I'm a leaky bucket; I run dry. But He stands ever ready to restore and renew. All it takes is a request.

Have You Thought? Lord, I'm empty and dry. Fill me again.

His Answer:
>   And now to him who can keep you on your feet, standing tall in his bright presence, fresh and celebrating—to our one God, our only Savior, through Jesus Christ, our Master, be glory, majesty, strength, and rule before all time, and now, and to the end of all time. Yes.

Jude 24-25
The Message

Day 155

Heartfelt

Thank You, Lord, that I don't have to compete with that really polished prayer someone prayed in church today. Honestly, my heart longs to pray that elegantly, but You want me to pray in my own way. No comparison or contest. In God's estimation it's sincere or it's not. Period. He accepts the heartfelt longings of His children at any level, wherever we are in our relationship with Him. He just wants us to *talk* to Him. Honestly and openly. With as much of our hearts as we can manage. He knows that our heart-space for Him will grow. It's just a function of time. Can I get an Amen?

Have You Thought? Lord, increase my heart-space for You.

His Answer:
> Since this is the kind of life we have chosen, the life of the Spirit, let us make sure that we do not just hold it as an idea in our heads or a sentiment in our hearts, but work out its implications in every detail of our lives. That means we will not compare ourselves with each other as if one of us were better and another worse. We have far more interesting things to do with our lives. Each of us in an original.

> Galatians 5:25-26
> The Message

Day 156

Backward Glances

Thank You, Lord, that prayer takes us past our past. It's time to expectantly look forward. If we only look in the rearview mirror when driving a car, we will eventually crash, won't we? It's the same with our lives. Sins, regrets or failures from long ago can restrain us with a control that is staggering. They become videotapes which Satan keeps on rewind in our minds in order to prevent us from moving on. I know those shackles. God wants to unlock them. Today, can we all allow Him to bring freedom where we have been handcuffed or muzzled? He remembers our sins no more (see Jer. 31:34 NIV). *No more.* No more backward glances!

Have You Thought? Forgiven. Is there any sweeter word?

His Answer:

> I'll be their God, they'll be my people. They won't go to school to learn about me, or buy a book called God in Five Easy Lessons. They'll all get to know me firsthand, the little and the big, the small and the great. They'll get to know me by being kindly forgiven, with the slate of their sins forever wiped clean. By coming up with a new plan, a new covenant between God and his people, God put the old plan on the shelf. And there it stays, gathering dust.

Hebrews 8:10-13
The Message

Day 157

Ordinary Lives

Thank You, Lord, that prayer also takes us past our present limitations. How often I need to remind myself of that! Your plans are not sidetracked one bit by my inadequacies… because it's not all about *me*! That's a big sigh of relief. When Satan insinuates, "God can't use you," I remember he is a liar. He's trying to derail God's purposes in my life because they squelch his influence in the world. God knows well how flawed we are. "Unadorned clay pots," Paul calls us. But filled with *His* brightness, the Light will shine through all of our chips. So, really, the more broken we are, the more radiantly He can shine in us. How cool is that?

Have You Thought? Shine through me today, Lord

His Answer:
If you only look at us, you might well miss the brightness. We carry this precious Message around in the unadorned clay pots of our ordinary lives. That's to prevent anyone from confusing God's incomparable power with us.

2 Corinthians 4:7
The Message

Day 158

Cherished

Thank You, Lord, You are always on my side. Psalms 56:9 (NKJV) says, "God is *for* me." I'll make it personal. You were for me when I wasn't for You! You left Heaven and came down to earth to buy me back. And now, You sit at the right hand of God, sticking up for me whenever the Accuser wags his bony finger in my direction. That makes me feel cherished, protected and loved. Lord, let me walk confidently in that unchanging fact today. Let that truth settle down in my soul and put a song in my heart that nothing and no one can drown out. Believing anything other than this would be a lie.

Have You Thought? No matter what the circumstances, God is still on my side.

His Answer:

What can we ever say to such wonderful things as these? If God is on our side, who can ever be against us? Since he did not spare even his own Son for us but gave him up for us all, won't he also surely give us everything else? Who dares accuse us whom God has chosen for his own? Will God? No! He is the one who has forgiven us and given us right standing with himself.

No, for the Scriptures tell us that for his sake we must be ready to face death at every moment of the day—we are like sheep awaiting slaughter; but despite all this, overwhelming victory is ours through Christ who loved us enough to die for us.

Romans 8:31-33, 36-37
The Living Bible

Day 159

Pardoned

Thank You, Lord, for the power of forgiveness. Not just that You forgive me, but that You enable me to pass it on to others. To overlook and give a second chance. To contemplate what could have caused such behavior…what pain, what empty places. To see with a caring heart instead of a cynical mind. That is what You do for me, Lord. You so quickly grant pardon to me. It's always a choice, isn't it? You chose to give me a reprieve. Help me today to decide to do the same for someone else, because when I do, I feel like Your child and I know Your joy.

Have You Thought? What freedom there is in forgiveness given or received.

His Answer:

If you forgive people when they sin against you, then your Father will forgive you *when you sin against Him and when you sin against your neighbor*. But if you do not forgive your neighbors' sins, your Father will not forgive your sins.

Matthew 6:14-15
The Voice

Day 160

Opening Up

Thank You, Lord, You know my wildest dreams and my deepest fears. You *know* them! Why am I so hesitant to talk to You about them? Isn't that what true intimacy with a best friend includes? Give me the courage to open up and share those fragile places, Lord. Then You can ignite those I-can't-believe-it possibilities and extinguish the worst-case-scenarios that I imagine on my own. What freedom! Forgive me for confessing Your Name but not totally confiding in You. You deserve my deepest trust. I'm beginning to enjoy this vulnerability with You, and I can only say "Thank You."

Have You Thought? Teach me the joy of being vulnerable with You.

His Answer:
> O Lord, please be merciful to me, as all day long I cry out to You.

> O Lord, You are good and ready to forgive; Your loyal love flows generously over all who cry out to You.

> When times of trouble come, I will call to You because *I know* You will respond to me.

> For You are great, and Your works are wondrous; You are the one True God.

Psalms 86:3, 5, 7, 10
The Message

Day 161

Visualize This

Thank You, Lord, that we don't have to spend our lives apologizing to You. We have all had those days where we feel You must be angry, or at the very least, disappointed in us. We regularly sense we have failed You, and "I'm sorry" becomes our only conversation with You. Lord, in Your mercy, show us today how wrong that thinking is, how absolutely opposite from Your understanding. We are accepted in Your Beloved, and can now live a new life—one built on joy, not guilt. God delights in us! He has things to do in and through us—and apologies are not on His mind at all!

Have You Thought? Acceptance, not apologies is what is on Your mind.

His Answer:
> *Visualize this:* His blood *freely flowing down the cross,* setting us free! We are forgiven for our sinful ways by the richness of His grace, which He has poured all over us.

> God of our Lord Jesus the Anointed, Father of Glory: *I call out to You on behalf of Your people.* Give them minds ready to receive wisdom and revelation so they will truly know You. Open the eyes of their hearts, *and let the light of Your truth flood in.* Shine Your light on the hope You are calling them to embrace. Reveal to them the glorious riches You are preparing as their inheritance.

> Ephesians 1:7-8, 17-18
> The Voice

Day 162

Biblical Design

Thank You, Lord, for the simplicity of godly parenting. Here's the gist of Your command to us: Teach Your children to love God first and love Him most. Then tell them, and even better, show them His importance in your own life. Profess His faithfulness, goodness and mercy whenever appropriate in the living of each day. This post-Christian world makes gods of education, materialism and careers, and leaves broken, empty people in the aftermath. God's biblical design brings true fulfillment, joy and blessing. It's never too late to start; today we can profess and live God's put-together plan for life.

Have You Thought? Let me profess Your Name with my life even more than my words.

His Answer:
Make the things I'm commanding you today part of who you are. Repeat them to your children. Talk about them when you're sitting together in your home and when you're walking together down the road. Make them the last thing you talk about before you go to bed and the first thing you talk about the next morning.

Deuteronomy 6:6-7
The Voice

Day 163

Looking to Him

Lord, when we pray You change our focus from our problems to the Answer, from the giant to the Giant-Slayer, from mortal man to the Most High. We remember who You are when we pray, which is why it overthrows Satan. No wonder he works so hard to keep us from looking to You! The act of prayer takes us from the turmoil of our circumstances to the peace of Your Presence. So Lord, wherever we are stressed, in sickness, in lack, in fear, in loneliness today, take us to our knees and help us turn our eyes to You, the Author of wholeness, plenty, peace, and security.

Have You Thought? Thank You, Lord, that You are my very own God.

His Answer:

> See, God has come to rescue me; I will trust *in Him* and not be afraid, for the Eternal, indeed, the Eternal is my strength and my song. My *very own* God has rescued me.
>
> Isaiah 12:2
> The Voice

Day 164

Doing Justice

Thank You, Lord, there is no one more powerful than You…and no one more gentle. You always called out of the crowds the children, the hurt, the isolated and the ignored. Your heart is for the hurting. When we are afraid, You help us to take that fearful, faltering first step. Then You beckon us to take another. If we fall down, You lovingly pick us up. We chide ourselves; You console us. So Lord, where our dreams are disintegrating or where we have lost our nerve, encourage us again. Give us Your strength and Your anointing to do all that You have gifted and empowered us to do.

Have You Thought? Your gentleness restores me.

His Answer:

Eternal One: Look here, let Me present My servant; I have taken hold of him. He is My chosen, and I delight in him. I have put My Spirit on him; by this he will bring justice to the nations.

What is bruised and bent, he will not break; he will not blow out a smoldering candle. *Rather, he* will faithfully *turn his attention to* doing justice.

Isaiah 42:1, 3
The Voice

Day 165

Regardless

Thank You, Lord, Your plans will prevail, despite any contradictory circumstances! So often we believe in the truth of our visible situation more than we believe in Your invisible character. A glitch, a detour, or an unforeseen problem, and we think God is undone. He is not. Nothing, not our unbelief, our sin, or even Satan himself can keep God's purposes from coming true. He sees every future crisis as if it happened yesterday, so He is never caught off guard. How comforting to know, at the end of our story and of the world's story, God wins—and so does everyone on His side!

Have You Thought? How awesome it is that nothing and no one can stop Your good plans and purposes, Lord.

His Answer:

Blessed be the name of God forever and ever, for he alone has all wisdom and all power. World events are under his control. He removes kings and sets others on their thrones. He gives wise men their wisdom and scholars their intelligence. He reveals profound mysteries beyond man's understanding. He knows all hidden things, for he is light, and darkness is no obstacle to him.

Daniel 2:20-22
The Living Bible

Day 166

Imposter

Thank You, Lord, for boldly proclaiming the true character of Satan. He is a liar. You unmasked him as the impostor to keep us from being deceived as Eve was. His technique has not changed one iota since the time in the Garden. He still either makes us question who You are, who we are because of Your grace, or how true Your Word is. These should be easy ploys to recognize, but Lord, he can still trip us up! Uncover any lies that continue to blind us and bind us, and release us by Your Truth. Then give us discerning eyes to readily see and a courageous heart to take authority over those lies.

Have You Thought? Show me those place where I believe lies.

His Answer:
For…the devil…was a murderer from the beginning and a hater of truth—there is not an iota of truth in him. When he lies, it is perfectly normal; for he is the father of liars.

John 8:44
The Living Bible

And we know that Christ, God's Son, has come to help us understand and find the true God. And now we are in God because we are in Jesus Christ his Son, who is the only true God; and he is eternal Life. Dear children, keep away from anything that might take God's place in your hearts.

1 John 5:20-21
The Living Bible

Day 167

In the Nick of Time

Thank You, Lord, that You love to show Your power. What makes us crazy, though, is how You choose to wait until seemingly the last minute to bring about rescue! You love to wait until the situation is the direst before you break in, often with a solution never even imagined by us. We've all seen You do Your amazing feats. This morning, would You bring to our memories a situation where You proved that You rule and You reign over every circumstance and every crisis in our lives? Then let that remembrance reassure us that in our problems today, You will help us at just the right time.

Have You Thought? You never arrive late, Lord.

His Answer:
> The Lord says: You are my people and nation! So pay attention to me. My teaching will cause justice to shine like a light for every nation.
>
> Look closely at the sky! Stare at the earth. The sky will vanish like smoke; the earth will wear out like clothes. … But my victory will last; my saving power never ends.

Isaiah 51:4, 6
Contemporary English Version

Day 168

God All-Powerful

Thank You, Lord, You are the Marvelous Juxtaposition. You are Holy, Unapproachable, Consuming Fire, the Great I AM. But You are also the Here-and-Now Friend who sticks closer than a brother, Emmanuel, God-with-us. Help us to keep that fragile balance between revering You and running to Your arms, for You call us to do both. Turn our eyes to the stars or the sunset to remember how little we are and how big You are, Creator, Sustainer, and Ruler of the universe. Let Your glory fill our minds today as it forever does in Heaven where You are constantly worshiped and adored.

Have You Thought? I bow before You in grateful praise today.

His Answer:

May kindness and peace be yours from Jesus Christ, the faithful witness.

Jesus was the first to conquer death, and he is the ruler of all earthly kings. Christ loves us, and by his blood he set us free from our sins.

Look! He is coming with the clouds. Everyone will see him, even the ones who stuck a sword through him. All people on earth will weep because of him. Yes, it will happen! Amen.

The Lord God says, "I am Alpha and Omega, the one who is and was and is coming. I am God All-Powerful!"

Revelation 1:5, 7-8
Contemporary English Version

178

Day 169

Fellowship with Jesus

Thank You, Lord, You are not only a Holy God, but a Here-and-Now God. The disciple John experienced you as a Lean-Your-Head-On-My-Shoulder Lord. At the Last Supper, not only did the disciples have a meal with Jesus, He also washed their feet. Yes, He taught servanthood and a new type of love, but He also provided much needed comfort to their weary feet after a long day of plodding along dusty roads. He wants to do the same for us, if we will invite Him in to be with us. He wants to experience life with us, and refresh our souls. Do you hear Him knocking?

Have You Thought? Come in, Lord. The door of my heart is open.

His Answer:

"I know you well—you are neither hot nor cold; I wish you were one or the other!"

"Look! I have been standing at the door, and I am constantly knocking. If anyone hears me calling him and opens the door, I will come in and fellowship with him and he with me."

Revelation 3:15, 20
The Living Bible

Day 170

Return

Thank You, Lord, You are the God who reconciles us to Yourself and to others. You long to bring healing to our broken relationships. You even give us the method for repairing those places where walls have gone up and intimacy has gone down. To rediscover the joy, we are to *remember* the details of the closeness we once had, *repent* of our actions that have caused strife or separation, and *return* to our former conduct. Lord, help us remember, repent and return. Then by Your grace, reconcile Your people where we are estranged from You and from others.

Have You Thought? Lord, show me where I've lost my way and get me back to the godly way.

His Answer:
> This is what the Lord says: "Stop at the crossroads and look around. Ask for the old, godly way, and walk in it. Travel its path, and you will find rest for your souls."

Jeremiah 6:16
New Living Translation

Day 171

Two Blades

Thank You, Lord, that changing is not a work we have to do all on our own. No, it is a shared responsibility, like a pair of scissors. You hold one blade and we hold the other, and together, the transformation is done. Each blade must do its part, but only its part. We can't do God's job, nor will He do ours. But how very gracious He is with us, if we just take the smallest little step! Our loving Father encourages and enables us to do so much more than we ever thought we could do! So, wherever we know we need to change, let's tell God that we are willing to do our part, and He will do amazing things.

Have You Thought? Make me willing to do my part, Lord.

His Answer:

By his divine power, God has given us everything we need for living a godly life. We have received all of this by coming to know him, the one who called us to himself by means of his marvelous glory and excellence. And because of his glory and excellence, he has given us great and precious promises. These are the promises that enable you to share his divine nature and escape the world's corruption caused by human desires. In view of all this, make every effort to respond to God's promises.

2 Peter 1:3-5
New Living Translation

Day 172

Dream-Giver

Thank you, Lord, that we don't really miss out on anything when we follow You. Satan loves to make us think that we do…spinning fantastic dreams for us that sound wonderful, but are not attainable. And if they could be done, the cost to relationships and health would be way too high. He spins fantasies that are all about us, gratifying our desires and pride. The Lord is the true Dreamgiver. He gives us meaningful aspirations that can not only come true, but He uses our God-given gifts, bringing fulfillment to us, and blessing to others. Lord, be the Guider and Director of our dreams.

Have You Thought? Guide my dreams, Lord

His Answer:
> Eternal One: I am the Eternal One your God. I have given you My instruction for living well and right, leading you in how you should be and do. If only you had listened to My instruction, then you would have been flooded with peace; Your righteousness *would have risen and crested* like waves on the sea.

Isaiah 48:17-18
The Voice

Day 173

Lord of it All

Thank You, Lord, for the consistent, authentic life You lived on this earth. You modeled for us a life that had no separation between secular and holy—it was all holy. Everything You did reflected Your Father. We classify our lives into categories—those things that involve and relate to God, and those that don't. God is Lord of it all. I confess my ongoing inner struggle between feeling either hypocritical or holier-than-thou. Transform me, Lord. Make me really transparently Yours, regardless of where I am or what I am doing. Help me live to please You first and foremost.

Have You Thought? Lord, make my life authentically Yours.

His Answer:
> For my part, I am going to boast about nothing but the Cross of our Master, Jesus Christ. Because of that Cross, I have been crucified in relation to the world, set free from the stifling atmosphere of pleasing others and fitting into the little patterns that they dictate.

Galatians 6:14
The Message

Day 174

Compassionate One

Thank You, Lord, Your love is boundless, never ending, and impossible to overstep. Mine is not. You love with a pure love, one not tainted by selfish motives or unhealthy needs. You love unconditionally. I gladly pour myself into a relationship or a situation until I am spent, and then I am no longer loving and I can't continue to shower grace or mercy. I am so grateful that You can and You do, Lord. Love through me, Compassionate One. Fill me anew with Your wonderful mercies because I run dry. Let the world see and experience Your love manifested in me today. Be my Supply.

Have You Thought? Fill me with Your love again, Lord.

His Answer:

Living then, as every one of you does, in pure grace, it's important that you not misinterpret yourselves as people who are bringing this goodness to God. No, God brings it all to you. The only accurate way to understand ourselves is by what God is and by what he does for us, not by what we are and what we do for him.

Romans 12:3
The Message

Day 175

New Joys

Thank You, Lord, for ordaining and orchestrating seasons, not only on the earth, but in our lives. I enjoy each new season for its unique beauty. It is the transition between the seasons of my life that sends me to my knees. When I am mourning a time in my life that is drawing to a close, You tenderly give me glimpses of the new joys which await me in my new season. I remember once again that You order every day and every interval of my life. Comfort us where our lives are changing and we are grieving, Lord. You are a Constant God in an inconstant world.

Have You Thought? You have blessings for me in every season of my life.

His Answer:

Show me Your grace, Eternal One, for I am in a tight spot. My eyes are aching with grief; my body and soul *are withering with miseries.* My life is devoured by sorrow, and my years *are haunted* with mourning.

But I pour my trust into You, Eternal One. I'm *glad to* say, "You are my God!" I give the moments of my life over to You, *Eternal One.* Rescue me from those who hate me and who hound me *with their threats.*

Psalms 31:9-10, 14-15
The Voice

Day 176

Well Aware

Thank You, Lord, that Your love for us is not a blind love. You are totally aware of our idiosyncrasies, our faults, our obsessions. You are familiar with our past sins and also the ones we have yet to commit. Yet You love us passionately. Is there any other realization that equals the joy of knowing this? It is the eternal sigh of relief that in Jesus we are never despised, disallowed or discarded. No wrong turn or deliberate detour can ever diminish His love for us. In the midst of all the insecurities of this life Lord, the awareness of Your unfailing love is the Hallelujah which supersedes any circumstance.

Have You Thought? Lord, You know me the best and love me the most.

His Answer:
Your love, God, is my song, and I'll sing it! I'm forever telling everyone how faithful you are.

Blessed are the people who know the passwords of praise, who shout on parade in the bright presence of God. Delighted, they dance all day long; they know who you are, what you do—they can't keep it quiet!

Psalms 89:1, 15-16
The Message

Day 177

Set Free

Thank You, Lord, that You understand the wearisome weight of worry. That is why You *plead* with us not to be troubled. If only I would really believe that my concerns are Your concerns, and that in Your mind, they are already settled. Then, I would not obsess about them so much. Lord, forgive me for losing sight of this truth so easily. It is the heart of the Gospel—the Good News that we are not alone or on our own anymore. The Savior has come to pay our debts, bear our burdens and free us from fear. These shackles I wear are self-imposed. Set me free again, Lord. Be my Burden Bearer.

Have You Thought? Keep on setting me free, Lord from self-imposed shackles.

His Answer:

> "The Spirit of the Lord is upon me, for he has appointed me to preach Good News to the poor. He has sent me to proclaim that captives will be released, that the blind will see, that the downtrodden will be freed from their oppressors, and that the time of the Lord's favor has come."

Luke 4:18-19
New Living Translation

Day 178

Light-Bearers

Thank You, Lord, that Your idea of success is vastly different from mine. How often I get caught up in this world's view of achievement! I am too impressed by income, perks and power. You discount these things, knowing that in an instant You can take them away. What do You search for? True followers who shine Your light in this darkened world. In fact, You think this is our primary job, over and above any occupation we may have. Help me to brighten the hearts of all I meet today. Fill me with Your Spirit, because more than anything, I want my days to please You, Lord.

Have You Thought? Lord, help me spread Your Light wherever I go today.

His Answer:
And you, *beloved*, are the light of the world. A city built on a hilltop cannot be hidden.

You are like that illuminating light. Let your light shine everywhere you go, *that you may illumine creation,* so men and women everywhere may see your good actions, *may see creation at its fullest, may see your devotion to Me*, and may turn and praise your Father in heaven *because of it.*

Matthew 5:14, 16
The Voice

Day 179

Barricades

Thank You, Lord, that You came to break down all barriers to You. So, why do I sometimes feel as if You are so far away? Sadly, it is because *I* build back the walls. And it seems like the bricks of my partitions go up so quietly and quickly and almost without my realization. Usually I've either been running too hard, or holding onto something or someone too closely. But You faithfully reveal my problem and forgive me, even as You demolish my barricade! Jonah was right when he said that You are "sheer grace and mercy, not easily angered, rich in love" (Jonah 4:2, MSG). How true in my life!

Have You Thought? Draw me close again, Lord. Show me what keeps me from You.

His Answer:
> It isn't too late. You can still return to me with all your heart. Start crying and mourning! Go without eating. Don't rip your clothes to show your sorrow. Instead, turn back to me with broken hearts. I am merciful, kind, and caring. I don't easily lose my temper, and I don't like to punish.
>
> Joel 2:12-13
> Contemporary English Version

Day 180

Walk on Water

Thank You, Lord, that You still call us to walk on water. You want us to go to places and situations in our lives where we can't navigate on our own, where we need You before us, beckoning us to "Come." You want us to venture to areas in our lives that would frighten us if You were not there. I don't like those places—they are not safe places, and not in my comfort zone. You call us out in order to do Your perfect purposes that stretch us, scare us and make us trust. The good news is You enable and empower us, if we'll just say, "Yes!" So, Lord take our hands and calm the waves.

Have You Thought? Lord, show me my comfort zones and then lead me out of them.

His Answer:
> "Don't be afraid, I've redeemed you. I've called your name. You're mine. When you're in over your head, I'll be there with you. When you're in rough waters, you will not go down. When you're between a rock and a hard place, it won't be a dead end."

Isaiah 43:1-2
The Message

Day 181

Your Way

Thank You, Lord, You are the Designer and Director of our lives! We may take many detours from Your plan, either by not listening to Your instruction or by deliberately going another way. I've done them both, and lived to regret them. But, all it takes is a simple, "I'm sorry, Lord" and a, "You lead now, and I'll follow," to get back on the Perfect Plan again. So, be the Compass and Captain of my life's journey, please. Of course, I will want to know the entire course's directions, but You will only give me the next step. I'm trusting *Your* way, because I know it is the best.

Have You Thought? I've done it my way. Now show me Yours, Lord.

His Answer:

> The Eternal *is ready to* share His wisdom *with us,* for His words bring true knowledge and insight; He has stored up *the essentials of* sound wisdom for those who do right; He acts as a shield for those who value integrity. God protects the paths of *those who pursue* justice, watching over the lives of those who keep faith with Him.

> Proverbs 2:6-8
> The Voice

Day 182

God's Call

Thank You, Lord, that You give each of us specific gifts, abilities and interests in order to bless others and show Your love. Have you realized and embraced God's design for you? Years ago, God called me to encourage others, but I literally scoffed at that gift. God is merciful! After walking through breast cancer and receiving calls, meals, cards and rides to chemo, I realized the amazing power of encouragement. If you have never considered how the Lord has specifically equipped you to touch this hurting, broken world with His love, ask Him to show you today. There are people who desperately need your special touch.

Have You Thought? Lord, help me to embrace Your one-of-a-kind call on my life.

His Answer:
>   Let's just go ahead and be what we were made to be, without enviously or pridefully comparing ourselves with each other, or trying to be something we aren't. If you preach, just preach God's Message, nothing else; if you help, just help, don't take over; if you teach, stick to your teaching;
>
>   Love from the center of who you are; don't fake it. Run for dear life from evil; hold on for dear life to good.

Romans 12:6-7, 9
The Message

Day 183

True Fulfillment

Thank You, Lord, that You mean for each of us to find true fulfillment and lasting joy in our lives. You know exactly how You wired us, and what our gifts are. Your plan is for each of us to touch the lives of others with our unique personality and capabilities. How You love to bless us as we walk into that calling! Our job is to fully embrace those God-given talents and not envy someone else's—that only brings division, jealousy and sadness. Lord, help us to gladly accept our one-of-a-kind design, and wholly walk into it, giving thanks to You, the Grand Designer, for our Sovereign shaping.

Have You Thought? No wishing I had someone else's gift. That brings real heartache.

His Answer:
God's various gifts are handed out everywhere; but they all originate in God's Spirit.

Each person is given something to do that shows who God is: Everyone gets in on it, everyone benefits. All kinds of things are handed out by the Spirit, and to all kinds of people!

1 Corinthians 12:4-7
The Message

Day 184

Unbeatable

Thank You, Lord, You provide the power to accomplish everything You ask us to do. That is such good news! It is the affirmation we need when Satan tries to tell us that we are not enough: not smart enough, strong enough or committed enough. You raise Your Almighty Hand inside us as if to say, "Maybe not, but I AM," and we are encouraged and empowered. Our job is to keep listening and looking to You, as we take each step of our faith-walk. Show us today, Lord, in a tangible way that together we are an unbeatable team. Move in and through us with Your unquenchable Spirit.

Have You Thought? When I can't see, You can.

His Answer:

So don't be embarrassed to speak up for our Master or for me, his prisoner. Take your share of suffering for the Message along with the rest of us. We can only keep on going, after all, by the power of God, who first saved us and then called us to this holy work. We had nothing to do with it. It was all his idea, a gift prepared for us in Jesus long before we knew anything about it.

2 Timothy 1:8-9
The Message

Day 185

Not in the Dark

Thank You, Lord, that keeping our eyes firmly fixed on You and the truth of Your Word removes our fear of tomorrow's troubles. We are bombarded every day with bad news, worst-case scenarios and dire predictions on multiple forms of media. It can be very scary; and Satan would love for that fear to immobilize us. But, thanks be to God, we know the One Who has the Last Word. Everything in this world will pass away, but we've read the end of the Story, and our side—*His* side wins! So, Lord, help us to *live* in this world but set our *sights* on You, Jesus, our eternal and also our everyday hope!

Have You Thought? Dress me in faith, Lord.

His Answer:

> I don't think, friends, that I need to deal with the question of when all this is going to happen. You know as well as I that the day of the Master's coming can't be posted on our calendars.

> But friends, you're not in the dark, so how could you be taken off guard by any of this?

> 1 Thessalonians 5:1-2, 4
> The Message

Day 186

Beckoned

Thank You, Lord, that Christianity has always been, and will always be a relationship initiated by You. Our first stirrings toward You really began in Your heart. Each time we run back or draw nearer, Your Spirit has beckoned us. That truth is the core of our faith and the confidence of our hope. You desire us and descend to our level because of Your great love for us. How can we possibly resist this inexpressible offer of love? Draw us fully into this Real Life You offer us, Lord. No striving, no trying to earn our way to You, just a "Yes!" to Your amazing grace in the face of Your Son.

Have You Thought? I want to live freely and lightly, Lord.

His Answer:
> "Come to me and I will give you rest—all of you who work so hard beneath a heavy yoke. Wear my yoke—for it fits perfectly—and let me teach you; for I am gentle and humble, and you shall find rest for your souls; for I give you only light burdens."

Matthew 11:28
The Living Bible

Day 187

Search Me

"Search me, O God, and know my heart…see if there is any wicked way in me," says Psalm 139:23-24 (NKJV). *Who* is doing the searching and seeing? *God.* I thought self-scrutiny was my job. I would come red-faced to the Cross time and time again with my conscience-stricken confessions. Not the case. The Holy Spirit reveals and realigns, but He restores too. What good news! Thank you, Lord, for this new understanding for me and hopefully, for others. Lord, will You continue to show me where You want me to be made new? Clean out my ears so I can hear Your voice. Remake me.

Have You Thought? You gently, graciously realign me.

His Answer:

> Search me, O God, and know my heart; test my thoughts. Point out anything you find in me that makes you sad, and lead me along the path of everlasting life.
>
> Psalms 139:23-24
> The Living Bible

Day 188

Rock-Solid Guarantee

I thank You today, Lord, that my feelings do not determine Your faithfulness. I know mine are as shifting as the sands. One day I feel as if I could reach out and take Your Hand, and the next I cry, "Where are You, God?" How grateful I am for Your steadfast love. Your character and Your promises stand. They are fixed, eternal and abiding. My emotions are temporary, changeable and unpredictable. So why do I listen to them? Lord, make me aware of my moods, but help me be not governed by them. Let my faith rest in Your constant, consistent, changeless character, which never fails. Amen.

Have You Thought? You always make good on Your promises.

His Answer:

When God made his promise to Abraham, he backed it to the hilt, putting his own reputation on the line.

When people make promises, they guarantee them by appeal to some authority above them so that if there is any question that they'll make good on the promise, the authority will back them up. When God wanted to guarantee his promises, he gave his word, a rock-solid guarantee—God *can't* break his word. And because his word cannot change, the promise is likewise unchangeable.

Hebrews 6:13, 15-18
The Message

Day 189

Wonderworking God

You are the miracle working God! Nothing is too hard for You. How about flasks of oil that never run dry, the sun standing still for a day, advancing armies that self-destruct, rocks that bring forth water, sticks turning into snakes or prophets taken to Heaven in chariots of fire? The really fun part of this truth is there is no extreme miracle that puts God to the test. There's no line in the sand that becomes unmanageable for Him. The next time you are in need of a wonder-working God, recall His past supernatural acts, and say "Thank you" in advance to show your trust.

Have You Thought? Your rescuing hand never tires.

His Answer:

Then Joshua explained again the purpose of the stones: "In the future," he said, "when your children ask you why these stones are here and what they mean, you are to tell them that these stones are a reminder of this amazing miracle—that the nation of Israel crossed the Jordan River on dry ground! Tell them how the Lord our God dried up the river right before our eyes and then kept it dry until we were all across! It is the same thing the Lord did forty years ago at the Red Sea! He did this so that all the nations of the earth will realize that Jehovah is the mighty God, and so that all of you will worship him forever."

Joshua 4:21-24
The Living Bible

Day 190

Tell Your Story

Lord, You understand the power of Story. You could have designed Your Word very differently, but You chose to fill it with the drama of individual lives. You wanted Your people to proclaim Your glory to others. You still do. The details of our lives are meant to be the salvation saga for others—how You saw us, stooped down and saved us, and set us free. Because each of our stories is unique, the telling is always fresh and alive. Help each of us to always be ready to share our one-of-a-kind God-Story with others. Just like the man in Mark's Gospel, we want to be Your talk of the town, Lord.

Have You Thought? Make me quick to share what Jesus has done for me.

His Answer:
When they arrived at the other side of the lake, a demon-possessed man ran out from a graveyard...

Then Jesus spoke to the demon within the man and said, "Come out, you evil spirit."

And a large crowd soon gathered where Jesus was; but as they saw the man sitting there, fully clothed and perfectly sane, they were frightened.

So he got back into the boat. The man who had been possessed by the demons begged Jesus to let him go along. But Jesus said no. "Go home to your friends," he told him, "and tell them what wonderful things God has done for you; and how merciful he has been." So the man started off to visit the Ten Towns of that region and began to tell everyone about the great things Jesus had done for him; and they were awestruck by his story.

Mark 5:2, 7, 15, 18-20
The Living Bible

Day 191

Dressed in Jesus

Today is a part of the God-Story of my life. I will never have this day again. Will I notice what You are showing me before the sun sets? Will my eyes see Your wonders today? If life storms threaten to blow across my path, will I trust You to speak Your Peace in the midst of them? Will my lips speak Your praise? Can I take a short moment to share a smile with a stranger or words of life with my family? Lord, I can't live my life in a way that pleases You without Your help. Live Your life through me today. Let's walk this day together, Lord. I want to be dressed in Jesus.

Have You Thought? Let me not be oblivious to God-incidences today.

His Answer:

But make sure that you don't get so absorbed and exhausted in taking care of all your day-by-day obligations that you lose track of the time and doze off, oblivious to God. The night is about over, dawn is about to break. Be up and awake to what God is doing. God is putting the finishing touches on the salvation work he began when we first believed.

Get out of bed and get dressed! Dress yourselves in Christ, and be up and about!

Romans 13:11-12, 14
The Message

Day 192

Not the Same

Lord, no miracle You do for us can ever surpass the one You did in us. You willingly chose to leave Heaven where You were constantly worshiped and adored, to come to earth where You were hated, betrayed and crucified—all because of Your intense love for us. That once-for-all salvation has become the high point of our lives as Christians, and the pivotal event of all history. This truth should be the essence of who we are and the guideline for every action we take. Jesus bought us a new life, a new start and a new identity. *Nothing* is the same—it's miraculous in every way!

Have You Thought? Is knowing Jesus the highpoint of my life?

The Answer:

> After saying all these things, Jesus looked up to heaven and said, "Father, the hour has come. Glorify your Son so he can give glory back to you. For you have given him authority over everyone. He gives eternal life to each one you have given him. And this is the way to have eternal life—to know you, the only true God, and Jesus Christ, the one you sent to earth. I brought glory to you here on earth by completing the work you gave me to do. Now, Father, bring me into the glory we shared before the world began.

John 17:1-5
New Living Translation

Day 193

Frazzled and Frantic

You are a God of order. You spoke forth creation in a precise way. While on this earth, You *walked*, You didn't run…and You got everything done. You left out nothing and regretted nothing. Some days my life feels chronically past due and a dollar short. Frazzled and frantic, I'm tempted to pick up my pace even more. What I need is to slow down and be still and spend time in Your Presence. You allow me to sigh, You quiet my breathing, and I wonder once again why I don't do this every day. Maybe today I will learn that a day ordered by You is a day with heavenly direction.

Have You Thought? Give me Your heavenly direction, Lord.

His Answer:

Let me see *clearly* so that I may take in the amazing things coming from Your law.

I have admitted my ways *are wrong*, and You responded; now help me learn what You require.

Eliminate faithlessness You find in my step, be gracious, and give me Your guidance. I have decided to take the path of faith…

Psalms 119:18, 26, 29-30
The Voice

Day 194

Within Us

You are the Ultimate Encourager! You delight to see us use our talents and tendencies. Cheers ring from heaven when we decide to take those first steps, trying something new and scary, something perhaps dreamed of for a long time. You bolster us when we are blue; provide new opportunities when we meet obstacles. You know how the world is languishing to hear our own God-song rising up. Lord, let today be an eye-opening, heart-lifting, thank-you-Jesus day for the unique way You knit us together. Revive us, renew us and let us bring You glory!

Have You Thought? Revive and renew me today, Lord.

His Answer:

I ask him to strengthen you by his Spirit—not a brute strength, but a glorious inner strength—that Christ will live in you as you open the door and invite him in. And I ask him that with both feet planted firmly on love, you'll be able to take in with all the Christians the extravagant dimensions of Christ's love.

God can do anything you know—far more than you could ever imagine or guess or request in your wildest dreams! He does it not by pushing us around but by working within us, his Spirit deeply and gently within us.

Ephesians 3:16-18, 20
The Message

Day 195

Abundant Grace

Thank You, Lord, for meeting me right where I am. I don't have to dress up or get myself together to come to You. Dirty hands, a disheveled life, even a sin-stained heart won't turn You away. You call me to come even as You sweep away the dust from the latest wall I have built between us. I can't comprehend Your love! But I have a choice. I can either allow Satan to keep me in my guilty, feeling-awful-about-myself state, or I can accept Your incomprehensible forgiveness so lavishly offered. Unending guilt and shame or everlasting mercy and grace. Lord, I choose grace…Your abundant grace.

Have You Thought? Lord, help me to be inside-out honest with You.

His Answer:
> You're the One I've violated, and you've seen it all…You have all the facts before you; whatever you decide about me is fair. What you're after is truth from the inside out. Enter me, then; conceive a new, true life.
>
> Psalms 51:4-6
> The Message

Day 196

The Last Word

Lord, You always have the last word! Satan distorts and deceives, but even he knows that his doom is sure. We don't have to wait for eternity to see God's victory, though. He daily delights in putting the devil in his place and making him eat his words. Just think of your most recent fears that did not come true. Or your last challenges that, by God's grace, you met and overcame. The Father of Lies speaks dismay, doubt and death. Jesus says, "I am the Way, the Truth, and the Life." Let the First and the Last, the Alpha and the Omega have the last word in our lives today.

Have You Thought? I want to walk within Your plans.

His Answer:
> The Lord All-Powerful has made this promise: Everything I have planned will happen just as I said.
>
> Isaiah 14:24
> Contemporary English Version

Day 197

Heaven

Thank You, Lord, Your Last Word is Heaven! You are Three-in-One: our Ticket to get there, the Guide to point the way, and the Host to welcome us in. That upcoming trip should thrill our imaginations, but instead, it consumes us with fear. How can that be? Is it because our minds are so immersed in this throwaway world that we never take the time to contemplate our forever Home? The Bible gives us so many clues of Heaven's beauty, joy, and fellowship. Lord, interrupt each one of our small, this-world-focused lives today with Your permanent Paradise point of view.

Have You Thought? Help me be a little less this-world focused today, Lord.

His Answer:
> Don't let this throw you. You trust God, don't you? Trust me. There is plenty of room for you in my Father's home. If that weren't so, would I have told you that I'm on my way to get a room ready for you? And if I'm on my way to get your room ready, I'll come back and get you so you can live where I live.
>
> Jesus said, "I am the Road, also the Truth, also the Life. No one gets to the Father apart from me."

John 14:1-4, 6
The Message

Day 198

The Heart of Man

Thank You, Lord, You have always understood the heart of man. The lessons in your Word continue to instruct and convict us because our weaknesses never change. The Israelites whined for the good bread they had in Egypt, so You gave them Bread from Heaven. They called it manna—translated "What is it?" They didn't understand Your provision for them. We are prone do the same thing. You long to teach us trust even in the midst of turmoil. Help us to place our confidence in You today, regardless of any confusion we have about Your plan for us.

Have You Thought? Lord, don't let me test You.

His Answer:

They tested God in their *stubborn* hearts by demanding whatever food they happened to be craving. Then they challenged God: "Can God fill a table *with food* in the *middle of the* desert?

He split open the rock, and water gushed out; streams *and rivers* were overflowing! But can He also provide us with bread? Can He supply meat to His sons and daughters?" When the Eternal heard these words, He was furious; His fiery anger erupted against Jacob; His wrath grew against Israel.

Nevertheless, He gave instructions to the clouds in the sky and swung open heaven's doors;

(*In that day* mortals ate the bread of heavenly messengers.) God provided them with plenty of food.

Psalms 78:18-21, 23, 25
The Voice

Day 199

Yes!

Lord, since I belong to you, my identity is in You alone. That lesson takes a lifetime to learn. I am not defined by my past mistakes or my future hopes. Nor am I simply my husband's wife or my children's mother. I am a new creation in Christ and I am inextricably linked to Him. The Lover of my soul determines my significance. Yes, He gives each one of us relationships to enjoy, but He longs for us to find our worth and meaning in Him alone. So, Lord, where we have forgotten this, speak Your words of affirmation deep into our hearts today. Yell a loud "Yes!" over each one of us.

Have You Thought? Add my yes to Yours, Lord.

His Answer:
> Whatever God has promised gets stamped with the Yes of Jesus. In him, this is what we preach and pray, the great Amen, God's Yes and our Yes together, gloriously evident. God affirms us, making us a sure thing in Christ, putting his Yes within us. By his Spirit he has stamped us with his eternal pledge—a sure beginning of what he is destined to complete.

2 Corinthians 1:20-22
The Message

Day 200

Unique Beauty

You are the Divine Horticulturist, and in Your Word you liken us to gardens. In a garden there are infinite varieties in the types of plantings, but each has its own distinct loveliness. A field of daisies has a relaxed, breezy charm while a formal rose garden has elegant grace. They are both beautiful to You. As Your showpiece of all creation, we need to learn this lesson. How untrue and unfair it is when we compare ourselves to others and find ourselves lacking. Lord, help us to gratefully and gracefully be full of the unique beauty You designed us to be.

Have You Thought? Let Your beauty be gracefully displayed in me.

His Answer:

I will sing for joy in GOD, explode in praise from deep in my soul! He dressed me up in a suit of salvation, he outfitted me in a robe of righteousness, as a bridegroom who puts on a tuxedo and a bride a jeweled tiara. For as the earth bursts with spring wildflowers, and as a garden cascades with blossoms, so the Master, GOD, brings righteousness into full bloom and puts praise on display before the nations.

Isaiah 61:10-11
The Message

Day 201

Color to Our Days

Thank You, Lord, for bringing color to our days. You paint the physical world, but You also color our emotional landscapes, when we allow You to show Your redeeming grace. Some days just seem dull and drab. Everything feels gray. Relationships may be on edge, finances stretched to the limit, or health issues arise. Those are the realities of this broken world. But we have a choice to let the dazzling brilliance of the Lord in to shine into the depths of our bleak circumstances. He stands ready to brush His glorious heavenly hues on those black clouds. Lord, give us eyes to see!

Have You Thought? Give me eyes to see.

His Answer:
> Wilderness and desert will sing joyously, the badlands will celebrate and flower—bursting into blossom, a symphony of song and color. God's resplendent glory, fully on display. God awesome, God majestic.
>
> Springs of water will burst out in the wilderness, streams flow in the desert.

Isaiah 35:1-2, 6
The Message

Day 202

Gone

Thank You, Lord, for the cleansing power of Your Blood. Our sins are washed away, and we are white as snow. They are not just barely covered either; not even a hint of a stain remains. That's the view from Heaven, anyway. Our eyesight often needs correction, for we see shadows of our offenses still. We pick up Satan's spectacles and believe his lies. Jesus offers His God-shaped glasses, to see ourselves as purged, purified and on the road to Paradise, by the grace of God and the shed Blood of His Son. From defiled to delivered—it doesn't get any better than that. Believe it!

Have You Thought? Lord, make me quick to confess.

His Answer:

What happiness for those whose guilt has been forgiven! What joys when sins are covered over! What relief for those who have confessed their sins and God has cleared their record. There was a time when I wouldn't admit what a sinner I was. But my dishonesty made me miserable and filled my days with frustration. All day and all night your hand was heavy on me. My strength evaporated like water on a sunny day until I finally admitted all my sins to you and stopped trying to hide them. I said to myself, "I will confess them to the Lord." And you forgave me! All my guilt is gone.

Psalms 32:1-5
The Living Bible

212

Day 203

Finest Treasure

Thank You, Lord, for the treasure of Your Word. In this unreliable, unpredictable, ever-changing world, Your Word stands firm and keeps us grounded. When we base our lives on its truth, it provides stability and a security of which this world knows nothing. It is Life and Light and Wisdom and Salvation— and it is easily ignored in our day-to-day lives. Lord, give us a new thirst for Your Living Water that quenches the dryness in our souls. Open our eyes to see and our minds to understand Your Love Letter written to us. Incline our hearts to search it as if we are finding the finest treasure.

Have You Thought? Incline my heart to You today, Lord

His Answer:

Every word you give me is a miracle word—how could I help but obey? Break open your words, let the light shine out, let ordinary people see the meaning. Mouth open and panting, I wanted your commands more than anything. Turn my way, look kindly on me, as you always do to those who personally love you. Steady my steps with your Word of promise so nothing malign gets the better of me.

Smile on me, your servant; teach me the right way to live.

Psalms 119:129-133, 135
The Message

Day 204

Live in Me

Thank You, Lord, Your ways are so much deeper and more meaningful than mine. Mine impact today—Yours bear fruit forever. My to-do list the other day was barely touched, and I was frustrated at getting "nothing" done. You were thrilled! Time after time, You revised my laid-out schedule and added in people who needed a word of hope. You interrupted my plans and caused me to think and act just a little bit more like You. Everyone won because of those agenda changes. Lord, today, by Your grace, help me to be a blessing to those who are on my to-do list, as well as those who are not. Re-arrange my day.

Have You Thought? Rewrite my to-do list, Lord.

His Answer:

"Take care to live in me, and let me live in you. For a branch can't produce fruit when severed from the vine. Nor can you be fruitful apart from me."

"You didn't choose me! I chose you! I appointed you to go and produce lovely fruit always, so that no matter what you ask for from the Father, using my name, he will give it to you."

John 15:4, 16
The Living Bible

Day 205

Mine Alone

Thank You, Lord, for Your Big Picture. What a comfort to know You have every moment of our lives planned. Nothing we do, and nothing that happens to us surprises You. As human beings, we are subject to physical influences such as gravity and time. God is not. We live in a right-here-and-now present dimension. God has a much different view. If life were a parade, He'd be in the blimp overhead, looking at the beginning and the end all at once. We're stuck on the curb, watching each attraction as it passes. Considering that, isn't He worthy of our complete trust?

Have You Thought? I give You the glory, Lord.

His Answer:
> Eternal One: In times long past, I determined and announced the things that would come. Then suddenly I acted, and they indeed happened.
>
> You've heard what I foretold; now you've seen what has happened—do you agree *that I'm God?* Well, from this moment, I am telling you new things, secrets hidden that no one has known. They are created now—brand new, never before announced, never before heard. So you can't claim, "Look, I already knew them."
>
> But it is all on account of Me, *not of you,* that I act, that I retain honor, that My glory is Mine alone, and not sullied.
>
> Isaiah 48:3, 6-7, 11
> The Voice

Day 206

Spectator

Thank You, Lord, for Your daily direction. So often, I relegate You to the role of Spectator in my life...and that breaks Your heart. You designed us to be in the closest possible relationship, where every little detail of our lives is brought before You and guided by You. Instead, I bring *my* plans to You and ask for Your blessing on them, but not Your input or correction. And then, I wonder why they don't prosper! Lord, would You change my heart today, and make me only want those plans which line up with Yours? Help me to truly long for Your daily direction, follow it, and realize the full life You mean for me.

Have You Thought? Be more than a spectator in my life, Lord.

His Answer:

> The Eternal One will never leave you; He *will* lead you *in the way that you should go.* When you feel dried up *and worthless,* God will nourish you and give you strength. And you will grow like a garden *lovingly* tended; you will be like a spring whose water never runs out.

Isaiah 58:11
The Voice

Day 207

Remembering

Lord, Your Word is a testimony of Your deeds. You call us to continue that witness...to record and retell the times when You showed Your strength on our behalf. Why? Because You understand the strength and stability found in remembering those miracles. In crisis, how comforting it is to recall Your faithfulness in a past difficulty. Our memories get fuzzy without a written reminder. So impress on us today a method to celebrate Your goodness: a blessing box, a journal, a Facebook post. The spiritual markers noted today will determine the depth of our faith tomorrow.

Have You Thought? Lord, let my memories of Your goodness never fade.

His Answer:

I recall the many miracles he did for me so long ago. Those wonderful deeds are constantly in my thoughts. I cannot stop thinking about them. O God, your ways are holy. Where is there any other as mighty as you? You are the God of miracles and wonders! You still demonstrate your awesome power.

Psalms 77:11-14
The Living Bible

Day 208

One Person at a Time

Thank You, Lord, You are the God who cares about us individually. Your eternal Story is written one person at a time, until collectively, the Kingdom is realized. But we are all players in that Good News saga for the salvation of the world. We each have our specific parts to play. The pivotal factor is not our eligibility, but rather, our availability. One day we will know how that kind word, merciful deed, or testimony of God's grace impacted someone's life—for a day or forever. Keep us ever ready to show Your heart in some way to that one person for whom You died. All of heaven will rejoice.

Have You Thought? Use me, Lord.

His Answer:
> So Jesus used this illustration: "If you had a hundred sheep and one of them strayed away and was lost in the wilderness, wouldn't you leave the ninety-nine others to go and search for the lost one until you found it?"

> "Well, in the same way heaven will be happier over one lost sinner who returns to God than over ninety-nine others who haven't strayed away!"

Luke 15:3-4,7
The Living Bible

Day 209

Road Tested

When we are at the end of our strength, You can begin to show Yours. Why don't we rely on You sooner? So often we fool ourselves into believing we are self-sufficient. What a lie that is, and the Lord calls it *pride*! On our "I've got it, Lord" days, remind us every breath we take and everything we have is a gift from You. When we feel overwhelmed, overburdened, helpless or hopeless, show Your strength on our behalf. Direct us where we are lost, steady our weary feet, and hold our shaky hands, most gracious Lord. We'll gladly sing Your praise!

Have You Thought? Lord, give me Your God-directions today.

His Answer:
> What a God! His road stretches straight and smooth. Every GOD-direction is road-tested. Everyone who runs toward him makes it. Is there any god like GOD? Are we not at bedrock? Is not this the God who armed me, then aimed me in the right direction?
>
> You protect me with salvation-armor, you hold me up with a firm hand, caress me with your gentle ways. You cleared the ground under me so my footing was firm.
>
> That's why I'm thanking you, GOD, all over the world. That's why I'm singing songs that rhyme your name.

Psalms 18:30-32, 35-36, 49
The Message

Day 210

Kind Deeds

Thank You, Lord, You rule and reign, even over our hardest days. When our every thought is a question, and nothing seems certain. Even when chaos seems to be brewing in our lives or our hearts…You are still Sovereign. It is Your great delight to involve Yourself in our conflicts and unforeseen circumstances, revealing that you are Lord of all. All. No exceptions. Nothing is past Your redemption or Your lavish compassion. Show us Your power again today when we feel out of Your reach. Remind us of Your unanticipated and not-even-dreamed-of past solutions.

Have You Thought? Your kindness never ends, Lord.

His Answer:

> I will tell about the kind deeds the Lord has done. They deserve praise! The Lord has shown mercy to the people of Israel; he has been kind and good. The Lord rescued his people, and said, "They are mine. They won't betray me." It troubled the Lord to see them in trouble, and his angel saved them. The Lord was truly merciful, so he rescued his people. He took them in his arms and carried them all those years.

Isaiah 63:7-9
Contemporary English Version

Day 211

Overriding Purposes

Lord, if we truly want to do Your will, no mistake we make will prevent Your plans or hinder Your work in our lives. Often, God's will is brought about despite our bad moves. Why? Because God has anticipated and taken into account long before our birth our every possible detour from His road. How comforting to know, if we truly are God-followers, we can't deter or override His purposes. That gives me great hope and a sure confidence to just take that next step, believing that if I am going the wrong way, He will let me know. What a relief!

Have You Thought? You have accounted for my every possible detour.

His Answer:
>Our Lord, you always do right, and you make the path smooth for those who obey you.

>You are the one we trust to bring about justice; above all else we want your name to be honored.

>Isaiah 26:7-8
>Contemporary English Version

Day 212

Impulsive and Impatient

Thank You, Lord, You are not impulsive or impatient. I am both. I want my problems fixed quickly and my prayers answered even faster. I realize the only way to get that kind of speed is to have only superficial change—band-aids—on the situation instead of deep healing. Your Heavenly Remedy brings true repentance and perfect redemption. I need to learn to wait for Your timing, and that requires Your work in my heart. So, Lord, here's another prayer request: make me a more patient, trusting daughter. Teach me to wait on You and Your timing, so you can do Your thorough work.

Have You Thought? Make me a more patient, trusting daughter.

His Answer:
Listen, GOD, I'm calling at the top of my lungs: "Be good to me! Answer me!" When my heart whispered, "Seek God," my whole being replied, "I'm seeking him!" Don't hide from me now! You've always been right there for me, don't turn your back on me now. Don't throw me out, don't abandon me, you've always kept the door open.

I'm sure now I'll see God's goodness in the exuberant earth. Stay with GOD! Take heart. Don't quit. I'll say it again: Stay with GOD.

Psalms 27:7-9, 13-14
The Message

Day 213

Don't Forget

Thank You, Lord, for the joy of remembering what You did for us on the Cross. You said "Remember" when You gave the bread and the wine. Paul, who was not there for the Last Supper, but who was instructed about it personally by Jesus, reminds us how serious this is. Communion or the Eucharist is celebrated in many ways, but the Greek meaning of the words stays the same. *Eucharisteo* means "to give thanks." The word "remember" is *anamnesis* (*ana* meaning "not," and *amnesis* meaning "forget"). The body and the blood…given for you. Eat it in holy awe for the love poured out. Give thanks… and don't forget.

Have You Thought? Let me never forget what You did for me on the Cross.

His Answer:

The Master, Jesus, on the night of his betrayal, took bread. Having given thanks, he broke it and said, This is my body, broken for you. Do this to remember me. After supper, he did the same thing with the cup: This cup is my blood, my new covenant with you. Each time you drink this cup, remember me…

Anyone who eats the bread or drinks the cup of the Master irreverently is like part of the crowd that jeered and spit on him at his death. Is that the kind of "remembrance" you want to be part of? Examine your motives, test your heart, come to this meal in holy awe.

I Corinthians 11:23-25, 27-28
The Message

Day 214

Zoe Life

Thank You, Lord, You are the God of Life. You've offered life in two forms to each of us, totally determined by our choice. All human beings have *bios* life—the breathing air, taking-up-space version of living. But there is a higher call extended—*zoe* life—the God-breathed, Pentecost-born, full-of-the-Holy Spirit life. It is a radical departure from the ho-hum walking around existence. This can-you-believe-it, *new* life transformed the disciples from the doors locked, scared-out-of-their-wits followers of Jesus into set-the-world-on-fire apostles. I want that *zoe* life, Lord. Fill me anew today.

Have You Thought? Lord, I want to be known as Your companion, too.

His Answer:
"By what power, or by whose authority have you done this?" the Council demanded. Then Peter, filled with the Holy Spirit, said to them, "Honorable leaders and elders of our nation, if you mean the good deed done to the cripple, and how he was healed, let me clearly state to you and to all the people of Israel that it was done in the name and power of Jesus from Nazareth, the Messiah, the man you crucified—but God raised back to life again. It is by his authority that this man stands here healed!

There is salvation in no one else! Under all heaven there is no other name for men to call upon to save them." When the Council saw the boldness of Peter and John and could see that they were obviously uneducated non-professionals, they were amazed and realized what being with Jesus had done for them!

Acts 4:7-10, 12-13
The Living Bible

Day 215

Lonely for You

Thank You, Lord, that You "put eternity in our hearts" (Ecclesiastes 3:11 NKJV). You purposely designed a longing for You in each one of us. That's why our running around, doing everything but being still before You leaves us, well…lonely. We try to find fulfillment in all our other relationships, but, ultimately, Your friendship and companionship is what we need. Some days just end up frantic despite our best efforts. There are also those times when we willingly run hard and fast right past You, ignoring Your gentle gaze. Lord, slow us down on those days. Make us lonely for You, Lord, above all.

Have You Thought? Lord, fill that longing in me.

His Answer:
> The Lord alone is God! He created the heavens and made a world where people can live, instead of creating an empty desert. The Lord alone is God; there are no others. The Lord did not speak in a dark secret place or command Jacob's descendants to search for him in vain. The Lord speaks the truth, and this is what he says to every survivor from every nation: "Gather around me! Learn how senseless it is to worship wooden idols or pray to helpless gods."

> "I invite the whole world to turn to me and be saved. I alone am God! No others are real."

> Isaiah 45:18-20, 22
> Contemporary English Version

225

Day 216

Real with You

Prayer is not being nice in front of You, Lord, it is about being real with You. As in any healthy parent/child relationship, You want to hear our true hearts, not just receive our lip service. Why else did You allow so many of David's impertinent psalms if not to show us You care about both the boring details and the emotional drama of our everyday lives? You take this prayer-life seriously, Lord. We fool ourselves into thinking You are unaware of our human experiences. Open us up and lay us bare before You today. Our uncovered inner souls are safe in Your gentle Hands.

Have You Thought? You know everything about me Lord… and I'm safe with You.

His Answer:

I call out loudly to the Eternal One; I lift my voice to the Eternal begging for His favor. I let everything that's going wrong spill out of my mouth; I spell out all my troubles to Him.

You are the One I called to, O Eternal One. I said, "You're the *only* safe place I know; You're all I've got in this world."

Psalms 142:1-2, 5
The Voice

Day 217

Piled on Him

I thank You, Lord, that there are no scales in Heaven. No balances weighing what we did right versus what we did wrong. No accounting of Sunday school attendance, Bible verses memorized or number of lies told. Why? Because Jesus allowed God to pile the weight of our sins on His shoulders, so our score with God would be settled *forever*. Instead of scales in Heaven, there is a Shepherd, counting His sheep…those included in His Fold because they followed His Voice. Jesus set the scales right for us, and then banished them forever. What a relief—what a redemption!

Have You Thought? All my sins were piled on You, Jesus.

His Answer:
> He took on our sins in His body *when He died* on the cross so that we, being dead to sin, can live for righteousness. *As the Scripture says,* "Through His wounds, you were healed." For there was a time when you were like sheep that wandered from the fold, but now you have returned to the Shepherd and Guardian of your lives.

> 1 Peter 2:24-25
> The Voice

Day 218

In Need of a Savior

Thank You, Lord, not only are You our Shepherd; You are our Savior. We need rescuing regularly. Life runs smoothly for a season, and then, out of the blue, we are brought to our knees and reminded again we don't have it all together. We can't solve every problem on our own. We need a Savior. In every relationship or situation in our lives, we are in need of prayer, despite the claims to the contrary by our self-reliant nature. Where has life shown you today that You are in need of a Savior? He is ready and waiting to act on your behalf when you call on Him.

Have You Thought? Act on my behalf today, Lord.

His Answer:

I have not forgotten your Law! Look at the trouble I am in, and rescue me.

You are merciful, Lord! Please do the right thing and save my life.

You give peace of mind to all who love your Law. Nothing can make them fall. You are my only hope for being saved, Lord, and I do all you command.

Psalms 119:153, 156, 165-166
Contemporary English Version

Day 219

Trustworthy

Lord, Your ability to help us is not determined by the level of our difficulty. You are mighty to save in *any* situation. Sometimes we don't act as if we believe that. If the cancer is stage one or two, we are hopeful. If it is stage four, we wonder if You can intervene. Really? Does the enormity of the situation restrain God's Hands? When can you remember God not being able to keep His Word? Is there a point when He says, "Sorry, this one is too big for Me"? Lord, we make You too small. Enlarge our view of You today in a way we can't miss. You are GOD.

Have You Thought? Your promises have no limitations.

His Answer:
>   I promise in my own name: Every word out of my mouth does what is says. I never take back what I say. Everyone is going to end up kneeling before me. Everyone is going to end up saying of me, "Yes! Salvation and strength are in GOD!"

Isaiah 45:23-25
The Message

Day 220

Direction and Deliverance

Thank You, Lord, You died to free us from all the baggage of life that we strap onto our backs. You know…that backpack chock-full of life's memories, on replay over and over in our minds. The ones we wish could stop because they remind us of words said or actions taken that caused pain or regret. Whether they were sins committed or sins inflicted, You came to break those chains. You understand how they weigh down our hearts and sap our joy, Lord. Help us to begin to recognize and hand over our troubled places to You today, so that we can walk in Your true freedom.

Have You Thought? Unlock any chains that bind me, Lord.

His Answer:
> Commit your path to the Eternal; *let Him direct you.* Put your confidence in Him, and He will follow through *with you.*
>
> The Eternal saves His faithful; He lends His strength in hard times…

Psalms 37:5, 39
The Voice

Day 221

For All the Saints

Thank You, Lord, for the saints in the Bible who encouraged and guided the lives of Your people as they lived in a world saturated by idol worship. You graciously continue to place mentors in our midst, because we are still getting battered around and beaten down in this God-deficient world. On a grand scale, You gave us Billy Graham and Beth Moore, but You also give each of us men and women who lovingly counsel and guide us along our way. Lord, bless them richly, and help each of us to joyfully continue the tradition of boosting others who are new on this God-path.

Have You Thought? Lord, help me to pass on what I have received.

His Answer:

> And now, friends, we ask you to honor those leaders who work so hard for you, who have been given the responsibility of urging and guiding you along in your obedience. Overwhelm them with appreciation and love!…Gently encourage the stragglers, and reach out for the exhausted, pulling them to their feet. Be patient with each person, attentive to individual needs.

> 1 Thessalonians 5:12-14
> The Message

Day 222

Who We Love

Lord, You personally came to earth to show us once and for all that You are on our side. That age-old concept of the angry, vengeful God was put to death on Calvary. Then why is fear our default mode whenever we feel as if we've failed You? Why do we expect Your retaliation? Our perfection was never the rule for our admission into heaven. God thought that was Jesus' job. In fact, not one person has ever asked for God's forgiveness and been refused. Getting into Heaven is not about what we do, but about Who we love, and Who madly loves us! It's called amazing grace!

Have You Thought? God's kindness rules.

His Answer:

> Everyone was going to be punished because Adam sinned. But because of the good thing that Christ has done, God accepts us and gives us the gift of life.

> The Law came, so that the full power of sin could be seen. Yet where sin was powerful, God's kindness was even more powerful. Sin ruled by means of death. But God's kindness now rules, and God has accepted us because of Jesus Christ our Lord. This means that we will have eternal life.

Romans 5:18, 20-21
Contemporary English Version

Day 223

Even If

Thank You, Lord, that whenever Satan screeches, "What if?," You gently whisper, "Even if." There is no situation which is out of Your glance, Your provision, or Your redemption. The Devil delights in causing us panic, and deliberately tries to keep us frenzied and fearful. No wonder Jesus tells us "Fear not" three hundred and sixty-six times in the Bible. He understands where we are easy prey. Well, I refuse to be Satan's target practice for his deceptive darts anymore! Lord, help me to discern and dismiss quickly his hallucinations from Hell, and cling to the fact that You forever hold me fast.

Have You Thought? Even if…

His Answer:
> Sit down and rest, everyone. Recover your strength. Gather around me. Say what's on your heart. Together let's decide what's right.
>
> I pulled you in from all over the world, called you in from every dark corner of the earth, Telling you, "You're my servant, serving on my side. I've picked you. I haven't dropped you." Don't panic. I'm with you. There's no need to fear for I'm your God. I'll give you strength. I'll help you. I'll hold you steady, keep a firm grip on you.

Isaiah 41:1, 9-10
The Message

Day 224

Ongoing Conversation

Thank You, Lord, for the simplicity of prayer. It's just an ongoing conversation between a Loving, Good, Wise Father and a trusting child. Satan would have us believe that it takes great spiritual insight and practice. He distorts the truth because he understands its power: a simple, sincere prayer shakes the gates of Hell and opens the windows of Heaven. Lord, forgive us for falling for his lies. Your ear is always listening and Your Hand forever ready to provide, any time of the day. May we diligently keep that God-dialog open on our end, for it is the only side that ever disconnects.

Have You Thought? Help me to keep my God-dialog open.

His Answer:
> Even before sunrise, I pray for your help, and I put my hope in what you have said. I lie awake at night, thinking of your promises.
>
> Psalms 119:147-148
> Contemporary English Version

Day 225

A Quiet Place

Lord, You lived a perfectly disciplined life. Why is that so hard for us? This crazy world embraces full-scale action, endless achieving, and rest only at the point of exhaustion and we buy into it. God calls us to live effective but balanced lives. Even when Jesus healed people, He left some untouched, because the Father ordered His day, and no one else. I want to listen to that Voice first and foremost, Lord. Give me wisdom as I walk through my days. Even when I am doing Your work, teach me to rest when You give the gentle command, so You can equip me for Your next move.

Have You Thought? Lord, give my life balance today.

His Answer:
> The apostles returned to Jesus from their ministry tour and told him all they had done and taught. Then Jesus said, "Let's go off by ourselves to a quiet place and rest awhile." He said this because there were so many people coming and going that Jesus and his apostles didn't even have time to eat. So they left by boat for a quiet place, where they could be alone.

Mark 6:30-32
New Living Translation

Day 226

Free From Death's Hold

I thank You, Lord, that You are our Sufficient, Supreme, Salvation Pioneer. You became human, endured temptation and took on suffering all for us, so You could become our salvation. You willingly became the perfect Lamb sacrificed to free us from the penalty of death. How Satan loves to use his scare tactics on us about death—as if he still has control of that anymore! The truth is Jesus won that victory triumphantly. The devil loves to growl, but has no teeth. So, Lord, wherever we allow that prowling lion to deceive or demoralize us, remind us death is simply You leading us to glory!

Have You Thought? How does God want to heal my view of death?

His Answer:

It makes good sense that the God who got everything started and keeps everything going now completes the work by making the Salvation Pioneer perfect through suffering as he leads all these people to glory.

Since the children are made of flesh and blood, it's logical that the Savior took on flesh and blood in order to rescue them by his death. By embracing death, taking it into himself, he destroyed the Devil's hold on death and freed all who cower through life, scared to death of death.

Hebrews 2:10, 14-15
The Message

Day 227

Disoriented

Thank You, Lord, You are the Way, but You also show the Way. How grateful I am that You never tire of redirecting me. I get off course so easily. Just the everyday business of living can disorient me, and it happens so unconsciously. It's a "Too busy for You today, Lord" one day, and a "Sorry, I've been so busy, Jesus" another, and all of a sudden, I don't like where I am. Sadly, though, I know how I've gotten there. So, once again, I pray, "Bring me back to You, Lord." Thank you for Your patience. You are always calling me back to You. Help me to hear Your voice this time.

Have You Thought? Lord, refocus me again today.

His Answer:
> The Lord is good and does what is right; he shows the proper path to those who go astray.

> My eyes are always on the Lord, for he rescues me from the traps of my enemies.

> Psalms 25:8, 15
> New Living Translation

Day 228

Wonders on Display

I thank You, Lord, for how You reveal Yourself in creation every day. Take my gaze from my cellphone, computer and other technology. They not only frustrate me, but even worse, keep me from focusing on experiences that You have planned for me...with others and with You. Give me eyes to see and a heart to rejoice in the natural beauty You designed for my enjoyment. A bird's song at dawn, a frog's croak at dusk, vibrant sunsets, chattering squirrels. You created these things for my joy. Heighten my delight in Your wonders on display. Let me please You with my praises, today and always.

Have You Thought? Lord, let me not miss Your glory today.

His Answer:

You are indeed great—You who are wrapped in glory and dressed in greatness. For covering, You choose light—Your clothes, *sunset and moonrise.* For a tent, You stretch out the heavens; *for Your roof, You pitch the sky.*

Meanwhile, the people take *to the fields and to the shops and to the roads,* to all the places that people work, until evening *when they rest.* There is so much here, O Eternal One, so much You have made.

Psalms 104:1-2, 23-24
The Voice

Day 229

A New Covenant

Thank You, Lord, that as Your New Covenant children, our hearts have become Your Home. Since *we* are Your new sanctuary now, we only need to go to a quiet place to commune with You. A designated building is not required to hold Your Glory. My sanctuary can often be my screened porch. I am surrounded by creation and can worship You who made it all, who made me. I read Your Word and lift up prayers, knowing that I have been in Your Presence and experienced Your Peace. What a joy. What a privilege. Where is your quiet place to hear your Prince of Peace? Go there today.

Have You Thought? Make me Your sanctuary, Lord.

His Answer:

At that time, you will call out for Me, *and I will hear.* You will pray, and I will listen. You will look for Me intently, and you will find Me.

Eternal One: Call to Me, and I will answer you. I will tell you of great things, things beyond what you can imagine, things you could never have known.

Jeremiah 29:12-13; Jeremiah 33:3
The Voice

Day 230

Jesus-Whispers

Lord, I thank you that the volume of Your voice is so different from the Devil's. Maybe I'm the last one to figure this out, but on one level, isn't it just a matter of distance? Because we belong to Jesus, His Spirit lives in us. Satan wants to be far away from anything related to God, so he keeps his space from God-dwellers. Simply because of that distance, he has to scream to make us hear him. God lives *in* us, so why would He shout? Because He is so very near, He can speak quietly and if we are listening, we will hear. Lord, help me to stay quiet enough to hear those Jesus-whispers.

Have You Thought? Let me hear You clearly today.

His Answer:

This is the God who made the universe and all it contains, the God who is the King of all heaven and all earth. It would be illogical to assume that a God of this magnitude could possibly be contained in any man-made structure, no matter how majestic.

His purpose in all this was that people *of every culture and religion* would search for this ultimate God, grope for Him *in the darkness, as it were*, hoping to find Him. Yet, in truth, God is not far from any of us. For *you know the saying*, "We live in God; we move in God; we exist in God." And still another said, "We are indeed God's children."

Acts 17:24, 27-28
The Voice

Day 231

Soul Soaring

Thank You, Lord, for the power of praise to lift our hearts and raise our eyes to Your Throne. Have you ever been so concerned about a situation or someone you love that you can't get that burden off your mind? Try as you might, you just can't leave it at the feet of Jesus. That's where I was this week. When I went before Him and lifted my weary, trembling voice in song to praise the Lord, I was brought face-to-face with His powerful mercy, love and redemption. Suddenly, though nothing had changed, my soul soared again. Lord, this praise-life is such a gift! Let me never neglect it!

Have You Thought? What a gift to praise You, Jesus!

His Answer:
> All who worship the Lord, now praise him! The Lord doesn't hate or despise the helpless in all of their troubles. When I cried out, he listened and did not turn away. When your people meet, you will fill my heart with your praises, Lord, and everyone will see me keep my promises to you.

Psalms 22:23-25
Contemporary English Version

Day 232

Just Ask

Thank You, Lord, for the provision You give when we pray. Yes, You know our every need and discern our thoughts before we ever think them, but You still expect us to seek You for our heart's desires. Why? Because You know if You gave us what we needed or longed for without our requests, You wouldn't hear from us very often. So sad! But stressing over something is not the same as seeking God for it. How often have I endlessly mulled over a situation, but later realized I had never made it a prayer request. That is crucial! Lord help us to *ask...* for You love to answer.

Have You Thought? Lord, make me persistent with my prayers.

His Answer:

Just ask and it will be given to you; seek after it and you will find. *Continue to* knock and the door will be opened for you. All who ask receive. Those who seek, find what they seek. And he who knocks, will have the door opened. Think of it this way: if your son asked you for bread, would you give him a stone? *Of course not—you would give him a loaf of bread.* If your son asked for a fish, would you give him a snake? *No, to be sure, you would give him a fish—the best fish you could find.* So if you, who are sinful, know how to give your children good gifts, how much more so does your Father in heaven, who is perfect, know how to give great gifts to His children!

Matthew 7:7-11
The Voice

Day 233

Little Choices

Lord, You long to guide all our choices, not just that big eternal one. We each have many options throughout our days, and You desire to be our Heavenly Micro-Manager. That term brings negative connotations to us, because as humans, we've seen it include manipulative control. Not so with You, Lord! Your ordering of the details of our days is kind, beneficial and a blessing to us and to others. And all it takes is a daily heart's cry: "Guide me today, Lord." This habit takes time to become a regular routine, but today is a great day to begin. Lord, begin with me!

Have You Thought? Breathe Your wisdom in me today.

His Answer:
> Train me in good common sense; I'm thoroughly committed to living your way. Before I learned to answer you, I wandered all over the place, but now I'm in step with your Word. You are good, and the source of good; train me in your goodness.

> Truth from your mouth means more to me than striking it rich in a gold mine. With your very own hands you formed me; now breathe your wisdom over me so I can understand you.

Psalms 119:66-68, 72-73
The Message

Day 234

I AM

Lord, I thank You that You are all that You say You are—Superlative and unrivaled forever. You are more than we could ever ask for and larger than we could ever imagine. Our minds can't grasp your enormity. You introduce yourself in Exodus by calling Yourself "I AM," forever allowing us to choose how to finish the rest of that sentence. Whatever we need on any given day, You are capable and willing to be for us. Can we ever say *thank you* enough? What has God been for you in just this past week? Has He been your Comforter? Deliverer? Counselor? Let's give Him thanks today.

Have You Thought? You are all I need.

His Answer:

Thank God because he's good, because his love never quits.

GOD's my strength, he's also my song, and now he's my salvation.

This is GOD's work. We rub our eyes—we can hardly believe it!

Psalms 118:1, 14, 23
The Message

Day 235

Erased

Thank You, Lord, that I am all You say I am—because of You. How differently You see me than the world does, or even than I do on many days. Your Word says because of Jesus' one-time sacrifice, God the Father considers me as already perfected. What? Even as I walk through His daily cleansing, God sees that job already accomplished. Since all my past and future sins have been covered by the blood of Jesus, the Father views me as blameless, even on my meanest, most impatient day. Believing that truth is life-changing. Give us eyes to see ourselves as You do, Lord!

Have You Thought? Lord, if You don't remember my sins, why should I?

His Answer:

I will erase their sins and wicked acts out of My memory *as though they had never existed.*

Since we have a great High Priest who presides over the house of God, let us draw near with true hearts full of faith, with hearts rinsed clean of any evil conscience, and with bodies cleansed with pure water. Let us hold strong to the confession of our hope, never wavering, since the One who promised it to us is faithful.

Hebrews 10:17, 21-23
The Voice

Day 236

Break Through

Thank You, Lord, that You designed light to always dispel darkness. You did it physically in Creation and You do it with the Presence of Jesus, the Light of the world. When Satan tries to darken our lives, You promise to break through with Your Radiance. Restore us to our God-designed selves and shed light on our path, Lord. In our dusky shadows of doubt, discouragement, disorder or even disinterest in You, bring Your Brilliance. In all the places where we are feeling the gloom encroaching upon our peace, our joy, our very lives, speak Your Words of Light and healing Life.

Have You Thought? Shine Your radiance in my life today.

His Answer:
Our Lord and God, you are my lamp. You turn darkness to light.

Your way is perfect, Lord, and your word is correct. You are a shield for those who run to you for help.

2 Samuel 22:29, 31
Contemporary English Version

Day 237

Tender Love

Thank You, Lord, that since Your righteous anger was satisfied by Your Son, we can now deal with You as our loving Abba, Daddy. It must grieve the Father that this truth gets either distorted or utterly ignored by many Christians. God's love is real and it is for us—all the time, in all of its fullness. If we could ever really comprehend this, we would not be fearful, envious, or insecure towards others. His infinite, unfailing passion would so fill our hearts and guide our actions. So, Lord, we pray, show us your affectionate, tender love today in a new and real way.

Have You Thought? More mercy, more peace, more love.

His Answer:
> I am writing to all who have been called by God the Father, who loves you and keeps you safe in the care of Jesus Christ. May God give you more and more mercy, peace, and love.

Jude 1-2
New Living Translation

Day 238

Unquenchable

Thank You, Lord, for Your unquenchable Light in the eyes of those who know You. Years ago, a friend and I visited an acquaintance who had undergone a bone-marrow transplant. Her body was ravaged by the cancer and the treatment and she was dying. We desperately wanted to know her relationship with the Lord, so I asked, "Do you know Jesus?" Just the sound of her Savior's name brought a beauty and a transformation to this precious woman's face that I can recall even now. When she triumphantly answered, "Oh, yes!," we saw that *true light* shining in her eyes. Hallelujah!

Have You Thought? Be the true light in my eyes.

His Answer:

Your strong love, O True God, is precious. All people run for shelter under the shadow of Your wings. In Your house, they eat and are full at Your table. They drink from the river of Your *overflowing* kindness. You have the fountain of life *that quenches our thirst*. Your light has opened our eyes *and awakened our souls*.

Psalms 36:7-9
The Voice

Day 239

Comments

Thank You, Lord, for Your prayer that we be unified as Your followers. I need that prayer daily, because I realize how often I can cause division. Any comment about another believer, any listing of their faults, is displeasing to You because it breaks unity. That changes my perspective on those "harmless" petty comments. Wow! Lord, forgive me for venting or picking up an offense so easily. How many times someone could point to flaws in me! Give me Your gracious, forgiving spirit to always see the good in others. Help me to uphold the unity of Your Church…Your Bride, for whom You died.

Have You Thought? May I always speak unifying words.

His Answer:

> "My prayer is not for the world, but for those you have given me, because they belong to you. All who are mine belong to you, and you have given them to me, so they bring me glory. Now I am departing from the world; they are staying in this world, but I am coming to you. Holy Father, you have given me your name; now protect them by the power of your name so that they will be united just as we are."

John 17:9-11
New Living Translation

Day 240

Thankless Thoughts

Thank You, Lord, for the true joy of a grateful heart. This world promotes comparison and competition; You call us to develop godly contentment. How winsome we are when we are thankful for the little and the truly important things. Lord, remove all thankless thoughts and attitudes from us today, for a dissatisfied, demanding frame of mind can sneak up on us so easily. Give us a consistent gratitude, not only in our relationship with You, but also in our encounters with each other. Make us like that one leper out of ten who came back to thank and worship You. You praised only *his* response.

Have You Thought? Lord, guard and guide my thoughts.

His Answer:

Yet true godliness with contentment is itself great wealth. After all, we brought nothing with us when we came into the world, and we can't take anything with us when we leave it. So if we have enough food and clothing, let us be content. But people who long to be rich fall into temptation and are trapped by many foolish and harmful desires that plunge them into ruin and destruction.

But you, Timothy, are a man of God; so run from all these evil things. Pursue righteousness and a godly life, along with faith, love, perseverance, and gentleness.

1 Timothy 6:6-9, 11
New Living Translation

Day 241

Seeds Planted

Thank You, Lord, for the priceless gift of Your Word. You compared it to seeds planted in the ground that need to be carefully tended. I know what happens to unkempt gardens—they become overgrown and don't yield much fruit. So it is with God's Word planted in my heart. I must lovingly hoe, mulch, and cultivate it in order to receive the harvest I want. But Lord, so many things can keep me from spending time in Your Word! So many weeds can choke the garden of my heart. Help me to make time in Your Word a higher priority, for the fruit of my labor is true life, joy, peace and security.

Have You Thought? Lord, make the soil of my heart fertile.

His Answer:

> This is the meaning of the parable: The seed is God's word. The seeds that fell on the footpath represent those who hear the message, only to have the devil come and take it away from their hearts and prevent them from believing and being saved. The seeds on the rocky soil represent those who hear the message and receive it with joy. But since they don't have deep roots, they believe for a while, then they fall away when they face temptation. The seeds that fell among the thorns represent those who hear the message, but all too quickly the message is crowded out by the cares and riches and pleasures of this life. And so they never grow into maturity. And the seeds that fell on the good soil represent honest, good-hearted people who hear God's word, cling to it, and patiently produce a huge harvest.

Luke 8:11-15
New Living Translation

Day 242

Envy

Thank You, Lord, that I can never overstep Your forgiveness, because I'm in need of it again. A good, hard look at my heart has exposed the envy there. Ugh! I've been down that wretched road before. It's a Garden of Eden, Cain-jealous-of-Abel sin, and we all know where that led—to murder. But, amazingly, Your mercy remains and Your cleansing renews and my heart is restored. Lord, make me quick to bring my every emotion to You. No dressing up or disguising my sins, just fervent prayers for Your help. You are ever Faithful to hear, to forgive, and to make me clean. I gratefully thank You.

Have You Thought? Lord, free me from the deadly emotion of envy.

His Answer:

But as for me, I almost lost my footing. My feet were slipping, and I was almost gone.

For I envied the proud when I saw them prosper despite their wickedness. They seem to live such painless lives; their bodies are so healthy and strong. They don't have troubles like other people; they're not plagued with problems like everyone else.

So I tried to understand why the wicked prosper. But what a difficult task it is! Then I went into your sanctuary, O God, and I finally understood the destiny of the wicked.

But as for me, how good it is to be near God! I have made the Sovereign Lord my shelter, and I will tell everyone about the wonderful things you do.

Psalms 73:2-5, 16-17, 28
New Living Translation

Day 243

Showing Your Love

Showing Your love preaches louder than any words I could ever say. You reminded me of that again recently. We all want, no need, the incredibly captivating grace of God. Wherever we are, whatever we have done, we desperately desire God's love…and He gives it. He may hate the choices we have made, or how far we have detoured from His path, but He loves *us* passionately. Showing the love of Christ makes it that much easier for someone to say "Yes" to God. I want to live my life like that—with my family, with my friends, with all who cross my path. Help me Lord.

Have You Thought? Help me be more loving, Lord.

His Answer:

Anyone who does not love does not know God, because God is love. Because of this, the love of God is a reality among us: God sent His only Son into the world so that we could find *true* life through Him.

So, my loved ones, if God loved us so *sacrificially*, surely we should love one another. No one has ever seen God *with human eyes*; but if we love one another, God *truly* lives in us. Consequently God's love has accomplished its mission among us.

1 John 4:8-9, 11-12
The Voice

Day 244

Perfect Clarity

Thank You, Lord, that you can't be manipulated. You are sovereign and You see the entire picture, from beginning to end. I see just this very moment, and I don't even view that with perfect clarity. Yet how often I try to bargain with You, reminding You of the benefits of *my* plan? As if You could possibly need one word of input or advice from me! Good and loving Father, convince me yet again today that Your plans and Your timing are always right. Help me to joyfully submit to Your instruction and Your plans more quickly instead of always having to take the roundabout route to obedience.

Have You Thought? Help me to submit to Your perfect plans, Lord.

His Answer:

I'm convinced: You can do anything and everything. Nothing and no one can upset your plans. You asked, "Who is this muddying the water, ignorantly confusing the issue, second-guessing my purposes?" I admit it. I was the one. I babbled on about things far beyond me, made small talk about wonders way over my head.

I'm sorry—forgive me. I'll never do that again, I promise! I'll never live on crusts of hearsay, crumbs of rumor.

Job 42:2-3, 6
The Message

Day 245

Connect the Dots

Lord, I thank You that You connect the dots in our lives and in human history. To continue our focus on praising God on purpose, we will focus on His Alpha and Omega, His Beginning-to-End Design. Genesis 1-2 and Revelation 21-22 are called the bookends of perfection in the Bible. These sacred writings keep our understanding of time in proper alignment. They tell of our origin and our destiny. In between them, though, is the sad story of sin and separation from God. For the next twelve days, we will look at God's glorious plan, its detour and its breathtaking resolution. Unraveling the end of this Story is momentous. Get ready to be amazed!

Have You Thought? You have breathtaking plans!

His Answer:
> "I'm Alive. I died, but I came to life, and my life is now forever. See these keys in my hand? They open and lock Death's doors, they open and lock Hell's gates. Now write down everything you see: things that are, things about to be."

Revelation 1:18-19
The Message

Heavens and Earth

Thank You, Lord, for creating the heavens and the earth. One day You will form a *new* Heaven and earth. Once again, You will bring a cosmos out of chaos, fullness out of emptiness and order from disorder, but this time there will be no one to ruin it. And one more thing...there will be no more sea! How odd that seems to us, because oceans are such a big part of the first creation. But, let's think of the spiritual meaning here. Oceans caused division; there will be none of that. Oceans can change quickly, causing fear, damage and loss. No more. We'll have a beautiful new creation from the One who "makes all things new" (see Rev. 21:5).

Have You Thought? You make all things new.

His Answer:

First this: God created the Heavens and Earth—all you see, all you don't see. Earth was a soup of nothingness, a bottomless emptiness, an inky blackness. God's Spirit brooded like a bird above the watery abyss.

I saw Heaven and earth new-created. Gone the first Heaven, gone the first earth, gone the sea.

Genesis 1:1-2; Revelation 21:1
The Message

Day 247

Light!

Thank You, Lord, that out of darkness You proclaimed light! The Hebrew translation of Genesis 1:3 says, "Light, Be!" John proclaims, "In You there is no darkness at all" (1 John 1:5 NKJV). Darkness has always been a potent biblical symbol of evil and wrong. Satan and his demons are called "rulers of this present darkness" in Ephesians 6:12 (AB). The Psalms say darkness brings fear, shame and weeping. How true! Satan bombards our wide-awake-and-mind-racing thoughts with fear and dread. One day, that will be history! The glory of the Lord fills Heaven, and night and darkness are no more! Woo-hoo!

Have You Thought? You fill the darkness in the world and in me with light, Lord.

His Answer:
> God spoke: "Light!" and light appeared. God saw that light was good and separated light from dark. God named the light Day, he named the dark Night. It was evening, it was morning—Day One.
>
> There won't be any night.
>
> Genesis 1:3-5; Revelation 21:25
> The Message

Day 248

Bright and Morning Star

Thank You, Lord, You are "a sun and a shield" (Psalms 84:11 NKJV). In the new Heaven and earth there will be no sun or moon. The Light of Heaven will be God, and Jesus will be the Lamp. And what that Lamp will do! Not only will He illuminate the exquisite beauty of Paradise, but those things we thought imperfect or flawed about ourselves will be transformed! This Bright and Morning Star, Jesus, will enthrall and captivate us for all eternity. He has chosen us, loved us, bought us, redeemed us, and He will then glorify us. No wonder we will be praising Him with our Hallelujahs!

Have You Thought? You will captivate us for all eternity.

His Answer:
> God made two big lights, the larger to take charge of Day, the smaller to be in charge of Night…God placed them in the heavenly sky to light up Earth.

> Genesis 1:16-17
> The Message

> And the city has no need of the sun nor of the moon to give light to it, for the splendor and radiance (glory) of God illuminate it, and the Lamb is its lamp.

> Revelation 21:23
> Amplified Bible

Day 249

No More Death

Thank You, Lord, that You will reverse every curse begun in the Garden of Eden in the garden called Paradise. How awesome is that! The first curse to be abolished is death. God told Adam and Eve not to eat of the Tree of Knowledge of Good and Evil, or they would die. They didn't listen, and death entered creation and aging and decay began. The consequences were not immediate, but they were certain, and we all deal with them. The promise we have though, is "He will swallow up death in victory; He will abolish death forever" (Isaiah 25:8 AB). Finally, life and life abundant (John 10:10)!

Have You Thought? Jesus, You bring victory over death.

His Answer:

> But of the tree of the knowledge of good and evil and blessing and calamity you shall not eat, for in the day that you eat of it you shall surely die.
>
> …for dust you are and to dust you shall return.
>
> Genesis 2:17, 3:19
> Amplified Bible
>
> And death shall be no more…
>
> Revelation 21:4
> Amplified Bible

Day 250

Satan Gone!

Thank You, Lord, that You redeem even global mess-ups! When Satan came into the Garden he was *not* the equal and opposite of God. He is just a creation of His…and a fallen one at that. Satan had a simple game plan. He sowed doubt, discouragement and diversion in Eve's mind. He made her question God's Word and His goodness; made her look at what she didn't have instead of her blessings; made her wrong desires seem right. He works the same way with us, but his days are numbered and his destiny is sure. He'll be *gone*!

Have You Thought? Can we even imagine life without his harassment? Hallelujah!

His Answer:

Now the serpent was more subtle and crafty than any living creature of the field which the Lord God had made. And he [Satan] said to the woman, Can it really be that God has said, "You shall not eat from every tree of the garden?"

Then the devil who had led them astray [deceiving and seducing them] was hurled into the fiery lake of burning brimstone…and will be tormented day and night forever and ever (through the ages of the ages).

Genesis 3:1, Revelation 20:10
Amplified Bible

Day 251

No More Lies

Thank You, Lord, that when Satan exits, so do his half-truths and lies. Eve fell for His deception, and his gifts to her were disgrace and dread. Ever been there? Yeah, you're in good company. Adam and Eve realized they were naked and they were ashamed. They tried to cover themselves with fig leaves. God made them tunics of animal skins—the very first sacrifice to cover sin. (Sounds like a Salvation Plan down the road, don't you think?) This Father of Lies and all his deceptions will be *toast* one day. Just look at the last two chapters of the Book. It has all been planned.

Have You Thought? No more deception, disgrace or dread.

His Answer:

> The serpent told the Woman, "You won't die. God knows that the moment you eat from that tree, you'll see what's really going on. You'll be just like God, knowing everything, ranging all the way from good to evil."

Genesis 3:4-5
The Message

> But there shall by no means enter anything profane, not one who causes an abomination or a lie.

Revelation 21:27
New King James Version

261

Day 252

Connected Again

Thank You, Lord, that one day our terrible sense that we are disconnected from You, or we don't hear You clearly will be gone forever. Poor Adam and Eve! What their sin cost them—intimacy with You, for starters! That perfect communication and closeness will one day be restored. The fulfillment in Revelation is nearly identical to the promise in Ezekiel 37:27 (MSG), "I'll live right there with them. I'll be their God! They'll be my people." Just as when Jesus walked this earth, we'll see "the glory with our own eyes, the one-of-a-kind glory, like Father, like Son…" (John 1:14 MSG). One day that will be the norm again. Unbelievable!

Have You Thought? Intimacy with God will forever be regained.

His Answer:
> When they heard the sound of God strolling in the garden in the evening breeze, the Man and his Wife hid in the trees of the garden, hid from God. God called to the Man: "Where are you?" He said, "I heard you in the garden and I was afraid because I was naked. And I hid."

Genesis 3:8-10
The Message

> I heard a voice thunder from the Throne: "Look! Look! God has moved into the neighborhood, making his home with men and women! They're his people, he's their God."

Revelation 21:3
The Message

Day 253

Prince of Peace

Thank You, Lord, that "the prince of the power of the air" will be grandly and decisively overthrown, though he is on the throne right now (Eph. 2:2 NKJV)! A quick look around our world today confirms "we are wrestling…against…the world rulers of this present darkness" (Ephes. 6:12 AB). Satan thought he had won when Adam and Eve joined his mutiny against God. But now he knows his doom is sure, and he's not happy and is working harder than ever. So don't be deceived. Despite the popular worldview, the Prince of Peace will one day regain His throne. And what a glorious Coronation it will be!

Have You Thought? Jesus will rule and reign once more.

His Answer:
> God told the serpent…"I'm declaring war between you and the Woman, between your offspring and hers. He'll wound your head, you'll wound his heel."

> Genesis 3:15
> The Message

> But the throne of God and of the Lamb shall be in it, and His servants shall worship Him [pay divine honors to Him and do Him holy service].

> Revelation 22:3
> Amplified Bible

Day 254

The New Order

Thank You, Lord, that sickness, sadness and stress belong only to this world. They came as unwelcome trespassers in the Garden. The so-sorry-I-ate-that-fruit aftermath became an ongoing friction between husbands and wives. One day that tension between the sexes will also be over. No more "Why don't you get this?" gender confrontations. How awesome will that be? Can you imagine not ever dealing with sickness, sadness and stress again? No death either. It is the promised new order of things. Punishment begun in Genesis will end in Revelation. Redemption will one day have its full sway, thanks to Jesus!

Have You Thought? Can you imagine? No more sickness, sadness or stress.

His Answer:

> To the woman He said, "I will greatly multiply your grief and your suffering in pregnancy and the pangs of childbearing; with spasms of distress you will bring forth children. Yet your desire and craving will be for your husband, and he will rule over you."

> God will wipe away every tear from their eyes; and death shall be no more, neither shall there be anguish (sorrow or mourning) nor grief nor pain any more, for the old conditions and the former order of things have passed away.

Genesis 3:16; Revelation 21:4
Amplified Bible

Day 255

No More Curses

Thank You, Lord, that the curses and consequences on creation will also be erased. Pain and sorrow weren't the only fallout from Adam and Eve's sin. They were cursed, but the ground was also cursed. Toil and sweat, thorns and thistles were the punishment. Think about Jesus' crucifixion. What did he have to wear on His head? A crown of thorns. He bore our curse… and not only ours, but creation's too. In Heaven, nothing will be cursed. Not the ground. Not the people. No frustrations, no disappointments, no failures. Multidimensional healing. So different from life now. This is no small salvation!

Have You Thought? No frustrations, disappointments or failures either.

His Answer:
He told the Man: "Because you listened to your wife and ate from the tree that I commanded you not to eat from…the very ground is cursed because of you; getting food from the ground will be as painful as having babies is for your wife; you'll be working in pain all your life long. The ground will sprout thorns and weeds, you'll get your food the hard way, planting and tilling and harvesting, sweating in the fields from dawn to dusk…"

The Tree of Life was planted on each side of the River, producing twelve kinds of fruit, a ripe fruit each month. The leaves of the Tree are for healing the nations. Never again will anything be cursed.

Genesis 3:17-18; Revelation 22:3
The Message

Day 256

Paradise Reopened

Thank You, Lord, one day we will be welcomed back into Paradise. You had prepared a perfect garden for Adam and Eve. Sin changed all that. You posted an angel with a flaming sword to guard the "Paradise Closed" sign. The only ray of hope? The Tree of Life inside the Garden remained. You didn't dig it up because You knew it would reappear in the new Paradise. One day we will experience the ultimate Welcome Home party thrown by our extravagant, extraordinary God. Here's the scoop: "No one's ever...so much as imagined anything quite like it" (1 Cor. 2:9 MSG).

Have You Thought? The Garden of Eden off limits no more!

His Answer:
> So GOD expelled them from the Garden of Eden and sent them to work the ground, the same dirt out of which they'd been made. He threw them out of the garden and stationed angel-cherubim and a revolving sword of fire east of it, guarding the path to the Tree-of-Life.

> Genesis 3:23-24
> The Message

> And the gates shall never be closed by day, and there shall be no night there.

> Revelation 21:25
> Amplified Bible

Day 257

Reunion

Thank You, Lord, for the coming reunion! It will be a final and ultimate redemption of that sin-moment when the world forever changed, and what was once perfect in design became horribly flawed. God and man together again in glorious harmony. A joyful-Prodigal-Son-ending for all who ask. We, who always wanted our own way in our own timing, then clothed in Family Robes. And the Party! It will be the Gala of all time. The invitations are still being sent by the One who gladly died to make the Reconciliation possible. But, one day, the guest list will be closed. Don't be left out.

Have You Thought? We'll be reconciled forever.

His Answer:
So [God] drove out the man…

Genesis 3:24
The Message

See! The abode of God is with men, and He will live (encamp, tent) among them; and they shall be His people, and God shall personally be with them and be their God.

They shall see His face, and His name shall be on their foreheads.

Revelation 21:3; 22:4
Amplified Bible

Unanswered Prayers

You are the God of the Big Picture. I get caught up in the individual steps to the long-term goal. You don't. When I despair that all is lost, You are simply building on Your previous work, setting the stage for the next answer to prayer. How grateful I am for all my "unanswered" prayers, when You did not do what *I* wanted, but rather what You knew would be infinitely better. You continue to bless me in spite of my tantrums when You override my suggestions. Thank You, Lord for Your sovereignty and patience. Teach me to trust You more readily every step of the way.

Have You Thought? How grateful I am for those prayers You denied.

His Answer:

I'm homesick—longing for your salvation; I'm waiting for your word of hope. My eyes grow heavy watching for some sign of your promise; how long must I wait for your comfort?

Save me! I'm all yours. I look high and low for your words of wisdom.

I see the limits to everything human, but the horizons can't contain your commands!

Psalms 119:81-82, 94, 96
The Message

Day 259

Divinely Extravagant Life

Thank You, Lord, for the gift of life. Each of us has a given number of years on this earth, and every so often, we need to remember they will end. We only have one go at this. I know we all want to get it right in all the ways You have ordained. So Lord, I give You my life again, and I ask You to make Your way plain to me, so that I can live in a manner that pleases You. Give me Your courage to go where You call, and Your heart to reach out to those whom You place in my path. Let me live the quiet but divinely extravagant life You have designed for me, for Your glory and my joy.

Have You Thought? Let it be true in my life, Lord.

His Answer:

What matters most to me is to finish what God started: the job the Master Jesus gave me of letting everyone I meet know all about this incredibly extravagant generosity of God.

Now I'm turning you over to God, our marvelous God whose gracious Word can make you into what he wants you to be and give you everything you could possibly need in this community of holy friends.

Acts 20:24, 32
The Message

Consuming Fire

Thank You, Lord, that You are not a lenient, lax God. You are a holy, righteous, consuming-fire God—but also a forgiving One. You didn't just let us slide or overlook our sins, You paid for them in full with Your own Son. This world has designed its own version of God, a permissive one who glosses over our misdeeds. The problem with that kind of god is He can't save us. I need and want to be saved. Our awesome Redeemer sent Jesus as our Substitute, not our Spoiler. He demands holiness, but He provides it too, out of His incredible love for us, and I gladly bow before Him.

Have You Thought? You were our perfect substitute, Jesus.

His Answer:

I love those who love me; those who search hard for me will find me.

So now listen to me, my children: those who live by my ways will find *true* happiness.

But *heed my warning:* the one who goes against me will only hurt himself, for all who despise me are *playing with fire and* courting death.

Proverbs 8:17, 32, 36
The Voice

Day 261

Humbling

Thank You, Lord, You love to empower us if we will just acknowledge our weakness. I do well with that unless I feel competent in my own abilities. In that case, those prayers for Your help never seem to get prayed…until I am totally spent. I just rush right into the task, confident my own strength is sufficient. But I am learning that either I humble myself, or You will. Why is it such a long process? You are teaching me that those places not surrendered to You can't be used for Your glory…they have already been used for mine. So, in Your mercy, help me to depend on You alone today.

Have You Thought? Lord, teach me to always ask for Your help.

His Answer:

Now you have every spiritual gift you need as you eagerly wait for the return of our Lord Jesus Christ. He will keep you strong to the end so that you will be free from all blame on the day when our Lord Jesus Christ returns. God will do this, for he is faithful to do what he says, and he has invited you into partnership with his Son, Jesus Christ our Lord.

1 Corinthians 1:7-9
New Living Translation

Day 262

On the Altar

Thank You, Lord, that I can trust my children to Your care. That's my hardest faith lesson. My stomach turns in knots every time I read the story of Abraham and Isaac. God also asks me if I love Him more than my children. No, He doesn't ask me to sacrifice them, but He does expect me to lay them at His feet. I have put each of them on the altar so many times, only to grab them back in my own arms, afraid that He might not guard them as well as I would. So, yet another time, Lord, I offer those whom You have given to me for a little while back to You for safekeeping.

Have You Thought? Lord, help me trust my children to You.

His Answer:
By faith Abraham, when he endured God's testing, offered *his beloved son* Isaac *as a sacrifice.* The one who had received God's promise was willing to offer his only son; God had told him, "It is through Isaac that your descendants will bear your name," and he concluded that God was capable of raising him from the dead, which, figuratively, is indeed what happened.

Hebrews 11:17-19
The Voice

Day 263

The Calm

Thank You, Lord, that when a storm is raging in my heart, You can already see the calm. When all I can see is the problem, the disaster, the gaping need, You already know the answer, the deliverance, the provision. In the midst of the pelting rain and crashing waves, You know that just Your Word will bring calm seas. If I could Velcro that truth to my heart for my next crisis, how much less turbulent my mind would be. Lord, would You fasten to my memory today Your actions and provisions in my past? Who-You-Were is also Who-You-Will-Be—faithful in all the storms of life!

Have You Thought? Thank You for Your Word that calms my storms.

His Answer:

One day Jesus said to his disciples, "Let's cross to the other side of the lake." So they got into a boat and started out. As they sailed across, Jesus settled down for a nap. But soon a fierce storm came down on the lake. The boat was filling with water, and they were in real danger. The disciples went and woke him up, shouting, "Master, Master, we're going to drown!" When Jesus woke up, he rebuked the wind and the raging waves. Suddenly the storm stopped and all was calm. Then he asked them, "Where is your faith?" The disciples were terrified and amazed. "Who is this man?" they asked each other. "When he gives a command, even the wind and waves obey him!"

Luke 8:22-25
New Living Translation

Day 264

Ever Deeper

Thank You, Lord, You are the God who reveals Yourself. It has been said we each have as much of God as we want. I need to reflect on that statement regularly. As this year progresses toward an end, have I grown closer to my Lord, or just coasted along on previous encounters with Him? Am I still living off my last spiritual high, or am I consistently asking God to deepen our relationship? Am I doing my part by spending quiet time with Him? God's love for us is constant and ours needs to be the same. Lord, forgive me for my roller coaster love. Make our relationship my number one priority.

Have You Thought? Don't allow me to coast along with You.

His Answer:

> How can men be wise? The only way to begin is by reverence for God. For growth in wisdom comes from obeying his laws. Praise his name forever.
>
> Psalms 111:10
> The Living Bible

Day 265

Intervention

Thank You, Lord, You are the God of intervention. When crises come, and they inevitably do, You are the Faithful One who steps in on our behalf. I'm thinking of Daniel's three Old Testament buddies in the fiery furnace. Do you know what was burned up in that inferno? Only the ropes that bound them and the guards who threw them in. They didn't even smell of smoke, because that fourth person seen in the furnace with them was the Lord. We all have fiery-furnace moments. Today, whatever your crisis, trust Your intervening God to act on your behalf. He is willing and He is waiting.

Have You Thought? You always act on my behalf.

His Answer:

So they tied them up and threw them into the furnace, fully dressed in their pants, turbans, robes, and other garments.

"Look!" Nebuchadnezzar shouted. "I see four men, unbound, walking around in the fire unharmed! And the fourth looks like a god!" Then Nebuchadnezzar came as close as he could to the door of the flaming furnace and shouted: "Shadrach, Meshach, and Abednego, servants of the Most High God, come out! Come here!" So Shadrach, Meshach, and Abednego stepped out of the fire. Then the high officers, officials, governors, and advisers crowded around them and saw that the fire had not touched them. Not a hair on their heads was singed, and their clothing was not scorched. They didn't even smell of smoke!

Daniel 3:21, 25-27
New Living Translation

Day 266

Wisdom Shared

Thank You, Lord, for gladly giving us Your wisdom when we ask for it. The asking part is our problem. Either we don't believe You will grant it, or we aren't willing to wait for Your answer. Perhaps we are too full of our own ideas and agendas to consider doing Yours. We lose in any of those scenarios. Last week I took on a suggestion to write down and date my most heartfelt problems that needed God's wisdom. Of the four I wrote, one has already been answered. God's counsel is accessible, and generously shared with those who ask. So, let's ask God today for *His* wise solutions!

Have You Thought? When I ask, You generously share.

His Answer:
> If you want to know what God wants you to do, ask him, and he will gladly tell you, for he is always ready to give a bountiful supply of wisdom to all who ask him; he will not resent it. But when you ask him, be sure that you really expect him to tell you, for a doubtful mind will be as unsettled as a wave of the sea that is driven and tossed by the wind; and every decision you then make will be uncertain, as you turn first this way and then that. If you don't ask with faith, don't expect the Lord to give you any solid answer.

James 1:5-8
The Living Bible

Day 267

Secret Miracles

Thank You, Lord, for all the times You protected, shielded or blessed me and I never even knew it. In studying Jesus' first miracle, I was struck by the fact that the bride and groom never realized what Jesus did for them that day. Jesus, His mother, the disciples, and the servants were the only ones aware of the need or the miraculous provision. I wonder how many times God performs "secret" miracles in each of our lives? With great awe and appreciation, I say "thank You" for all those rescues and other blessings. When I see You face to face, I will know and praise You for them.

Have You Thought? Your grace is so much larger than I can ever grasp, Lord.

His Answer:

> The next day there was a wedding celebration in the village of Cana in Galilee. Jesus' mother was there, and Jesus and his disciples were also invited to the celebration. The wine supply ran out during the festivities, so Jesus' mother told him, "They have no more wine."

> Jesus told the servants, "Fill the jars with water."

> When the master of ceremonies tasted the water that was now wine, not knowing where it had come from (though, of course, the servants knew), he called the bridegroom over. "A host always serves the best wine first," he said. "Then, when everyone has had a lot to drink, he brings out the less expensive wine. But you have kept the best until now!" This miraculous sign at Cana in Galilee was the first time Jesus revealed his glory. And his disciples believed in him.

John 2:1-3, 7, 9-11
New Living Translation

Day 268

A New Day

Thank You, Lord, You never have one of "those" days. You know the kind…where we check off the errands, put out the fires, and at the end of the day, we feel as if we have maneuvered totally on our knee-jerk instincts alone. For me, those are the days not begun with the Lord. There was no surrender, no request for guidance, and hardly even a nod to His existence in my life. I'm not proud of those days, and to add to that misery, I know they are totally my fault! But, today is a new day, and I choose You, Lord! Your will and Your way, bringing Your meaning and blessing to my day. Thank you, Jesus!

Have You Thought? Point the way today, Lord.

His Answer:

If you wake me each morning with the sound of your loving voice, I'll go to sleep each night trusting in you. Point out the road I must travel; I'm all ears, all eyes before you.

Teach me how to live to please you, because you're my God. Lead me by your blessed Spirit into cleared and level pastureland.

Psalms 143:8, 10
The Message

Day 269

RSVP

Thank You, Lord, for desiring time alone with me. Imagine that! You, the Infinite, Invincible, I AM, want to have one-on-one, sit-down-and-talk time with me every day! You send me a daily invitation to come and chat with You. Sometimes I accept it. Other times I don't even open the royal envelope. How sad to have the full attention of the Most High God focused on me—my dreams, my fears, my challenges—and choose to ignore it. I am so sorry, Lord. Thank You that You are patient, and Your invitation will come again tomorrow morning. I'm giving You my RSVP right now. *Yes!*

Have You Thought? Today I say, "Yes," Lord.

His Answer:
> Eternal One: If you are thirsty, come here; come, there's water *for all*. Whoever is *poor and* penniless can still come and buy *the food I sell*. There's no cost—here, have some food, *hearty and delicious*, and beverages, *pure and good*.

> *So turn your attention and* seek the Eternal One while it is still possible; call on Him while He is nearby. Let those who are busy plotting violence and doing wrong stop *right now*, turn, and do right. Let them turn *back* to the Eternal so they can experience His compassion. God will excuse our past wrongs. Our God's forgiveness is inexhaustible.

> Eternal One: My intentions are not *always* yours, and I do not go about things as you do.

Isaiah 55:1, 6-8
The Voice

Day 270

Spiritually Mature

Thank You, Lord, that You'll keep working in us until that moment when we step into Your presence. Some days we need to hear that encouragement. We compare ourselves to others who have walked with Jesus longer than we have, and wonder if we will ever become as spiritually mature as they are. But Jesus knows right where we are in our faith. He understands all of our faults, fears and failures, and He is growing us up in Him just as He promised. On those discouraging days, remember that the God who began His work in you, will finish it too. Obey Him, one day at a time, and watch Him work!

Have You Thought? What a comfort to know that You will finish Your work in me.

His Answer:

May God himself, the God who makes everything holy and whole, make you holy and whole, put you together—spirit, soul, and body—and keep you fit for the coming of our Master, Jesus Christ. The One who called you is completely dependable. If he said it, he'll do it!

The amazing grace of Jesus Christ be with you!

1 Thessalonians 5:23-24, 28
The Message

Day 271

You Chose Me

Thank You, Lord, that before we chose You, You chose us. You desired to make us Yours because of Your unrelenting, unsurpassed, incredible love for us. Do you remember the sense of relief that His forgiveness first brought to your heart? Transformed, and joyously so? Have you kept that breathtaking joy you felt when freedom first swept over you? If not, ask the Lord to restore that bubbling over joy that you felt when you first knew the saving grace of Jesus. Be amazed again at His wondrous gift of salvation, His love and grace. Let thanksgiving be your song again.

Have You Thought? Let my praises rise to You.

His Answer:

Shout with joy before the Lord, O earth! Obey him gladly; come before him, singing with joy. Try to realize what this means—the Lord is God! He made us—we are his people, the sheep of his pasture. Go through his open gates with great thanksgiving; enter his courts with praise. Give thanks to him and bless his name. For the Lord is always good. He is always loving and kind, and his faithfulness goes on and on to each succeeding generation.

Psalms 100:1-5
The Living Bible

Day 272

Baggage

Thank You, Lord, for gladly taking the baggage of our lives to the Cross with You, and that is where You intended it to stay. Why do we routinely pick it back up? Jesus bought us a new life, made us new creations and reckoned our sins as dead, through His sacrifice. Why would we want to "resurrect" those sins that were forgiven long ago? When we pick up the remnants of our old life instead of claiming His forgiveness, we are burdened and broken all over again. We can choose to give that baggage power over us again, or we can choose freedom in Jesus. Let's choose His perfect freedom!

Have You Thought? You have taken all my mistakes and regrets and laid them on the Cross.

His Answer:
> The Spirit of the Lord God has taken control of me! The Lord has chosen and sent me to tell the oppressed the good news, to heal the brokenhearted, and to announce freedom for prisoners and captives. This is the year when the Lord God will show kindness to us and punish our enemies.

> The Lord has sent me to comfort those who mourn, especially in Jerusalem. He sent me to give them flowers in place of their sorrow, olive oil in place of tears, and joyous praise in place of broken hearts. They will be called "Trees of Justice," planted by the Lord to honor his name.

> Isaiah 61:1-3
> Contemporary English Version

Day 273

The Spirit of God

Thank You, Lord, for the indwelling presence of Your Holy Spirit. So often that person of the Trinity is ignored, but it is through the Spirit and His anointing that we understand the Bible at all. Those "aha!" moments we occasionally have are all because the Spirit of God lives in us. You may think a preacher or a teacher has revealed new things to you, but God has given you the revelation. How cool is that? Doesn't that fill you with awe to think that God Almighty, the Ruler of Heaven and earth, whispers His truth to your heart by means of his Holy Spirit? What a gift this life in Christ is!

Have You Thought? Whisper Your Truth into my life, Lord.

His Answer:

We don't have to rely on the world's guesses and opinions. We didn't learn this by reading books or going to school; we learned it from God, who taught us person-to-person through Jesus, and we're passing it on to you in the same firsthand, personal way. The unspiritual self, just as it is by nature, can't receive the gifts of God's Spirit. There's no capacity for them. They seem like so much silliness. Spirit can be known only by spirit—God's Spirit and our spirits in open communion. Spiritually alive, we have access to everything God's Spirit is doing, and can't be judged by unspiritual critics. Isaiah's question, "Is there anyone around who knows God's Spirit, anyone who knows what he is doing?" has been answered: Christ knows, and we have Christ's Spirit.

1 Corinthians 2:13-16
The Message

Day 274

With-You-to-the-End Love

Thank You, Lord, for the unexpected blessings that You delight to give us. Just when we are about to throw in the towel, You revive us in such glorious ways that we know they are from You. You are not a distant, disinterested God, but One who sees and cares and steps in to help us. In our times of fatigue or frustration, You pour out Your grace for You understand our feelings. You've been tired and hurting; You've been looked down upon, and had friends desert You. Whatever we are feeling, You get it! Thank you, Lord, for Your I'm-with-you-to-the-end Love.

Have You Thought? It's awesome that whatever I'm feeling, You understand.

His Answer:
> I bow before your holy Temple as I worship. I praise your name for your unfailing love and faithfulness; for your promises are backed by all the honor of your name. As soon as I pray, you answer me; you encourage me by giving me strength.

> Though the Lord is great, he cares for the humble, but he keeps his distance from the proud.

Psalm 138:2-3, 6
New Living Translation

Day 275

Who I Am

Thank You, Lord, our foundation stands if it is built on You. Our lives encounter shaking, rattling, and even seismic reordering. If storms show us where our identity is wrongly placed, then they have done us a favor. Our relationships, economic status or health history may take on a new look. This may be uncomfortable to us, but doesn't affect who we *are*. Our value and meaning in life, if we are the Lord's, are dependent on one thing only—that we are *His*. Sometimes I forget that. Who I am is constant in Your eyes. Let it be that unshakable in mine too, Lord.

Have You Thought? Let my identity be solely based on Your love, Lord.

His Answer:
Those people who are listening to Me, those people who *hear what I say and* live according to My teachings—you are like a wise man who built his house on a rock, *on a firm foundation. When storms hit*, rain pounded down and waters rose, *levies broke* and winds beat all the walls of that house. But the house did not fall because it was built upon rock. Those of you who are listening and do not hear—you are like a fool who builds a house on sand. When a storm comes to his house, *what will happen?* The rain will fall, the waters will rise, the wind will blow, and his house will collapse with a great crash.

Matthew 7:24-27
The Voice

Day 276

Eternal Perspective

Thank You, Lord, You are the answer to every problem and every question in life. We look for solutions other places, but they don't satisfy for long. They're not meant to. You give explanations for the hardest questions, even if Your answer is simply, "You'll understand later." That's what you told the disciples (John 13:7), and You tell us that even now. It is much easier to understand life when we look back over it. It's said, "Life is like the Hebrew language. You only understand it when you read it backwards." When we don't understand, help us to trust *Your* eternal perspective for our lives.

Have You Thought? Help me to trust You when life doesn't make sense.

His Answer:

Let not the wise boast in their wisdom, nor the mighty in their strength, nor the rich in their wealth. Whoever boasts must boast in this: that he understands and knows Me. Indeed, I am the Eternal One who acts faithfully and exercises justice and righteousness on earth. These are the things that delight Me.

Jeremiah 9:23-24
The Voice

Day 277

Stillness

Thank You, Lord, for times of stillness. This world moves too fast, and I can get swept up in its frenzy. It drains me dry, wears me down and leaves me feeling fragmented. But You call me to so much more. You beckon me to life abundant in You, with You. Because only there You refresh and restore. You remind me that at the end of the day, it's just You and me, walking through life. Nothing else will remain except my relationship with You. Thank You, Lord, for those joyful times when my eyes are focused on You alone, and my ears are listening for Your whispers. Speak to me in my silence, Lord.

Have You Thought? Let me hear Your whispers today, Lord.

His Answer:

Take great joy in the Eternal! His gifts are coming, and they are all your heart desires!

Be still. Be patient. Expect the Eternal to arrive *and set things right*. Don't get upset when you see the worldly ones rising up the ladder. Don't be bothered by those who are anchored in wicked ways.

Wait for the Eternal. Keep to His path. *Mind His will.* He will *come for you*, exalt you; you will inherit the land. Before your very eyes you will see the end of the wicked.

Psalm 37:4, 7, 34
The Voice

Day 278

The Body of Christ

Thank You, Lord, that Your Cross makes a new family for me.
The Body of Christ is that eternal congregation that brings
together every color, nationality and economic strata on one
common ground—the Name of Jesus. How outrageously
delightful to meet new brothers and sisters here in this world
who will spend eternity with me! To regularly make those
connections and hear how the Lord won their hearts is such
a Holy-Spirit-Pentecost-born joy. Even if we meet for just a
moment, or enjoy a longstanding relationship, it's a wonder to
begin to live now as a part of that forever-as-one family.

Have You Thought? How exciting to have a forever-family
who all love You, Jesus.

His Answer:

I looked again. I saw a huge crowd, too huge to count.
Everyone was there—all nations and tribes, all races and
languages.

I heard a voice thunder from the Throne: "Look! Look!
God has moved into the neighborhood, making his
home with men and women! They're his people, he's
their God."

The Enthroned continued, "Look! I'm making everything
new. Write it all down—each word dependable and
accurate."

Revelation 7:9; Revelation 21:3, 5
The Message

Day 279

The Real Me

Thank You, Lord, for Your authenticity while You walked this earth. I am not nearly that genuine. Depending on my circumstances, I can hide behind many a mask, be anything but real. You were totally, truthfully *You*, regardless of Your audience. I want to become more of my true self, Lord. Would You prepare my heart to receive You in my deep, don't-let-anyone-see places? Heal me where I am broken? I want to live the courageous life that You desire. Make me into my God-begotten, child-of-God-self, by Your grace. Help me trust You as I open up to Your work in me.

Have You Thought? Make me into my true, God-begotten me, Lord.

His Answer:
> But to all who believed him and accepted him, he gave the right to become children of God. They are reborn—not with a physical birth resulting from human passion or plan, but a birth that comes from God.

John 1:12-13
New Living Translation

Day 280

Vast Love

Thank You, Lord, for the vastness of Your love shown so clearly at the Last Supper. Your interaction with Judas showed God's heart for all who don't believe. You offered him the Bread of Life. He took it in his hand, but didn't eat it. He was with the Light of the world, but chose to go out into the darkness, physically and spiritually. You also loved the other eleven, the believers, with a depth of compassion we can't imagine. You knew perfectly well that one would deny You and the rest would abandon You. You chose to die for them—and for us—anyway. Just a "Thank You" doesn't do that justice.

Have You Thought? You chose to die for *me*, Lord.

His Answer:

> After Jesus had said these things, he was deeply troubled and told his disciples, "I tell you for certain that one of you will betray me."
>
> Jesus answered, "I will dip this piece of bread in the sauce and give it to the one I was talking about." Then Jesus dipped the bread and gave it to Judas, the son of Simon Iscariot. Right then Satan took control of Judas. Jesus said, "Judas, go quickly and do what you have to do."
>
> Judas took the piece of bread and went out. It was already night.
>
> Peter asked, "Lord, why can't I go with you now? I would die for you!" "Would you really die for me?" Jesus asked. "I tell you for certain that before a rooster crows, you will say three times that you don't even know me."

John 13:21, 26-27, 30, 37-38
Contemporary English Version

Day 281

No Barriers

Thank You, Lord, for Your Church. It crosses every man-made barrier. Racially, ethnically and socially, we are one in You, regardless of external differences. The church at Philippi was the perfect example of this unity despite diversity. The New Testament mentions Asian, Greek and Roman members of this church. One was a businesswoman who sold purple cloth to the rich, another was a slave girl who had been delivered from demonic possession, and another was a jailer. Three different races and social ranks, but all sinners saved by the grace of God, living by His Spirit.

Have You Thought? What joy there is in having brothers and sisters in Christ.

His Answer:

Every time I think of you, I thank my God. And whenever I mention you in my prayers, it makes me happy. This is because you have taken part with me in spreading the good news from the first day you heard about it.

Philippians 1:3-5
Contemporary English Version

Day 282

Faithful Warrior

Thank You, Lord, that trusting You brings shelter, strength and stability even on topsy-turvy days. Your Presence makes all the difference, not only in eternity, but in this life, too. You bring peace in the midst of the chaos of our circumstances. Life is an emotional roller coaster, a free-for-all without Your steadying Hand. Remind us of the power and peace available to us every day, just for the asking. You long to fight our battles for us, but so often we go it alone, forgetting that God Almighty is just waiting for us. Those days drain and discourage us Lord, so come and be our faithful Warrior today.

Have You Thought? You are always on my side, ready to fight my battles.

His Answer:
> Just hold tightly to the Eternal One, your True God, as you always have…

> One of you can pursue a thousand because it is He who fights for you, just as He promised.

> Think back and you will know without a doubt that not one single good thing that the Eternal One, your God, promised you has been left undone. Not a single one.

Joshua 23:8, 10, 14
The Voice

Day 283

You Alone

Thank You, Lord, for Your merciful love and the faithful acts that You do in our lives for Your Name's sake, to show Your glory for all to see. Sometimes we usurp that glory, and make it more about ourselves and less about You. We are like the Greeks in the New Testament who believed that humility was a fault, and that it was a characteristic of a slave. The Greek definition of a slave (*doulos*) is "one who is subject to the will of his master." The Apostle Paul called himself a slave to God (Rom. 1:1). He was willing to be used for Jesus' sake. Lord, make me willing to be humble, like a slave, to show You alone are worthy of praise forever. Amen.

Have You Thought? Let the praise in my life always be for You.

His Answer:

Not for us, O Eternal One; this glory is not for us—but for Your name because of Your loyal love and truth.

Psalms 115:1
The Voice

Day 284

All My Detours

Thank You, Lord, for forgiving Peter. He denied You three different times. If I am honest, I do the same thing. I conveniently forget Your call on my life. I get engrossed in the gods of this world...its priorities and its pleasures. I think I deserve them, but how quickly these indulgences can become imprisonment. Lord, I confess them to You. Thank you that You forgive me as readily as You did Peter. Make my heart tender before You, Lord. Make me quick to realize my detours from You and Your ways, and eager to find the road back to Your side, as Peter joyfully did.

Have You Thought? Help me run quickly back to Your side.

His Answer:

The girl asked Peter, "Aren't you one of Jesus' disciples?" "No," he said, "I am not!" Meanwhile, as Simon Peter was standing by the fire, he was asked again, "Aren't you one of his disciples?" "Of course not," he replied.

But one of the household slaves of the High Priest—a relative of the man whose ear Peter had cut off—asked, "Didn't I see you out there in the olive grove with Jesus?" Again Peter denied it. And immediately a rooster crowed.

John 18:17, 25-27
The Living Bible

Day 285

Preconceived Notions

Thank You, Lord, You are the answer to life's most important questions. In Jesus' time, they asked, "Are you the King of the Jews?" but didn't understand His answer. He is the Truth, yet we ask, "What is truth?" just as Pilate did. They had preconceived notions of the type of king He would be. I do too. I expect superficial, earthly solutions to my problems, which He often gives, but He gives oh, so much more! Lord Jesus, in all the places where I don't understand who You really are, would You make Yourself more plain to me? Make Your Kingship and Truth more clear in my heart today.

Have You Thought? Make Yourself plain to me today.

His Answer:

Then Pilate went back into his headquarters and called for Jesus to be brought to him. "Are you the king of the Jews?" he asked him.

Jesus answered, "My Kingdom is not an earthly kingdom. If it were, my followers would fight to keep me from being handed over to the Jewish leaders. But my Kingdom is not of this world." Pilate said, "So you are a king?" Jesus responded, "You say I am a king. Actually, I was born and came into the world to testify to the truth. All who love the truth recognize that what I say is true." "What is truth?" Pilate asked.

John 18:33, 36-38
New Living Translation

Day 286

High Price Tags

Thank You, Lord, You want to be my best friend. You are always faithful, always available, always ready to see the best in me, and to use everything in my life for good. How could I ever ask for more? But I do. I ask for a lot more sometimes, and You actually give some of those things to me. But they don't satisfy for long. Not like You do. They tarnish, get used up and weigh me down. You bring joy, peace and fulfillment without the high price tags the world puts on its friendship. I need to be reminded of the true value of things again Lord. Thanks for Your patience.

Have You Thought? No friendship is like Yours, Lord.

His Answer:

So seek God and live! You don't want to end up with nothing to show for your life but a pile of ashes...

You're in a cosmos star-flung with constellations by God, A world God wakes up each morning and puts to bed each night. God dips water from the ocean and gives the land a drink. God, God-revealed, does all this.

...You talk about God, the God-of-the-Angel-Armies, being your best friend. Well, live like it, and maybe it will happen.

Amos 5:6, 8, 14
The Message

Day 287

Confusion

Thank You, Lord, for the prophet Habakkuk's total honesty with God. He took his confusion about his life to God. He told Him just how desperate his circumstances were, and then waited for God's answer and listened to what God said. Because of that, he gained the proper perspective on life. He knew, regardless of his circumstances, the "believing-in-God life, the steady trusting-in-God life" is the full life, the only *real* life. Thanks, Habakkuk.

Have You Thought? Lord, make me willing to wait. Willing to listen. Trusting always in You.

His Answer:

I listened and *began to feel sick with fear*, my insides churned…Now I wait quietly…

Even if the fig tree does not blossom and there are no grapes on the vines, If the olive trees fail to give fruit and the fields produce no food, If the flocks die *far* from the fold and there are no cattle in the stalls; then I will *still* rejoice in the Eternal! I will rejoice in the God who saves me!

Habakkuk 3:16-18
The Voice

Day 288

Night Watch

Lord, You "kept and preserved, guarded and protected" those the Father gave You. You prayed those words the night before You died for us. That same idea is in Phil. 4:7: *"And God's peace…shall garrison and mount guard over your hearts and minds in Christ Jesus"* (AB). God's peace is a guard around our hearts and minds, and has all the weight of heaven behind it. The world knows nothing of this comforting watch, so it scratches and claws to provide its own protection. When my mind races and my heart faints, Lord, remind me of Your care.

Have You Thought? Your peace is an amazing gift, Jesus.

His Answer:
> "As long as I was with them, I guarded them. In the pursuit of the life you gave through me, I even posted a night watch. And not one of them got away…"

John 17:12
The Message

Day 289

You Amaze Me

Thank You, Lord, for Your incredible love for us. You showed this by the words You laboriously prayed the very night You were betrayed. Immediately before You went with Your disciples to the Garden of Gethsemane, You thanked Your Father for all those who would believe because of the witness of Your disciples. That's *us*! Somehow, down the thousands of years, You could see each of us who would place our trust in You. It boggles my mind that You would pray for each of us as You walked to the place where You knew Your agony would begin. But everything about Your love amazes me, Lord.

Have You Thought? Your prayers uphold me, Lord.

His Answer:
"I am praying not only for these disciples but also for all who will ever believe in me through their message."

John 17:20
New Living Translation

Day 290

Bigger Than Any Bad Day

Thank You, Lord, Your grace is bigger than any bad day I may have. When nothing goes right, and my reactions make things even worse, Your grace still covers me. When I hardly resemble a child of Yours, the pardon remains. When I take two steps forward and three back, You love me still. Can I even conceive of such a forgiving Father? Wash me clean and dress me in Your righteousness again, Lord. Free me from that guilt-ridden, energy-sapping state of mind. Every day brings Your new mercies and new power. How I rejoice in that freedom purchased for me—for all time!

Have You Thought? Your unlimited pardon restores me, Lord.

His Answer:

That's all I ever think about, and I am depressed. Then I remember something that fills me with hope. The Lord's kindness never fails! If he had not been merciful, we would have been destroyed. The Lord can always be trusted to show mercy each morning. Deep in my heart I say, "The Lord is all I need; I can depend on him!"

Lamentations 3:20-24
Contemporary English Version

Day 291

Once, For All

Thank You, Lord, for Your once-for-all perfect Offering. No other eternal requirements need to be satisfied to gain us entry into Heaven. Salvation is pure gift, offered with divine delight. Remind me again today that Your life-plan for us is not a frantic exercise or a desperate attempt to win Your love, but rather a grateful, graceful response to that love. Not a life regulated by man-made rules but one reflecting Your grace, lived out in acknowledgment of our position in and through Christ. How wonderful to be able to really rest in the relationship of a God-begotten, God-delighted life! What a relief, Lord. Let me walk in that today.

Have You Thought? How wonderful not to have to win Your love.

His Answer:
>With a powerful hand, You drove the nations *from this land*, but then You planted our parents here. You fought for us against people of this land; You set our parents free *to enjoy its goodness.* They did not win the land with their swords. It wasn't their strength that won them victory. It was *Your strength*—Your right hand, Your arm, and the light of Your presence *that gave them success,* for You loved them.
>
>We shout Your name all day long; we will praise Your name forever!
>
>Psalms 44:2-3, 8
>The Voice

Day 292

Holy One of God

Thank You, Lord, that even when the people around You didn't understand who You were, the demons did! Whoa! And when the demons talked about Jesus coming to destroy them, they weren't just speaking of those evil spirits in that particular man. You were a threat to every satanic creature. Even those under the control of Satan himself called Jesus "the Holy One of God." Are there any places in my life where even the demons acknowledge the truth of Your Presence and Your Power more than I do? That thought makes me shudder! Show me quickly, and heal me there, Lord.

Have You Thought? Be Lord of every part of my life, Jesus.

His Answer:
> Suddenly a man with an evil spirit in him entered the meeting place and yelled, "Jesus from Nazareth, what do you want with us? Have you come to destroy us? I know who you are! You are God's Holy One." Jesus told the evil spirit, "Be quiet and come out of the man!" The spirit shook him. Then it gave a loud shout and left. Everyone was completely surprised and kept saying to each other, "What is this? It must be some new kind of powerful teaching! Even the evil spirits obey him." News about Jesus quickly spread all over Galilee.

Mark 1:23:28
Contemporary English Version

Day 293

Touched

Thank You, Lord, for the sweet grace of the leper story and Your redeeming love. You healed his body, removing all traces of the disease. That was miraculous enough. But You took the cure to a much deeper level…You touched the man. Can you even begin to understand the value of that touch? That poor man had been ostracized from the temple and shunned by every "clean" person in the world…except Jesus. I wonder how long it had been since he felt the touch of another human being? Since he wasn't greeted by shouts of "Unclean"? What joy that brought! Lord, go to our deepest hurts and bring healing there today.

Have You Thought? What deep hurts in my heart are in need of Your touch today?

His Answer:

A leper walked right up to Jesus, dropped to his knees, and begged Him for help.

Leper: If You want to, You can make me clean.

Jesus was powerfully moved. He reached out and actually touched the leper.

Jesus: I do want to. Be clean.

And at that very moment, the disease left him; the leper was cleansed *and made whole once again.*

Mark 1:40-42
The Voice

Day 294

God's Word

Thank You, Lord, for the value and benefits of the Word of God in our lives. Let's look at a bite-sized breakdown of the claims. It promises to give revelation to teach us, signposts to point the way, and a big-picture map to help keep us focused on the joyful journey's end. But promises are only trustworthy if the One making them is reliable. This Oath-Giver is treasured and esteemed more than pure gold, and His Warranty never runs out. So, why do I look for promises anywhere else but here? Lord, be my counsel above any other. I give You permission, once again, to guide my life by Your precious promises in Your Word.

Have You Thought? You are my ever-reliable Counsel. Let me listen to You today.

His Answer:

That's how God's Word vaults across the skies from sunrise to sunset, melting ice, scorching deserts, warming hearts to faith. The revelation of GOD is whole and pulls our lives together. The signposts of GOD are clear and point out the right road. The life-maps of GOD are right, showing the way to joy. The directions of GOD are plain and easy on the eyes. GOD's reputation is twenty-four-carat gold, with a lifetime guarantee. The decisions of GOD are accurate down to the nth degree.

Psalms 19:6-9
The Message

Day 295

See Through Me

Thank You, Lord, for the truth of our relationship with You. All You ask of us is to be attentive to You and Your Word, and available for Your work—You do all the rest. Listening ears and answering lips, that's our part. Then You come and fill each one of us full of the life-of-the-party joy of the deepest, most meaningful quality. You don't want me to bring You this crazy world's substitute for real sacrifice…shallow symbols in place of my sincere self. Make me real before You. I can even fool myself sometimes. See right through me. Keep me listening and responding so I can live the life that You desire.

Have You Thought? Help me be sincere before You, Lord.

His Answer:
> Doing something for you, bringing something to you—that's not what you're after. Being religious, acting pious—that's not what you're asking for. You've opened my ears so I can listen. So I answered, "I'm coming. I read in your letter what you wrote about me, and I'm coming to the party you're throwing for me." That's when God's Word entered my life, became part of my very being.

Psalms 40:6-8
The Message

Day 296

Unencumbered

Thank You, Lord, for making life a Great Adventure, not a monotonous drudgery. I know You want me to bury my old life forever and experience the life You bought for me. I don't step into that reality nearly deeply enough, Lord. You just wait for me to let go and open up to You on that level. Let me finally be liberated to jump in with abandon—unashamed and unrestrained in the joy of being Yours, Jesus. Help me to live Your extravagantly-alive resurrection life, unencumbered by what others think, and unafraid to walk through the doors You open for me. I want to live in Your powerful freedom.

Have You Thought? Lord, show me where I am not totally Yours.

His Answer:

Or didn't you realize we packed up and left there for good? That is what happened in baptism. When we went under the water, we left the old country of sin behind; when we came up out of the water, we entered into the new country of grace—a new life in a new land!

Don't even run little errands that are connected with that old way of life. Throw yourselves wholeheartedly and full-time—remember, you've been raised from the dead!—into God's way of doing things. Sin can't tell you how to live. After all, you're not living under that old tyranny any longer. You're living in the freedom of God.

Romans 6:3, 13-14
The Message

Day 297

A Face with a Name

Thank You, Lord, for coming to earth to make God clear to us, to put a Face with the Name. In Your dealings with the disciples You used "show and tell" stories of everyday occurrences to make Your points and explain Your heavenly mysteries. You patiently dealt with them at whatever level they could understand. Thank you, Lord, for still doing that with each of us. You know all those places where we don't understand You or Your ways, and You lovingly work with us right where we are. No exasperation. No irritated condescension. Just love and gentle patience. I am so very grateful.

Have You Thought? Lord, help me learn Your patient ways.

His Answer:
> Jesus used many other stories when he spoke to the people, and he taught them as much as they could understand. He did not tell them anything without using stories. But when he was alone with his disciples, he explained everything to them.

Mark 4:33-34
Contemporary English Version

Day 298

It's All There

Thank You, Lord, for Your Word so rich in multiple layers and meanings. Psalm 69 speaks of David's suffering yet also prophetically describes Jesus' crucifixion: the rejection by His Father, the parched throat and the vinegar, the beatings and taunting, the abandonment by all His friends—it's all there! He was the sinless Lamb on the altar, totally acceptable to the Father. Because of Him we God-seekers take heart! On the Cross Jesus thought about His followers, not wanting them to become discouraged and lose heart after the crucifixion. I stand in awe at the truth of Your suffering, Lord.

Have You Thought? Lord, Your willingness to suffer for me overwhelms me.

His Answer:

I'm hoarse from calling for help, Bleary-eyed from searching the sky for God.

Don't let those who look to you in hope be discouraged by what happens to me, Dear Lord! God of the armies! Don't let those out looking for you come to a dead end by following me—please, dear God of Israel!

I'm broken by their taunts, flat on my face, reduced to a nothing. I looked in vain for one friendly face. Not one. I couldn't find one shoulder to cry on. They put poison in my soup, vinegar in my drink.

Psalm 69:3, 6, 20-21
The Message

Day 299

Compassionate Correction

Thank You, Lord, for Your compassionate correction of my thinking yesterday. I was upset over the behavior of a friend. To be honest, my feelings were hurt. Then I heard Your tender voice. It was not condemning or angry, just truthful, and I had to consider it. "Linda, you've done that same thing to other people." Oh my. Now my finger of shame was pointing back at me. How many times must this happen before I realize I share the same faults as the person I am condemning? Lord, make me quick to analyze my own heart, and leave others' hearts to You.

Have You Thought? Lord, let me look within before I criticize others.

His Answer:
> Jesus: If you judge *other people*, then you will find that you, too, are being judged. Indeed, you will be judged by the very standards to which you hold other people.

> Matthew 7:1-2
> The Voice

Day 300

My Wanderings

Thank You, Lord, for Your pursuing love. "You number my wanderings," says Psalms 56:8 (NKJV). To think Jesus keeps such close track of me to even count all the times I stray away from His fold. He doesn't just keep track, but while I am wandering, chases after me in love. The Hebrew word used denotes an animal in pursuit. You truly are the Hound of Heaven! You track me down and woo me back when I have taken the bait of Satan and traveled into his quagmire. Those steps always take me to places I never wanted to go, but You find me even there. This is the Gospel Good News!

Have You Thought? You always woo me back, Lord.

His Answer:

Certainly Your faithful protection and loving provision will pursue me where I go, always, everywhere. I will always be with the Eternal, in Your house forever.

Psalms 23:6
The Voice

Day 301

No Band-Aids

Thank You, Lord, for pardoning us from the "continuous, low-lying cloud" that once covered our heads. You ushered in the "Spirit of Life" on that Resurrection Sunday. No more sacrificial Band-Aids placed on the altar of religion. You were the deep healing Offering that was accepted for all time. No more gloom of guilt. No more "not-good-enough" ever again. Those "get-your-act-together" ideas—pure lies! The truth is You came to save, not to condemn. No more striving. No more struggling. Just believing. We're blameless now, because of Jesus! Embrace it with paid-for-on-Easter eyes today! Woo-hoo!

Have You Thought? You give true deep healing, and I am so grateful.

His Answer:

With the arrival of Jesus, the Messiah, that fateful dilemma is resolved. Those who enter into Christ's being-here-for-us life no longer have to live under a continuous, low-lying black cloud. A new power is in operation. The Spirit of life in Christ, like a strong wind, has magnificently cleared the air, freeing you from a fated lifetime of brutal tyranny at the hands of sin and death.

And now what the law code asked for but we couldn't deliver is accomplished as we...simply embrace what the Spirit is doing in us.

Romans 8:1-4
The Message

Day 302

Tender Lullabies

Thank You, Lord, for Your works already accomplished in my life. Yesterday's miracles are etched on my mind. Sometimes those remembrances are all I have to keep me afloat. They are my anchor in today's boisterous seas. When sleep eludes me and questions distress my quiet thoughts, Your past faithfulness brings relief. I remember Your loyal love and Your tender answers to prayers long past. Never let me demand new proof of Your steadfastness or constancy, Lord. Coax me to sleep tonight with tender lullabies of Your love poured out richly over my life time and time again. Compose and calm this little lamb's restless heart, my Faithful Shepherd.

Have You Thought? My restless heart rests in You.

His Answer:

> I cry out to God; yes, I shout. Oh, that God would listen to me! When I was in deep trouble, I searched for the Lord. All night long I prayed, with hands lifted toward heaven, but my soul was not comforted.
>
> You don't let me sleep. I am too distressed even to pray! I think of the good old days, long since ended…
>
> But then I recall all you have done, O Lord; I remember your wonderful deeds of long ago.
>
> Psalm 77:1-2, 4-5, 11
> New Living Translation

Day 303

Excess Baggage

Thank You, Lord, that You promise to take the world off our shoulders if I only ask. I seem to carry all of my stress on my shoulders, everything I worry about, every fear I allow to grip my heart. Over and over, You remind me *You* were meant to carry those burdens. So why do I get weary from their load when Your strong stature was meant to bear them? Isaiah 9:6 (NKJV) says "the government will be upon *His* shoulder." Lord, I need to have a One-on-one, Heart-to-heart with You once again, to transfer that baggage I lug around to Your Mighty God shoulders. I don't want to pick it back up this time!

Have You Thought? Lord, let me transfer my worries and cares to Your shoulders today.

His Answer:
>   I removed the burden from your shoulders; I removed *heavy* baskets from your hands.
>
>   You cried out to Me, *I heard* your distress, and I delivered you; I answered you from the secret place, *where clouds* of thunder *roll.*
>
>   Psalms 81:6-7
>   The Voice

Day 304

Checklist

Thank You, Lord, for Your guidance when we face problems. The apostle Paul wrote a two-sentence exhortation to the church in Corinth—a church sitting in the center of an area well known for its immorality. Factions were arising and dividing the church. Do problems inside and outside the body of Christ sound familiar? That's why this timeless guidance is still a compelling checklist for Christ-like living. "Watch, stand fast in the faith, be brave, be strong. Let all that you do be done with love" (1 Cor. 16:13-14 NKJV). Lord, I need Your strength, but more than that, I need You to help me to love without stopping.

Have You Thought? I really need Your help with this, Lord.

His Answer:
> LISTEN, stay alert, stand tall in the faith, be courageous, and be strong. Let love prevail in your life, words, and actions.
>
> 1 Corinthians 16:13-14
> The Voice

Day 305

Victorious Shoes

Thank You, Lord, for calling us to do so much more than we can do in our own power. You call us to do more than our natural abilities or giftings and more than we could ever ask or think—but in Your power. I've tried to do it on my own too many times. My pink prissy shoes won't go the distance. Either they wear out, or my feet do, but the result is the same. I fall flat on my face. Help me to ask for Your power and Your guidance more and more. Replace my human prissy shoes with Your *nike*, victorious, overcoming ones. (In Greek *nike* means overcoming and victorious!)

Have You Thought? At the Throne there is undeserved kindness and help.

His Answer:

> We have a great high priest, who has gone into heaven, and he is Jesus the Son of God. That is why we must hold on to what we have said about him. Jesus understands every weakness of ours, because he was tempted in every way that we are. But he did not sin! So whenever we are in need, we should come bravely before the throne of our merciful God. There we will be treated with undeserved kindness, and we will find help.

Hebrews 4:14-16
Contemporary English Version

Day 306

Two Things

Thank You, Lord, that You are the One who empowers us. You see our weariness as we anticipate a job ahead or chores to be done. You care when there is no job at all. You know the fears as bills pile up and due dates pass. You understand the heartbreak of headstrong children or fractured relationships. But, hallelujah, when every earthly hope has faded, You are our Hope. Where we are broken, You bring healing. Where we are fearful, courage. In our weakness, You show Your Power. So, come into every place of need, and be our Source-of-Strength-God in the midst of our daily lives today.

Have You Thought? You are amazingly powerful and kind.

His Answer:

Only God gives inward peace, and I depend on him. God alone is the mighty rock that keeps me safe, and he is the fortress where I feel secure. God saves me and honors me. He is that mighty rock where I find safety.

I heard God say two things: "I am powerful, and I am very kind."

Psalms 62:5-7, 11-12
Contemporary English Version

Day 307

Lackadaisical Nod

Thank You, Lord, that no matter how tiring or disappointing a day may be, there are still a million reasons to praise You. Could I possibly walk through a day and never speak one "Thank you" to You? Not even one? Am I not grateful You allowed me to wake up this morning? Do I not realize my heart is kept beating by Your merciful Hand? To see a sunset, hear a bird sing or enjoy my family and friends, these are all gifts from You. Forgive me for my lackadaisical nod to Your blessings showered on me daily. I am grateful. Make praise my perpetual language to You, Lord.

Have You Thought? Make praise my perpetual language.

His Answer:

All day long I will tell the wonderful things you do to save your people. But you have done much more than I could possibly know. I will praise you, Lord God, for your mighty deeds and your power to save.

Psalms 71:15-16
Contemporary English Version

Day 308

My God-Box

Thank You, Lord, that You always get to the bottom line—who You are, and who I am. I may try to fool myself, but the truth is I have my own downsized version of You, a way-too-small God-box into which I try to fit You. It never works. Thank goodness! Just because You've answered a prayer in one way doesn't mean You'll always do it that way. You delight in bursting my "this-is-how-God-works" bubble! You stretch me over and over, so that my next estimation of You is a little bit larger. Make me ready today for a new revelation of all that You are. Uncover another misconception, dear Lord.

Have You Thought? Don't let me have a downsized version of You, Lord.

His Answer:
> Jesus and his disciples went to the villages near the town of Caesarea Philippi. As they were walking along, he asked them, "What do people say about me?" The disciples answered, "Some say you are John the Baptist or maybe Elijah. Others say you are one of the prophets." Then Jesus asked them, "But who do you say I am?" "You are the Messiah!" Peter replied.

Mark 8:27-29
Contemporary English Version

Day 309

Not Just in Theory

Thank You, Lord, Your gentle whispers of peace can actually speak louder than the incessant mental chatter of our own fretfulness. You, who are our Refuge, our Fortress, and our Strength long for us to know Your peace, not only in theory, but in practice. It is easy to say we trust You when life is calm. It is in the times of crisis that the real truth reveals itself. God wasn't just watching Daniel in the fiery furnace, He was in there with him. Be that real to us, Lord, in our trials. Give us a new, deeper sense of Your Presence that compels us to praise You because of Your promises.

Have You Thought? You always do what is good for me, Lord.

His Answer:

Mercy. May Your mercy come to me, O God, for my soul is safe within You, *the guardian of my life*. I will seek protection in the shade of Your wings until the destruction has passed.

I cry out to God, the Most High, to God who always does what is good for me. Out of heaven my rescue comes. He dispatches His mercy and truth And goes after whoever tries to run over me.

Psalms 57:1-3
The Voice

Day 310

To-Do Lists

Thank You, Lord, that You are never overwhelmed with all that You have to do. I am. So guide my agenda, Lord. Show me what You want me to do, and reveal to me those things I have impetuously signed up for, but have no business doing. You did everything Your Father told You to do, and You did it perfectly. Help me to do Your will for this day, equipped with Your power. Change my to-do list wherever You desire. Help me to pare down and walk purposefully. Tomorrow will be a new day, and Your mercies will be new all over again. Today, let me focus on today.

Have You Thought? Let me walk purposefully today, Lord.

His Answer:

And now may the God of peace, who brought again from the dead our Lord Jesus, equip you with all you need for doing his will. May he who became the great Shepherd of the sheep by an everlasting agreement between God and you, signed with his blood, produce in you through the power of Christ all that is pleasing to him. To him be glory forever and ever. Amen.

Hebrews 13:20-21
The Living Bible

Day 311

Ambassadors

Thank You, Lord, for giving each of us a story of hope to tell: a here's-what-God-did-for-me account that has been handwritten throughout our lives. It's easy for us to tell this story because it really happened to us! How many people are dying to hear some good news today? Or be reminded that He cares? A word of our unique Jesus-story could mean so much. To know the Lord can and will comfort and restore the broken places in a life would be huge! So help us to "always be ready to give a…reason for the hope within us" (1 Peter 3:15), as Your ambassadors of life-giving Hope.

Have You Thought? Give me Your beautiful fragrance today, Lord.

His Answer:

> Yet I am so thankful to God, who always marches us to victory under the banner of the Anointed One; and through us He spreads the beautiful fragrance of His knowledge to every corner of the earth. *In a turbulent world* where people are either dying or being rescued, we are the sweet smell of the Anointed to God *our Father*. To those who are dying, they smell the stench of death in us. And to those being rescued, we are the unmistakable scent of life.

2 Corinthians 2:14-16
The Voice

Day 312

Keep it Simple

"Just keep it simple," was Paul's four-word command about proclaiming the Good News of Jesus to others. Nothing is more winsome, harder to resist than hearing a heartfelt, "I was... blind...deaf...broken in some way...but Jesus made me whole!" Lord, help me to always be quick to say how You have changed my life, how You have brought freedom, joy and peace. Who doesn't want those things? May I always "keep it simple" when I tell others what You have done for me.

Have You Thought? Don't let me ever quit, Jesus.

His Answer:
> ...so proclaim the Message with intensity; keep on your watch....Don't ever quit. Just keep it simple.

> 2 Timothy 4: 2
> The Message

Day 313

Just Respond

Thank You, Lord, that my relationship with You began in Your heart, not in mine. We don't have to pursue or strive to please You, but only respond to Your relentless call to us. You woo us to Your side in every possible way, until our very last breath. We are Your delight, Your beloved, Your treasure. We don't always believe those truths, so You pursue. Zealously. And even better, regardless of our present level of intimacy with You, there is always that next level that You long for us to enter. We can't even comprehend Your intense desire to be close to us. Draw us deeper into Your adventure in love, Lord!

Have You Thought? Take me to that next level, Lord.

His Answer:

For it's by God's grace that you have been saved. You receive it through faith. It was not *our plan or* our effort. It is God's gift, *pure and simple.* You didn't earn it, *not one of us did,* so don't go around bragging *that you must have done something amazing.*

Ephesians 2:8-9
The Voice

Day 314

Adopted

You have "designs on us for glorious living," (Eph. 1:11 MSG). Embracing the made-new me requires me letting go of the old that's-just-how-I-am me! Why? Because He adopted us into His family through Jesus. In ancient Rome, an adopted son had all the rights of a son physically born into the family. What characteristics of Jesus would you most like to see lived out in your life? Let's search our hearts for attributes that God might long to breathe into us next. He'll make it clear if we just ask. Thank you that we are *"believers cleaned up by Jesus and set apart for a God-filled life!"* (1 Cor. 1:2 MSG).

Have You Thought? Thank You for my new life in Your family, Jesus.

His Answer:

So, my brothers and sisters, you owe the flesh nothing! You do not need to live according to its ways, *so abandon its oppressive regime.*

If the Spirit of God is leading you, then *take comfort in knowing* you are His children. You see, you have not received a spirit that returns you to slavery, so you have nothing to fear. The Spirit you have received adopts you *and welcomes you* into God's own family. That's why we call out to Him, "Abba! Father!" *as we would address a loving daddy. Through that prayer,* God's Spirit confirms in our spirits that we are His children.

Romans 8:12, 14-16
The Voice

Day 315

Changed

Just being in Your Presence changes me, Lord. You rub off on me in the very best way...when I stand close enough to You. This is so much better than the world's self-help philosophy! I give up very quickly when I try to do the renovations-to-me on my own. Totally frustrating! But You understand me and why I am the way that I am. And the best part of being transformed by being in Your Presence is the gentle way You do it. Your Plan doesn't usually change me overnight. You just keep polishing and refining, knowing exactly how You want me to end up. Keep working, Lord!

Have You Thought? Rub off on me today, Lord.

His Answer:

There has never been the slightest doubt in my mind that the God who started this great work in you would keep at it and bring it to a flourishing finish on the very day Christ Jesus appears.

Philippians 1:6
The Message

Day 316

Involved

Thank You, Lord, that You are not only informed about our lives, but Your greatest desire is to also be involved in them. And even better, You delight in giving us wisdom about our choices and decisions. You have a perfect plan for our lives and You long to share it with us. But often, I get so caught up in my *own* plans, that instead of asking You for Yours, I just ask You, please, please, please, to bless *mine*! Eventually, I am always sorry. So Lord, change my tendency, and draw me closer to seek Your face, to desire Your will for my life, and then gratefully, joyfully walk in Your ways.

Have You Thought? Tighten my grip on Your will, Lord.

His Answer:
> Hear my words, my son, and take them in; *let them soak in* so that you will live a long, *full* life. I have pointed you in the way of wisdom; I have steered you down the path to integrity.
>
> *So get going.* And as you go, *know this: with integrity* you will overcome all obstacles; even if you run, you will not stumble. Tighten your grip around *wise* advice; don't let it slip away. Protect Wisdom, for without her, life isn't worth living.

Proverbs 4:10-13
The Voice

Day 317

Two Unchanging Things

Thank You, Lord, that not one single event in our lives is outside Your sovereign ability to turn around into a blessing. Even in the midst of difficult circumstances, You are still our Intercessor and Deliverer. When life feels topsy-turvy, You provide peace. Circumstances only tell part of the story. You reach past what appears to be to change events at Your command. At this very moment, Jesus, our Great High Priest, is praying for each of us. At *any* moment of *any day*, He prays for us. Help us to hang our hats in that calm place instead of dwelling in chaos, Lord.

Have You Thought? Steady my restless soul today, Lord.

His Answer:

So God has given us two unchanging things: *His promise and His oath.* These prove that it is impossible for God to lie. As a result, we who come to God for refuge might be encouraged to seize that hope that is set before us. That hope is real and true, an anchor to steady our *restless* souls, a hope that leads us back behind the curtain *to where God is (as the high priests did in the days when reconciliation flowed from sacrifices in the temple)* and back into the place where Jesus, who went ahead on our behalf, has entered since He has become a High Priest forever…

Hebrews 6:18-20
The Voice

Day 318

The Core

Thank You, Lord, Your desire is to lift up our head and lighten our hearts as we walk through our days. Life can stoop our shoulders, strain our nerves and sap our energy. You long for us to live above our circumstances by entering into the practice of praise, even when our days have been challenging. You are faithful to show us Your goodness in the midst of our daily problems. Help us to live in the joy of today, thanking You for its blessings, leaving tomorrow to You, trusting in Your faithful care for that day when it comes. Let praise be the core of our being, not fretful worrying.

Have You Thought? Let praise become my practice.

His Answer:
> Don't fret or worry. Instead of worrying; pray. Let petitions and praises shape your worries into prayers, letting God know your concerns. Before you know it, a sense of God's wholeness, everything coming together for good, will come and settle you down. It's wonderful what happens when Christ displaces worry at the center of your life.

Philippians 4:6-7
The Message

Day 319

Make-Me-Smile Gifts

Thank You, Lord, for the every day make-me-smile gifts You shower on us: the sweet touch of a child's hand, the fragrant narcissus, the graceful neck of a heron, the splendor of fall's crisp colors, the beauty of creation, and the joy of love. Have I thanked Him for all this recently? He could have made His Creation in black and white. He didn't. He knew we'd enjoy His artistry and brilliant hues. He could have made us more robotic, incapable of deep feelings. No. Scratch that. God is highly relational and He made us like Himself. Today, I choose to notice the little things designed to brighten my day. I will be blessed, and God will be pleased.

Have You Thought? Let me notice Your gifts today, Lord.

His Answer:

So, my very dear friends, don't get thrown off course. Every desirable and beneficial gift comes out of heaven. The gifts are rivers of light cascading down from the Father of Light.

James 1:16-17
The Message

Day 320

Razor-Sharp Word

Thank You, Lord, for Your razor-sharp Word that either pierces or pacifies my heart, depending on my soul-need at that moment. When I need to be convicted, it pierces me, exposing sin. When I require comfort, it pours tender mercies over my wounded spirit. It is the Great Revealer of Your amazing love and of my amazing need of it. Countless believers in other countries risk their lives to read it, yet we are so nonchalant about it here. That privilege may not always stand. Lord, give us a fresh love and a holy hunger for Your precious Word. Engrave it on our hearts from constant use.

Have You Thought? Help me get in Your Word today, Lord.

His Answer:

> God means what he says. What he says goes. His powerful Word is sharp as a surgeon's scalpel, cutting through everything, whether doubt or defense, laying us open to listen and obey. Nothing and no one is impervious to God's Word. We can't get away from it—no matter what.
>
> Hebrews 4:12-13
> The Message

Day 321

God-Glasses

Thank You, Lord, that You see me and love me the same way every day. How different Your love is from my fickle affection. Your relentless passion for me remains constant whether I act right or I act out. It's hard to fathom, but I am certainly grateful for Your constancy. You have clothed me in Your Righteousness, and nothing, *nothing* can change that. In Your God-glasses, I am flawless, because of the blood of Your Son. Loved from everlasting to everlasting. Lord, as only You can do, persuade each of us again today of Your unfailing, unchanging love. Let it be the very core of our identity. The world screams a different refrain.

Have You Thought? I can't resist Your unchanging love, Lord.

His Answer:
"I've never quit loving you and never will. Expect love, love, and more love!"

Jeremiah 31:3
The Message

Day 322

Finger Wagging

Thank You, Lord, for not condemning the woman caught in "an act of adultery." Did you notice her name was not given? To the Pharisees, she was known only by her sin. How cruel! They belittled and condemned her to death by stoning. Jesus viewed her differently. To *Him*, she was one in need of life-changing forgiveness. He challenged the Pharisees to look at their own lives. "The sinless one among you, go first." One by one, they all walked away. Remind me of Your forgiveness in my life, Lord. May I never wag my finger at another, but joyfully pass on the same forgiveness I have received.

Have You Thought? Help me pass on Your forgiveness today.

His Answer:

As he was speaking, the teachers of religious law and the Pharisees brought a woman who had been caught in the act of adultery. They put her in front of the crowd. "Teacher," they said to Jesus, "this woman was caught in the act of adultery. The law of Moses says to stone her. What do you say?" They were trying to trap him into saying something they could use against him, but Jesus stooped down and wrote in the dust with his finger. They kept demanding an answer, so he stood up again and said, "All right, but let the one who has never sinned throw the first stone!" Then he stooped down again and wrote in the dust. When the accusers heard this, they slipped away one by one, beginning with the oldest, until only Jesus was left in the middle of the crowd with the woman.

John 8:3-9
New Living Translation

Day 323

Not Alone

Thank You, Lord, for telling us, "I am with you!"—four of the most beautiful words in the English language. In the crazy rush of this life, it is easy to feel alone, even when surrounded by others. Your Presence changes that. Unlike earthly friends, You have all the time in the world for a relationship. No limit to the conversation. Never a "Sorry, I've got to go!" You are loyal, persistent, unwavering in Your never-ending support. You understand how the highs of one day can descend to the depths the next, and You empathize with our emotions. You are our Anchor in the storm and our Good Shepherd when we have lost our way. You are all I want, Lord Jesus!

Have You Thought? No one understands me like You.

His Answer:
But even so, you love me! You are holding my right hand! You will keep on guiding me all my life with your wisdom and counsel, and afterwards receive me into the glories of heaven! Whom have I in heaven but you? And I desire no one on earth as much as you!

Psalms 73:23-25
The Living Bible

Day 324

In My Corner

Thank You, Lord, You remain changeless when our worlds change or even fall apart. What a comfort. When everything, or even just one thing in my life, alters, ends or feels threatened in some way, Satan tries to rock my world. Temporarily. But then I remember that You remain the same, and even more, You remain in the same position—in my corner. You are always ready to listen and act on my behalf; never weary of hearing my endless requests or complaints. Why? Because if it matters to me, then it matters to You. No one else in my world is that unshakably for me. Just You.

Have You Thought? Everything that matters to me, matters to You, Lord.

His Answer:
> You will keep the peace, a perfect peace, for all who trust in You, for those who dedicate their hearts *and minds* to You. So trust in the Eternal One forever, for He is like a great Rock—*strong, stable, trustworthy, and* lasting.

Isaiah 26:3-4
The Voice

Day 325

Misfits

Thank You, Lord, for coming to earth to be one of us. Really. Thank you. Do you know why I say that? Because while Jesus was here, there were times He felt like an outcast, a misfit, not part of the "in" crowd. So I know He relates to me and to everyone else on this planet who, at some point (or even, regularly), feel left out, insecure, or out of place. Maybe God likes that vulnerable place in all of us. It makes us more real; more open to Him. Because that's the only place where He can meet us and re-fill us with the courage and confidence we need to get up again. Lord, give us a fresh heart today so we can put on a fresh face and restart.

Have You Thought? How comforting that You understand my insecurities, Lord.

His Answer:
> May Jesus himself and God our Father, who reached out in love and surprised you with gifts of unending help and confidence, put a fresh heart in you, invigorate your work, enliven your speech.
>
> 2 Thessalonians 2:16-17
> The Message

Day 326

Face to Face

Thank You, Lord, that one day I will see You "face to face" (1 Cor. 13:12 NKJV). I'll see those winsomely kind eyes in person… the ones I saw in a dream as a very young girl. I can't even imagine. There will be so many more real faces—and oh, the stories! To hear how Jesus transformed Mary Magdalene's life; to ask Lazarus what it felt like to be brought back from the dead! Or chat about life on an ark or inside a whale's belly or in the Garden of Eden. I don't contemplate these things often, but today, it's kind of fun. It is our promised future as believers. Let it fill you with awe and excitement now!

Have You Thought? How amazing to contemplate Heaven.

His Answer:
> We don't yet see things clearly. We're squinting in a fog, peering through a mist. But it won't be long before the weather clears and the sun shines bright! We'll see it all then, see it all as clearly as God sees us, knowing him directly just as he knows us! But for now, until that completeness, we have three things to do to lead us toward that consummation: Trust steadily in God, hope unswervingly, love extravagantly.

1 Corinthians 13:12-13
The Message

Day 327

Not a Beggar

Thank You, Lord, for answering my prayers! You have shown me countless times how You change hearts, order circumstances, and even bring about downright miracles. So why do I sometimes come into Your gracious presence like a beggar? How many times will You have to prove Your generosity to me? I would totally lose patience. But You just wait for me to finally come dressed in the family garments You died to buy for me. Teach me to approach Your throne as a child of the King, unafraid and uninhibited, trusting You with all my needs, certain of Your loving answer.

Have You Thought? You chose me. I am Your beloved child.

His Answer:

> Long ago, even before he made the world, God chose us to be his very own through what Christ would do for us; he decided then to make us holy in his eyes, without a single fault—we who stand before him covered with his love. His unchanging plan has always been to adopt us into his own family by sending Jesus Christ to die for us. And he did this because he wanted to! Now all praise to God for his wonderful kindness to us and his favor that he has poured out upon us because we belong to his dearly loved Son.

> Ephesians 1:4-6
> The Living Bible

Day 328

A Child in Need

Thank You, Lord, for the many examples in the Gospels of Your love for children. To the man seeking help for his demon-possessed son, You said, "Bring him to Me" (Mark 9:19 NKJV). I need to remember that Divine command because You understood the father's distraught plea. Haven't you been there? I have. As parents, nothing else consumes and breaks our hearts like a child in need. No prayers are more heartfelt than those for a wayward or a hurting child. Lord, I'm asking as a mom, would You emboss this prescription for peace on my heart? Be the first One I run to when one of my children is in need. The first.

Have You Thought? Let me run to You first.

His Answer:
Father *(in the crowd)*: Teacher, I have brought my son to You. He is filled with an unclean spirit. He cannot speak, and when the spirit takes control of him, he is thrown to the ground *to wail and moan*, to foam at the mouth, to grind his teeth, and to stiffen up. I brought him to Your followers, but they could do nothing with him. *Can You help us?*

Jesus: O faithless generation, how long must I be among you? How long do I have to put up with you? Bring the boy to Me.

Mark 9:17-19
The Voice

Day 329

Relationship

Thank You, Lord, that You long for my company. Sometimes I can hardly wrap my mind around that truth. When I mistakenly view my quiet times with you as only beneficial to me, I totally miss the relational aspect of those precious encounters. You desire to hear my heart, Lord. You are High and You are Holy, but You are also Best Friend and Abba, Daddy. Make me more and more comfortable in Your Presence. Teach me to run to Your arms, joyfully and unashamedly. Incline my heart to confide the events and emotions of my day with you, my ever-waiting-to-hear Heavenly Father.

Have You Thought? Lord, let me share my heart with You.

His Answer:

O True God, You are my God, *the One whom I trust.* I seek You *with every fiber of my being.* In this dry and weary land with no water in sight, my soul is dry and longs for You. My body aches for You, *for Your presence.* I have seen You in Your sanctuary and have been awed by Your power and glory. Your steadfast love is better than life itself, so my lips will give You *all my* praise.

You have been my *constant* helper; therefore, I sing for joy under the protection of Your wings.

My soul clings to You; Your right hand *reaches down and* holds me up.

Psalms 63:1-3, 7-8
The Voice

Day 330

Crazy Love

Thank You, Lord, for the most famous Bible verse of all time, John 3:16. Maybe we've heard it too many times. Maybe we don't really hear it anymore. Sometimes familiarity does that. Today, let's try to embrace this cornerstone truth of the Bible: God loved us enough to send His only Son to die in our place, so we could be back in relationship with Him. That's the perspective of the Father. What about the Son? He agreed to this crazy-out-of-your-mind Love Story. He said "Yes" to the Plan that would take Him from the "Hallelujahs" of Heaven to the "Crucify Him" of earth. For you. For me. Even on our worst days. Crazy love. Get it today.

Have You Thought? I'm so grateful I'm part of Your love story.

His Answer:
> For God expressed His love for the world in this way: He gave His only Son so that whoever believes in Him will not face everlasting destruction, but will have everlasting life. Here's the point. God didn't send His Son into the world to judge it; instead, He is here to rescue a world *headed toward certain destruction.*

John 3:16-17
The Voice

Day 331

Our Inheritance

Lord, Your salvation is real and it cost You everything. This world preaches "a god without wrath bringing men without sin to a kingdom without judgment, and a Christ without a cross." Thank you for the real truth of our inheritance—God's wrath was paid for in full on the cross, redeeming us from the judgment for sin and ushering us into a new life. Not a life of obeying rules, but about enjoying a relationship. One that transforms our here-and-now life, not just the by-and-by in the hereafter existence. Draw me closer to You today, Lord, because of that Jesus-bought friendship.

Have You Thought? May my worship be honest and true.

His Answer:

So the religious leaders asked him, "Why don't your disciples follow our age-old customs? For they eat without first performing the washing ceremony." Jesus replied, "You bunch of hypocrites! Isaiah the prophet described you very well when he said, 'These people speak very prettily about the Lord but they have no love for him at all. Their worship is a farce, for they claim that God commands the people to obey their petty rules.' How right Isaiah was! For you ignore God's specific orders and substitute your own traditions."

Mark 7:5-8
The Living Bible

Day 332

Amazed Beyond Belief

Thank you Lord for the many layers of Your salvation. The Greek word for salvation, *soteria*, means "deliverance." It's so much more than just a get-out-of-Hell-free ticket, You bought us *release* from the guilt of our sin. (Whether we still cling to that shame is another matter entirely!) You often bring *reconciliation* along the way with unexpected healings, harmony where there once was discord, peace instead of brokenness. One day, You will bring *restoration* to that original Garden of Eden plan for us. Maybe today our quickly muttered thanks need to change to amazed-beyond-belief and breathless-with-delight exclamations of praise!

Have You Thought? Let my praise never end.

His Answer:

Come, let's shout praises to GOD, raise the roof for the Rock who saved us! Let's march into his presence singing praises, lifting the rafters with our hymns! And why? Because GOD is the best, High King over all the gods.

Psalms 95:1-3
The Message

Day 333

Plans Fulfilled

Thank You, Lord, Your plans are perfect. Your perfect plan of salvation was always "for the Jew first and also for the Greek" (Rom. 1:16 NKJV). Did you know that there were *two* miraculous feedings? The first was mostly a Jewish crowd, and the leftovers filled twelve *small* baskets. Hmm… there were twelve tribes of Israel. The second crowd was chiefly Gentiles, and there were seven *large* baskets collected… the number of completion. Small baskets for the Jews; large baskets for the Gentiles. Sounds like the demographics for Christianity today—mostly Gentile, with a few Messianic Jews. Your plans fulfilled, God!

Have You Thought? Everything is falling into Your plan.

His Answer:

Jesus *(overhearing them)*: Why are you focusing on bread? Don't you see yet? Don't you understand? You have eyes—why don't you see? You have ears—why don't you hear? Are you so hard-hearted? Don't you remember when I broke the five rounds of flatbread among the 5,000? *Tell Me*, how many baskets of scraps were left over? Disciples: Twelve. Jesus: And how many were left when I fed the 4,000 with seven rounds? Disciples: Seven. Jesus: And still you don't understand?

Mark 8:17-21
The Voice

Day 334

Divine Design

Thank You, Lord, that your large Plan for history is unfolding even as I immerse myself in the day-in-and-day-out occurrences of my own life. Whether I focus on it or not, You are still working out Your divine design for all creation. Every God-promise ever spoken will be fulfilled, whether it is recognized as Your Hand at work or not. The blessings spoken in the Old Testament ultimately all point to Jesus, the Lion of Judah, who waged war and won the victory. If I keep Your triumphant return firmly in mind, I will gain the proper perspective for every event in time, whether it's worked out in my life or in all of mankind's story.

Have You Thought? Your promises will all come true.

His Answer:

…Your hand will *firmly* grasp the neck of your enemy, and your brothers will bow down before you *in respect*.

…Until the One comes to whom true royalty belongs, all people will *honor and* obey him.

Genesis 49:8, 10
The Voice

Day 335

Lowing of Cattle

Thank You, Lord, for all that You gave up…and all You took on, to bring us Christmas. Your coming was recklessly premeditated and outrageously purposeful. You joyfully laid down Your preeminence over all the universe to put on fragile skin. You once received unending Hallelujahs but arrived to hear the lowing of cattle. I gladly ponder Your coming and take time to celebrate You breaking into our world to save us from it. You knew You would not only be disregarded, but disobeyed. Shunned and spurned. Renounced and rejected. Yet, You came. Let me hold these things dear and deep within.

Have You Thought? Let me not disregard all that You began for me with Your birth.

His Answer:

But the angel said, "Don't be afraid! I have good news for you, which will make everyone happy. This very day in King David's hometown a Savior was born for you. He is Christ the Lord. You will know who he is, because you will find him dressed in baby clothes and lying on a bed of hay." Suddenly many other angels came down from heaven and joined in praising God. They said: "Praise God in heaven! Peace on earth to everyone who pleases God."

But Mary kept thinking about all this and wondering what it meant.

Luke 2:10-14, 19
Contemporary English Version

Day 336

Lovingly Ordained

Thank You, Lord, that this Christmas story was etched on Your heart ages ago. Jesus, the babe in Bethlehem, is the fulfillment of promises God began in the Garden of Eden. Doesn't that give you hope? You and I, as God's own, are a part of, and in the midst of, His wonderful work in the world. Nothing in your life is random or accidental; it is all ordained and lovingly planned by Your Heavenly Father. My life is guided and ordained by You. If I can trust You for the salvation of the world, I can trust you for the daily details of my life. Thanks be to God!

Have You Thought? How comforting that my daily and eternal care are ordered by my most gracious God.

His Answer:

Brothers—you sons of Abraham, and also you God-fearing Gentiles—this message of salvation has been sent to us!

And now we are here to bring you this Good News. The promise was made to our ancestors, and God has now fulfilled it for us, their descendants, by raising Jesus.

Acts 13:26, 32-33
New Living Translation

Day 337

Not Looking

Thank You, Lord, for the Advent lesson we learn from the shepherds.
And what a wonderful word it is: God reveals Himself to those
who are not looking for Him. Those sheepherders were just
taking turns protecting their flocks from wolves or bandits,
totally engrossed in their everyday existence. They certainly
did not expect an angelic visitation or a celestial choir. Many
of our lives were just like that—we weren't looking for Jesus,
and possibly weren't the least bit interested in Him. But God
intersected and interrupted our lives as He did the shepherds
that night, and nothing is the same.

Have You Thought? You intersected our lives when we weren't
looking for You.

His Answer:

> That night some shepherds were in the fields outside the
> village, guarding their flocks of sheep. Suddenly an angel
> appeared among them, and the landscape shone bright
> with the glory of the Lord. They were badly frightened…

> When this great army of angels had returned again to
> heaven, the shepherds said to each other, "Come on!
> Let's go to Bethlehem! Let's see this wonderful thing
> that has happened, which the Lord has told us about."

Luke 2:8-9, 15
The Living Bible

Day 338

Sincerely Looking

Thank You, Lord, for the Advent lesson we learn from the Magi:
God also reveals Himself to those who *are* looking for Him…
even pagan astrologers from the East. Jeremiah 29:13 says,
"And you will seek Me and find Me, when you search for Me
with all your heart." God used a star from His creation to lead
these men to Bethlehem, to the newborn King of the Jews.
Their gifts symbolized everything Jesus would be for us: gold
for His royalty as King, frankincense for His divinity as God,
and myrrh for His humanity in His death. His Gift is offered
to us all, looking for Him or not.

Have You Thought? Those who search for You always find
You.

His Answer:

> Jesus was born in the town of Bethlehem, in Judea,
> during the reign of King Herod. At about that time
> some astrologers from eastern lands arrived in Jerusalem,
> asking, "Where is the newborn King of the Jews? for we
> have seen his star in far-off eastern lands and have come
> to worship him."

> After this interview the astrologers started out again.
> And look! The star appeared to them again, standing
> over Bethlehem.

> Matthew 2:1-2, 9
> The Living Bible

Day 339

The Great Arranger

Thank You, Lord, for the Advent lesson we learn from You, the Great Arranger. It had been hundreds of years since the prophecies about the Messiah. But God wasn't *procrastinating,* He was *preparing* every little detail. Listen to Micah 5:2, 4: "But you, Bethlehem, David's city...from you will come the leader who will shepherd-rule Israel." The plan: God used Quirinius, a pagan governor, to call for a census. By Jewish custom, every man had to register in his ancestral home, so Joseph and Mary traveled from Nazareth to Bethlehem. Promise fulfilled. Awesome, sovereign God.

Have You Thought? Your delays are not procrastination, but preparation.

His Answer:

About that time Emperor Augustus gave orders for the names of all the people to be listed in record books. These first records were made when Quirinius was governor of Syria. Everyone had to go to their own hometown to be listed. So Joseph had to leave Nazareth in Galilee and go to Bethlehem in Judea. Long ago Bethlehem had been King David's hometown, and Joseph went there because he was from David's family.

Luke 2:1-4
Contemporary English Version

Day 340

No Limits

Thank You, Lord, for the Advent lesson we learn from Matthew's lineage of Jesus: God's amazing grace has no limits. It was unusual to include women in a Jewish geneology, but to include women such as Tamar, Rahab, Bathsheba, and Ruth was outrageous. Tamar was part of a sexual scandal, Rahab was a Caananite prostitute, Bathsheba was David's mistress, and Ruth, although she led an exemplary life, was a Moabitess. But, they were included in the ancestry of Jesus! God lifted up these lowly women, and placed them in the royal line—just as He does with each of us.

Have You Thought? You certainly are a God of redemption.

His Answer:
These are the ancestors of Jesus Christ, a descendant of King David and of Abraham:

Abraham was the father of Isaac; Isaac was the father of Jacob; Jacob was the father of Judah and his brothers. Judah was the father of Perez and Zerah (Tamar was their mother...

Salmon was the father of Boaz (Rahab was his mother); Boaz was the father of Obed (Ruth was his mother); Obed was the father of Jesse; Jesse was the father of King David. David was the father of Solomon (his mother was the widow of Uriah);

Jacob was the father of Joseph (who was the husband of Mary, the mother of Jesus Christ the Messiah).

Matthew 1:1-3, 5-6, 16
The Living Bible

Day 341

Questions Allowed

Thank You, Lord, for the Advent lessons we learn from Mary. First, she taught us that God accepts our questions. He doesn't get angry, as we often fear. The angel Gabriel explained that the Holy Spirit would bring about the conception. Mary showed no disrespect or disbelief, just her confusion, since she was a virgin. She also taught us our second lesson: total acceptance of His will, even with incomplete understanding. A model of faith to those of us who want full explanations! God knew her humble, trusting heart…it's why He chose her. Lord, make me more like Mary.

Have You Thought? Lord, make my heart as trusting as Mary's heart.

His Answer:
>Messenger: Mary, don't be afraid. You have found favor with God. Listen, you are going to become pregnant. You will have a son, and you must name Him "Savior," *or* Jesus.

>Mary: But I have never been with a man. How can this be possible?

>Messenger: The Holy Spirit will come upon you. The Most High will overshadow you. That's why this holy child will be known, *as not just your son, but also* as the Son of God.

>So the impossible is possible with God.

Luke 1:30-31, 34-35, 37
The Voice

Day 342

Immediate Obedience

Thank You, Lord, for the Advent lesson we learn from Joseph. Mary wasn't the only one whose life had changed dramatically! When Mary conceived, Joseph had two choices under Jewish law: to divorce her publicly or just privately dismiss her in front of two witnesses. Mercifully, he chose the private route. An angel told him in a dream to marry Mary and he obeyed. In fact, every time God gave him directions, he immediately complied. When God reveals something to me, asking me to do a task that seems illogical, I pray I obey as quickly as Joseph did!

Have You Thought? Lord, make my heart as open to Your plans as Joseph's heart.

His Answer:

This is how Jesus the Messiah was born. His mother, Mary, was engaged to be married to Joseph. But before the marriage took place, while she was still a virgin, she became pregnant through the power of the Holy Spirit. Joseph, her fiancé, was a good man and did not want to disgrace her publicly, so he decided to break the engagement quietly. As he considered this, an angel of the Lord appeared to him in a dream. "Joseph, son of David," the angel said, "do not be afraid to take Mary as your wife. For the child within her was conceived by the Holy Spirit. And she will have a son, and you are to name him Jesus, for he will save his people from their sins."

When Joseph woke up, he did as the angel of the Lord commanded and took Mary as his wife. But he did not have sexual relations with her until her son was born. And Joseph named him Jesus.

Matthew 1:18-21, 24-25
New Living Translation

Day 343

Underestimating God

Thank You, Lord, for the Advent lesson we learn from Zachariah. God honored Mary's questions, why did Zachariah displease Him? Zachariah didn't take into account two very important facts. First, he did not consider the divine messenger who was speaking to him. Gabriel was sent by God Almighty to give him this great news; he should have been respected. Secondly, he should have remembered the many other Old Testament examples of childless couples who miraculously conceived—like Abraham and Sarah! Lord, as we live our lives, help us never forget Your miracles in our past!

Have You Thought? Let me never cause Your punishment by my unbelief.

His Answer:

Zacharias: How can I be sure of what you're telling me? I am an old man, and my wife is far past the normal age for women to bear children. *This is hard to believe!*

Messenger *(sternly)*: I am Gabriel, the messenger who inhabits God's presence. I was sent here to talk with you and bring you this good news. Because you didn't believe my message, you will not be able to talk—not another word—until you experience the fulfillment of my words.

Meanwhile the crowd at the temple wondered why Zacharias hadn't come out of the sanctuary yet. It wasn't normal for the priest to be delayed so long. When at last he came out, *he* was making signs with his hands to give the blessing, but he couldn't speak. They realized he had seen some sort of vision.

Luke 1:18-22
The Voice

Day 344

New Life

Thank You, Lord, for the second Advent lesson we learn from Zechariah: Your touch brings new life and results in praises to Your Name. The infant was not the only new birth in the lives of this couple. At his birth, God also brought forth a new creation in Zechariah, a new God-praising, God-honoring life. He went from a man who declared disbelief to one who professed praises and prophecies. What an encouragement to us! God continues to mold and remold us, regardless of our age. If we are fully yielded to His Hand on us, He will continue in His wonderful re-creation of our hearts.

Have You Thought? Mold and remold me all my life, Lord.

His Answer:

> *As was customary,* eight days after the baby's birth the time came for his circumcision *and naming.* Everyone assumed he would be named Zacharias, like his father. Elizabeth *(disagreeing):* No. We will name him John. Her Relatives *(protesting):* That name is found nowhere in your family. They turned to Zacharias and asked him what he wanted the baby's name to be. He motioned for a tablet, and he wrote, "His name is John." Everyone was shocked *by this breach of family custom. They were even more surprised when,* at that moment, Zacharias was able to talk again, and he shouted out praises to God.

> Luke 1:59-64
> The Voice

Day 345

Filled

Thank You, Lord, for the Advent lesson we learn from Elizabeth. You changed her life from barren to blessed. We all have barren, dry or unfruitful places...in relationships, jobs, or even in our walks with You. That is why Jesus came, to fill every longing in our lives. He understands our brokenness and our need for refilling and refreshing. Possibly you just need some time alone with Him for renewal. Elizabeth certainly understood the value in that...she retreated for five months! Rest is in short supply this season, but just ask for His filling, and receive His gifts to you, as Elizabeth did.

Have You Thought? Where I am empty, fill me, Lord.

His Answer:

> When Zechariah's week of service in the Temple was over, he returned home. Soon afterward his wife, Elizabeth, became pregnant and went into seclusion for five months. "How kind the Lord is!" she exclaimed. "He has taken away my disgrace of having no children."

> For nothing is impossible with God.

Luke 1:23-25, 37
New Living Translation

Day 346

Wonder

Thank You, Lord, for the Advent lesson we learn from those who observe. The shepherds observed Mary, and Elizabeth's neighbors observed her. Their response was praise, holy fear and wonder, when they saw God's miracles in each of these women's lives. They were also quick to tell others of all that they had seen or heard. What an example for us! Certainly we have each seen God's Hand moving in our own lives or in the lives of others…delivering, forgiving, answering prayers. Have we told anyone? The shepherds and neighbors spread the Good News. Lord Jesus, make us as quick to tell of Your works.

Have You Thought? Fill my heart with wonder at Your ways, Lord.

His Answer:

The shepherds told everyone what had happened and what the angel had said to them about this child. All who heard the shepherds' story expressed astonishment…

By now Elizabeth's waiting was over, for the time had come for the baby to be born—and it was a boy. The word spread quickly to her neighbors and relatives of how kind the Lord had been to her, and everyone rejoiced.

Wonder fell upon the whole neighborhood, and the news of what had happened spread through the Judean hills.

Luke 2:17-18, 1:57-58, 65
The Living Bible

Day 347

No Room

Thank You, Lord, for the Advent lesson we learn from the innkeepers. There was no room in the inn. No place for baby Jesus. Unfortunately, that "Not Welcome Here" sign happened even more in people's hearts during Jesus' life. In His hometown, he was hailed at one moment as being wise, and then ridiculed the next for just being a carpenter, the son of Mary. On a deeper level, where do I do that? Do I say, "Maybe I'll let You in there, Jesus, but there is no room here, Lord." Show me those areas in my life where I don't welcome You, Jesus. I want You to be at home everywhere in my heart.

Have You Thought? Where don't I welcome You into my life, Jesus?

His Answer:
And while they were there, the time came for her baby to be born. She gave birth to her first child, a son. She wrapped him snugly in strips of cloth and laid him in a manger, because there was no lodging available for them.

Luke 2:6-7
New Living Translation

Day 348

Still Sovereign

Thank You, Lord, for the Advent lesson we learn from Herod and the chief priests: You are sovereign even over those who hate You. Herod the Great was a violent, cruel king, whose fury was kindled by this impending birth of the "King of the Jews." He gathered the chief priests to inquire about this One who might usurp his throne, and they told him the Micah 5:2 prophecy of Jesus' birth in Bethlehem. How ironic that these men who later would defy and crucify Jesus now disclosed His foretelling! Then and now, every event is under God's direction; His will and His way prevail.

Have You Thought? Your rule and reign extends everywhere, Lord.

His Answer:

King Herod was deeply disturbed when he heard this, as was everyone in Jerusalem. He called a meeting of the leading priests and teachers of religious law and asked, "Where is the Messiah supposed to be born?" "In Bethlehem in Judea," they said, "for this is what the prophet wrote: 'And you, O Bethlehem in the land of Judah, are not least among the ruling cities of Judah, for a ruler will come from you who will be the shepherd for my people Israel.'" Then Herod called for a private meeting with the wise men, and he learned from them the time when the star first appeared. Then he told them, "Go to Bethlehem and search carefully for the child. And when you find him, come back and tell me so that I can go and worship him, too!"

Matthew 2:3-8
New Living Translation

Breathtaking

Thank You, Lord, for the Advent lessons we learn from the five dreams of divine guidance in the Nativity story. Again, Your Lordship is proclaimed over all the events of the earth. First, Joseph's dream to marry Mary (Matt. 1:20), then the dream warning the wise men not to return to Herod with news of the Christ child (Matt. 2:12). Later, three more dreams for Joseph, telling him to quickly flee to Egypt to escape Herod's fury, instructing him of Herod's death, allowing him to return to Israel, and the fifth dream leading him to Nazareth (Matt. 2:13-23). What a breathtaking God!

Have You Thought? Lord, Your details astound me.

His Answer:
When it was time to leave, they returned to their own country by another route, for God had warned them in a dream not to return to Herod. After the wise men were gone, an angel of the Lord appeared to Joseph in a dream. "Get up! Flee to Egypt with the child and his mother," the angel said. "Stay there until I tell you to return, because Herod is going to search for the child to kill him." That night Joseph left for Egypt with the child and Mary, his mother, and they stayed there until Herod's death. This fulfilled what the Lord had spoken through the prophet: "I called my Son out of Egypt."

When Herod died, an angel of the Lord appeared in a dream to Joseph in Egypt. "Get up!" the angel said. "Take the child and his mother back to the land of Israel, because those who were trying to kill the child are dead."

Then, after being warned in a dream, he left for the region of Galilee. So the family went and lived in a town called Nazareth.

Matthew 2:12-15, 19-20, 22-23
New Living Translation

Day 350

Expectation

Thank You, Lord, for the Advent lesson about expectation we learn from Simeon and Anna. Simeon was told by the Holy Spirit that He would not die until he had seen the Lord's Christ. As he held Jesus, he proclaimed that God could now take him, for He had brought forth His promise. Anna arrived and confirmed all that Simeon had said. They had both been looking for and anticipating a deeper, more intimate revelation of God, and their hopes were answered. That makes me wonder…am I looking for an even deeper walk with God? Lord, raise my expectations of You.

Have You Thought? Raise my expectations of an ever-deepening walk with You.

His Answer:

Now there was a man named Simeon who lived in Jerusalem…

The Holy Spirit had revealed to him that he would not die until he had seen the Lord's Messiah. That day the Spirit led him to the Temple. So when Mary and Joseph came to present the baby Jesus to the Lord…Simeon was there. He took the child in his arms and praised God, saying… "Lord, now I can die in peace! As you promised me… I have seen the Savior…you have given to all people.

Anna, a prophet, was also there in the Temple.

She came along just as Simeon was talking with Mary and Joseph, and she began praising God…

Luke 2:25, 27-31, 36, 38
New Living Translation

Day 351

Anxiously Waiting

Thank You, Lord, for the Advent lesson we learn from Mary's delivery of Jesus: it was in God's timing. "The time came," means just that. Time was needed for Jesus' body to form in the womb, and for Mary's body to deliver Him safely. Our lives run the same way. I try to rush God, and bring myself much stress in the process. What are you anxiously waiting for today? The answer might not be "No." There may just be work to do in the situation, or in *you*, to make you ready to receive the blessing. Let God do His perfect work to bring forth the birth of your heart's desire in *His* timing.

Have You Thought? Lord, let me not run ahead of You.

His Answer:
> While they were there, the time came for her to give birth.

Luke 2:5-6
The Message

Day 352

Wave After Wave

Thank You, Lord, for the Advent lesson we learn from Mary's song of praise. We see why God chose this young girl to birth the Savior of the world. He was pleased with her realization that she brought nothing to this divine encounter except an empty womb and a willing heart. Every Jewish girl had certainly dreamed of being in her place, so her humble heart is a lesson to me. I sometimes forget what she knew—that this is *all* grace. I deserve *none* of it; I bring God nothing. It is the Gift beyond measure, bringing light for my darkness, grace for my sin, and hope for my longings. My soul sings!

Have You Thought? Your mercy flows in on me, wave after wave.

His Answer:

And Mary said, "I'm bursting with God-news; I'm dancing the song of my Savior God. God took one good look at me, and look what happened—I'm the most fortunate woman on earth! What God has done for me will never be forgotten, the God whose very name is holy, set apart from all others. His mercy flows in wave after wave on those who are in awe before him."

Luke 1:46-50
The Message

Day 353

The Lord Saves

Thank You, Lord, for the Advent lesson we learn from the name of Jesus. His name means, "The Lord Saves." God's Son has many names, and for the next few days we will explore them. Jesus is His human name and also His mission. The angel proclaimed it to Joseph before Jesus' birth. Jesus embraced it as He walked into His ministry, saying, "For the Son of Man has come to seek and to save that which was lost" (Luke 19:10 NKJV). How sweet to contemplate the freedom, the release of that salvation. Thank You again for doing for me what I could never do—save myself. What mercy!

Have You Thought? You did for me what I could never do, Lord.

His Answer:

"Christ Jesus came into the world to save sinners." This saying is true, and it can be trusted. I was the worst sinner of all! But since I was worse than anyone else, God had mercy on me and let me be an example of the endless patience of Christ Jesus. He did this so that others would put their faith in Christ and have eternal life.

1 Timothy 1:15-16
Contemporary English Version

Day 354

Immanuel

Thank You, Lord, for the Advent lesson we learn from the name Immanuel—God with us. The name Jesus satisfies our heavenly need, salvation from our sins. Immanuel meets our earthly needs. Jesus, our Savior, set us free once and for all, and Immanuel, God with us, sustains us day by day. He *became* us, to be *with* us. He humbly walked away from Heaven to become one of us. Augustine says that He was born of a mother whom He created; carried by the hands He formed. Lord, I want to honor You with all that I am, because You gave all that You were to become as I am.

Have You Thought? You gave up Heaven for us—what a thought!

His Answer:
> He had equal status with God but didn't think so much of himself that he had to cling to the advantages of that status no matter what. Not at all. When the time came, he set aside the privileges of deity and took on the status of a slave, became human! Having become human, he stayed human. It was an incredibly humbling process. He didn't claim special privileges. Instead, he lived a selfless, obedient life and then died a selfless, obedient death.

Philippians 2:5-8
The Message

Day 355

Like Father, Like Son

Thank You, Lord, for the Advent lesson that You are the Messiah— the Revealer of God and the Reality of God. Jesus, You are the answer to our question, "What is the Father like?" You came as His spitting image, with skin on. You told Your disciples if they had seen You, they had seen the Father. Forget the misconception of an Old Testament angry God or a New Testament nice one. In Your short life on earth, we saw Your compassion and forgiveness, Your goodness and mercy—and Your holiness. Like Father, like Son…You showed us the very heart of God. Thank You, Lord.

Have You Thought? Keep showing me the Father's heart, Jesus.

His Answer:

Jesus replied, "Don't you even yet know who I am, Philip, even after all this time I have been with you? Anyone who has seen me has seen the Father! So why are you asking to see him? Don't you believe that I am in the Father and the Father is in me? The words I say are not my own but are from my Father who lives in me. And he does his work through me."

John 14:9-10
The Living Bible

Day 356

The Coming One

Thank You, Lord, for the Advent lesson we learn from John the Baptist: You are the Christ, the Anointed One. John knew well the prophecies of old about the Coming One. He could probably recite them line-by-line. But he was in prison, and things weren't looking good for him. He needed assurance from his cousin that He really was the Christ. There is a wonderful little interchange between Jesus and John's disciples. Jesus sends them back to John with the words of Isaiah 61. He wanted those words to be imprinted on John's heart and mind. He wants the same thing for each of us today.

Have You Thought? Lord, You fulfilled every prophecy about You.

His Answer:
> John the Baptist, who was now in prison, heard about all the miracles the Messiah was doing, so he sent his disciples to ask Jesus, "Are you really the one we are waiting for, or shall we keep on looking?" Jesus told them, "Go back to John and tell him about the miracles you've seen me do—the blind people I've healed, and the lame people now walking without help, and the cured lepers, and the deaf who hear, and the dead raised to life; and tell him about my preaching the Good News to the poor. Then give him this message, 'Blessed are those who don't doubt me.'"

Matthew 11:2-6
The Living Bible

Do You Like My Gift?

Thank You, Lord, for the Christmas lesson we learn from the heart of the Father. On a very minuscule level we know His feeling on Christmas morning. A loved one opens our gift, and every fiber of our being wants to respond, *"Do you like my gift?"* That is the heart of the Father. He waits with longing for our response to Jesus. From before time began, He has anticipated the unwrapping of His Gift. With great joy He has anticipated all those who will accept His Gift beyond measure. How will we answer Him? All of heaven is waiting, so say "yes!" to Him.

Have You Thought? This is the most important question in life. How will I answer?

His Answer:

And what is it that God has said? That he has given us eternal life and that this life is in his Son. So whoever has God's Son has life; whoever does not have his Son, does not have life. I have written this to you who believe in the Son of God so that you may know you have eternal life.

1 John 5:11-13
The Living Bible

Day 358

Discipleship

Thank You, Lord, for the Christmas lesson we learn from Mary's continuing journey of faith with her Son. For Jesus grew up, became a man, and walked into His mission and ministry. Mary grew up in her faith, too. Have you ever thought of Mary as Jesus' very first disciple? Her journey of faith walks her through many phases and all the changes in her life as His mother. He matures her in her faith. He wants to do the same thing with each of us. Every day, the discipleship question remains, "Where are you *now* with the Lord?" Keep us ever growing up and growing closer to You.

Have You Thought? Where am I *now* with the Lord?

His Answer:

Every year Jesus' parents went to Jerusalem for Passover. And when Jesus was twelve years old, they all went there as usual for the celebration. After Passover his parents left, but they did not know that Jesus had stayed on in the city.

When they could not find him with their relatives and friends, they went back to Jerusalem and started looking for him there. Three days later they found Jesus sitting in the temple, listening to the teachers and asking them questions.

Jesus went back to Nazareth with his parents and obeyed them. His mother kept on thinking about all that had happened.

Luke 2:41-43, 45-46, 51
Contemporary English Version

Day 359

Repentance

Thank You, Lord, for the Christmas lesson we learn from John the Baptist. He had begun his ministry of preaching repentance. This voice in the wilderness was shaking up Judea, telling everyone that God was breaking in. After centuries of silence, John screamed out for all to make a change! Bring the deadwood in your life to Jesus. Your attitudes, lifestyles and baggage; all the old and stale, worthless and the empty things in our lives to which we cling. Bring them to Jesus, and let them stay there. Repentance is freedom, and it's just the beginning. The joyful ending comes tomorrow. Just wait!

Have You Thought? I'm grateful for the freedom you bring, Lord.

His Answer:
Years later, John the Baptist started preaching in the desert of Judea. He said, "Turn back to God! The kingdom of heaven will soon be here." John was the one the prophet Isaiah was talking about, when he said, "In the desert someone is shouting, 'Get the road ready for the Lord! Make a straight path for him.'"

An ax is ready to cut the trees down at their roots. Any tree that doesn't produce good fruit will be chopped down and thrown into a fire.

Matthew 3:1-3, 10
Contemporary English Version

Day 360

The Real Action

Thank You, Lord, for the Christmas lesson we learn about grace. The word is *chesed* in Hebrew, meaning "God's immense lovingkindness." This time of year, we look back on all that we've done and been and sometimes there are regrets... situations we would have done differently if we could... words we would gladly have never spoken. Peter understood this better than anyone. He must have relived his denial of Christ thousands of times in his mind, wishing he had done and said things very differently. But, he understood the grace of the Gospel of Christ, that through Him, we can be made clean. Do we?

Have You Thought? Have Your way in me, Lord.

His Answer:

I'm baptizing you here in the river, turning your old life in for a kingdom life. The real action comes next: The main character in this drama...will ignite the kingdom life within you, a fire within you, the Holy spirit within you, changing you from the inside out. He's going to clean house—make a clean sweep of your lives. He'll place everything true in its proper place before God; everything false he'll put out with the trash to be burned.

Matthew 3:11-12
The Message

Changed Identity

Thank You, Lord, for the Christmas lesson we learn from Peter about our true identity. Jesus saw who Peter would ultimately become. Not Simon, his original name, but rather Peter. Changed name, changed identity. His true identity. What a victory! If Satan had had his way, Peter would have never rallied from that dreadful I-don't-know-Him night. He could have been lost in that guilt-ridden prison forever. But Jesus' forgiveness and restoration freed him. Are there any prisons from this year that He needs to unlock for you? He is waiting to give you your freedom and your new identity. Be made new.

Have You Thought? Lord, You see me as I will be one day.

His Answer:

> Simon Peter answered, "You are the Messiah, the Son of the living God." Jesus replied, "You are blessed, Simon son of John, because my Father in heaven has revealed this to you. You did not learn this from any human being. Now I say to you that you are Peter (which means 'rock'), and upon this rock I will build my church, and all the powers of hell will not conquer it."

Matthew 16:16-18
New Living Translation

Day 362

How I Live

Thank You, Lord, for the Christmas lesson we learn about the Coming King. No more sweet little baby in the manger, Jesus will return as Victorious Ruler. For now there is just the waiting, mindful I will face Jesus one-on-One, one way or another. I don't want to be embarrassed when my life is on display before Him. I know He has covered all my sins completely with His blood. But, am I living my life according to His plans for me? Or my own plans? Have I obeyed all that He has called me to do? Lord, order and anoint my steps in this next year. It matters to You how I live.

Have You Thought? Lord, help me live wisely as I wait for Your return.

His Answer:

Don't overlook the obvious here, friends. With God, one day is as good as a thousand years, a thousand years as a day. God isn't late with his promise as some measure lateness. He is restraining himself on account of you, holding back the End because he doesn't want anyone lost. He's giving everyone space and time to change.

Interpret our Master's patient restraint for what it is: salvation.

Grow in grace and understanding of our Master and Savior, Jesus Christ. Glory to the Master, now and forever! Yes!

2 Peter 3:8-9, 15, 18
The Message

Day 363

Train Me

Thank You, Lord, for the Christmas lesson we learn from the entire Nativity cast of characters. They walked out their lives, as crazy as they were, trusting in God's leading and provision. And He was always faithful. How do you view the coming year? With trepidation? With a stacked up pile of "What if?" scenarios? Those imagined fears totally leave God out of the equation! He worked in our past; He will continue in our future. Whatever the year may hold, God will be there… to guide, restore, intervene, and to bring blessings. Let's allow God to truly be the God of our lives in the coming year.

Have You Thought? Keep me on Your trail.

His Answer:
> Because you have satisfied me, GOD, I promise to do everything you say. I beg you from the bottom of my heart: smile, be gracious to me just as you promised. When I took a long, careful look at your ways, I got my feet back on the trail you blazed. I was up at once, didn't drag my feet, was quick to follow your orders…Your love, GOD, fills the earth! Train me to live by your counsel.

Psalms 119:57-60, 62, 64
The Message

Day 364

Old History

Thank You, Lord, You always call me to look forward. Satan beckons me to the past…not only to rehearse my old sins, but also to agonize over the seasons in my life that are done or no longer true. Sadly, I have fallen for his schemes. But, no more! The Lord is a promise-keeping, forward-looking God. Yes, He allows changes, but He is faithful to bring fresh joys in those altered situations. He has blessings left in His bag. His lovingkindness has not all been spent. So, I will look up and trust God for every new turn in my life, thanking Him that His blessings never end.

Have You Thought? You are a forward-looking God.

His Answer:

Forget about what's happened; don't keep going over old history.

Don't be afraid, and don't worry: Haven't I always kept you informed, told you what was going on? You're my eyewitnesses: Have you ever come across a God, a real God, other than me? There's no Rock like me that I know of.

Isaiah 43:18; Isaiah 44:8
The Message

Day 365

Salvation

Thank You, Lord, that You are consistently and unconditionally faithful to me even when I am repeatedly fickle in my dealings with You. Never, when I lose my bearings, do You require me to grovel or beg for entrance back into Your Presence. Instead, You receive me back with open arms and shower me with love. How grateful I am for Your steadfast lovingkindness. I have proven my need for it repeatedly in my life. I guess Your name isn't Redeemer for nothing! You are the setting free, salvaging, and safeguarding God of Salvation, and I give You grateful praise. How You have rescued me!

Have You Thought? Your arms are always open to me.

His Answer:

> "If you'll hold on to me for dear life," says GOD, "I'll get you out of any trouble. I'll give you the best of care if you'll only get to know and trust me. Call me and I'll answer, be at your side in bad times; I'll rescue you, then throw you a party. I'll…give you a long drink of salvation!"

Psalms 91:14-16
The Message

May Jesus Himself and God our Father, who reached out in love and surprised you with gifts of unending help and confidence, put a fresh heart in you, invigorate your work, enliven your speech.

2 Thessalonians 2:16-17
The Message

Index

Contact Information

To order additional copies of this book,
please visit www.redemption-press.com.
Also available on Amazon.com and
BarnesandNoble.com or by calling toll
free 1 (844) 2REDEEM (273-3336).

Visit Linda's website at www.lindagrabeman.com

Share your thoughts with Linda at:
linda@lindagrabeman.com

2/1/19

Elizabeth enjoy reading
this devotional everyday
to give you strength and
love of God!

love,
Margie